IMAGES
of America

GRANDFATHER MOUNTAIN

On the Cover: Watauga County resident Bob Davis built the Davis Special in 1951. It was constructed from several different cars and trucks. Winston-Salem driver Ed Welch drove the car to victory one year at the Grandfather Mountain Sports Car Hill Climb. The car was sold and wrecked in a Burnsville race; then, after spending more than two decades in a junkyard and passing through a couple more owners, it was restored in 2013. (Courtesy of Patricia Combs.)

IMAGES
of America

GRANDFATHER MOUNTAIN

Michael C. Hardy

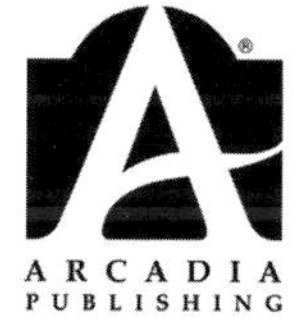

ISBN 978-1-4671-2104-0

Published by Arcadia Publishing
Charleston, South Carolina

Printed in the United States of America

Library of Congress Control Number: 2013946860

For all general information, please contact Arcadia Publishing:
Telephone 843-853-2070
Fax 843-853-0044
E-mail sales@arcadiapublishing.com
For customer service and orders:
Toll-Free 1-888-313-2665

Visit us on the Internet at www.arcadiapublishing.com

For all those who have visited Grandfather Mountain over the last 200 years and for all those to come who will fall under his gentle gaze

Contents

Acknowledgments

There are many, many people who graciously dug through old photographs to contribute to this project. Their names are noted accordingly at the end of each caption. There are a few people to whom I would like to extend an even greater acknowledgment. Levin Sudderth generously granted me access to the photographs of the Grandfather Mountain Highland Games and the real treasures within. Heather South guided me through various collections at the Western Office, North Carolina Department of Archives and History in Asheville. Ranger Jonathan Bennett, Blue Ridge Parkway, was always around to field questions and usually came up with some pretty good answers. Jackie Holt graciously allowed me to search through the files of the Blue Ridge Parkway Office in Asheville. Suzanne Tucker not only provided a few of her own photographs, but also encouraged her family members to scan their photographs. I think we are all the richer for her work. Susan McBean, superintendent at the Grandfather Mountain State Park, provided photographs from its collection. Ike Forester and Becky Phillips gave valuable assistance in my attempts to sort out the facts in the early ownership of Grandfather Mountain. Colin Foust of the Caldwell Heritage Museum sent photographs from its collection. I sincerely appreciate the support of the Grandfather Mountain Stewardship Foundation and the great work the group does. And to all of my "friends" on Facebook—thanks for sharing in the journey of putting this book together. We have all grown and benefitted from our shared journey up Grandfather Mountain together. A special thanks goes to my readers, Levin Sudderth and Elizabeth Baird Hardy.

INTRODUCTION

Sometime during the Civil War, an anonymous prisoner penned the following lines: "I'd ruther be on the Grandfather Mountain / A-taking the snow and rain / Than to be in Castle Thunder / A-wearin' the ball and chain." Grandfather Mountain had already begun gaining notoriety by the 1860s when the prison-bound soldier recorded his longing, but he could not possibly have imagined the fame and recognition that the old mountain has since garnered.

Miles Tager, in his 1999 book, *Grandfather Mountain: A Profile*, noted that while we often define Grandfather Mountain as just the attraction and the state park, stretching from Linville Peak to Calloway Peak, the whole mountain is much larger. Tager argues that the mountain is actually 10 miles long and 3 miles wide, stretching from Price Park to the Linville Gorge along the Blue Ridge Parkway, encompassing some 150 square miles, or about 100,000 acres. There is a wealth of history in those 100,000 acres.

Geologists consider Grandfather Mountain one of the oldest mountains in North America, arguing that 750 million years ago, the rock that became Grandfather Mountain began forming as sediment after the breakup of the supercontinent Rodinia. Between 460 million and 270 million years ago, several land masses collided, and Grandfather Mountain was formed. In the collision, the older rock of our Grandfather Mountain was thrust on top of much younger rock before the land masses gradually separated. The mountain was once much taller, up to 10 miles in height. Over time, erosion has diminished its size, but not its impressive geology, which includes a variety of rocks. Near the Grandfather Nature Museum and the Split Rock are metamorphosed conglomerates. Along the ridgeline are phyllite or metasiltstone rocks, while the Mile-High Swinging Bridge is erected on granular pebble conglomerate rocks. Though the rock faces are streaked with quartz, there are very few minerals or precious gems found within the Grandfather Mountain area. This is one of those odd quirks of geology, as just a few miles away is the Spruce Pine Mining District, an area 25 miles long and 10 miles wide, containing at least 57 minerals, including mica, feldspar, quartz, emeralds, and aquamarine.

The distinct geology, along with the flora and fauna, has long drawn many to the Grandfather Mountain area. Native American sites abound in the high country. Archaeologist Stanley South documented 27 sites in Watauga County in 1952. On the mountain itself, in 1951, a cave used by Native Americans was explored. Now known as Indian House Cave, the large cavern contained numerous points, stone axes, and pottery shards. Alex McRae claimed to have found the cave in 1892 while searching for some sheep. According to an article in the *Greensboro Daily News*, he kept the location a secret but would visit the cave every so often, gathering artifacts to sell to tourists. A few of the remaining artifacts were saved to be examined by experts, but the real history of the site was lost.

European explorers first started arriving in the 16th century. Hernando de Soto was in Western North Carolina in 1540, and Juan Pardo led expeditions in the 1560s. Historians and archaeologists believe that Pardo and his men visited the area during these expeditions. More than a century later, English naturalist Mark Catesby explored the area in 1722, recording the various types of flora and fauna he found. His published volumes included 220 plates of birds, reptiles and amphibians, fish, insects, mammals, and plants.

André Michaux was a French explorer and botanist who spent a great deal of time trekking through the mountains of Western North Carolina, making observations and gathering specimens. In 1794, his travels brought him to the vicinity, and his journal entry on August 26, 1794, records his scaling of the mountain as follows: "Started for Grandfather Mountain, the most elevated of all those which form the chain of the Alleghanies and the Appalachians." He reached the foot of the mountain the next day, "the rocks" on the 28th, and continued his "herborization" on August 29. On August 30, Michaux recorded that he "climbed to the summit of the highest mountain of all North America, and with [his] companion and guide sang the hymn of the Marseillaise, and cried 'Long live America and the Republic of the French! Long live Liberty!'"

Settlement in Western North Carolina, beyond the crest of the Blue Ridge, largely took place in the years following the colonies' declaration of independence from Great Britain. The King's Proclamation of 1763 prohibited European settlement west of the Appalachian Mountains in the valleys of the Holston, Watauga, and Nolichucky Rivers. There were colonists already living along the Watauga River, and in 1772, they organized the Watauga Association and drafted a constitution. They originally leased their land from the Cherokee and in 1775 purchased the property outright for the sum of 2,000 pounds. The lands stretched to the headwaters of the Watauga River.

There are actually several rivers that originate on Grandfather Mountain. The Eastern Continental Divide tracks along US 221 from the north, crossing the Blue Ridge Parkway near Green Mountain Creek, and following the mountain up Calloway Peak. From there, the divide heads down the mountain, along Little Grassy Creek, before crossing NC 105 at Linville Gap. The Watauga River flows to the north and includes feeder streams, like Green Ridge Branch and Shanty Spring Branch. The Watauga River flows through Watauga County and into east Tennessee. These waters eventually flow into the Holston and thence into the Mississippi River and Gulf of Mexico. To the south of Linville Gap is the Linville River. This river continues through Avery County and the Linville Gorge, known as the "Grand Canyon of the South," before joining the Catawba River. On the eastern side of Grandfather Mountain are Andrew Creek, Stack Rock Creek, Linn Cove Branch, and Little Wilson and Wilson Creeks. These primarily empty into Johns River, which itself empties into the Catawba River. These all eventually make their way to the Atlantic Ocean.

Early settlers found these creeks and bottoms inviting places and settled there first. Much of the good land was quickly granted to farmers willing to attempt taming the wilderness. The first land grant related to Grandfather Mountain was made in 1788 to Waightstill Avery for 200 acres "between the Grandfather and Grand Mother Mountain and the head of a branch of Linville." Avery was the first attorney general for North Carolina, and in the same year he received the grant, he fought a duel with future president Andrew Jackson. This land grant was recorded in Burke County and is probably the earliest official reference to the area being called "Grandfather Mountain."

Others who were awarded land grants include William White, who was the biggest land grant owner. In 1790, he was granted 300 acres "under the N.E. end of Grandfather Mountain" and 1,877 acres "[o]n head of Watauga River lying Between the Fair Mt. and Grand Father Mt." James Aldridge was granted 100 acres in 1828, which "Beg. at a sugar tree at the Big Branch of Grand F. Mt." Tobias Long was granted 70 acres in 1829, which "Beg. on the Top of Grand Father Mountain (E. along the top of Blue Ridge.)" James W. McCleaird and David Sands in 1847 were granted 100 acres "on head Watauga River E. (to include land on side next to Grandfather Mt." William A. Lenoir was granted 640 acres "[o]n Grandfather Mnt." in 1853.

Eventually, most of the property at Grandfather Mountain passed into the hands of the Lenoir family. When William A. Lenoir died in 1861, his Grandfather Mountain land went to his brothers and sisters. William's brother Walter purchased this land and added to it, purchasing additional lands and even obtaining an additional land grant for 100 acres in 1885. By the time of his death, Walter owned 17,500 acres of land in the area.

Walter Lenoir was a Confederate officer during the Civil War. While Grandfather Mountain was sparsely populated in the 1860s, local dissidents and escaped Federal prisoners of war found it a welcoming haven from the local home guard. Watauga County dissidents Keith and Malinda Blalock were chased up the mountain in late 1862, finding refuge in a hog pen. After fleeing to east Tennessee, they returned as guides for many crossing through the area to the safety of Federal lines.

When the end of the war brought an uneasy peace to Western North Carolina, new families began to arrive. Walter Lenoir spent more time at his home on the Watauga River. He greatly admired Grandfather Mountain and wanted to see it turned into a park. Lenoir brought in a shepherd from Scotland, Alexander MacRae, to tend his sheep.

Others found the Grandfather Mountain area attractive as well. In 1885, Shepherd Monroe Dugger and his brother-in-law J. Erwin Calloway opened the Grandfather Hotel, "a white house nestling so near the evergreens that the sweet odor of the balsams is wafted through the doors." Located near Linville Gap, the hotel had a 30-by-30-foot room used for dances, and Dugger himself frequently guided groups up the rocky slopes of the mountain.

Samuel T. Kelsey came about the same time. Kelsey had founded the town of Highlands and was hoping to repeat the successful venture in the Linville Valley. In 1887, Kelsey shared with Lenoir his ideas regarding a town, and by 1888, he had acquired options on most of Lenoir's land. At some point, Kelsey, undoubtedly looking for investors, talked with Donald MacRae of Wilmington. It was the habit of the MacRae family to vacation at Cloudland, found on top of Roan Mountain, and at the Cranberry Hotel. Donald's son Hugh MacRae, a graduate of the Massachusetts Institute of Technology, was working at various local mica mines and explored the area on behalf of his father. In 1888, the Linville Land, Manufacturing, and Mining Company was formed, with Donald MacRae as president and Kelsey as vice president and general manager. Soon thereafter, Hugh MacRae replaced his father as president. The name of the company was changed in 1889 to the Linville Improvement Company.

To generate income, the Linville Improvement Company set up a sawmill. However, to be successful, the lumber mill needed a railroad. In 1890, Hugh MacRae proposed the Cranberry & Linville Railroad to the owners of the East Tennessee & Western North Carolina Railroad. They declined. With no rail connection, the company, trying to also develop the new town of Linville, chose to build a road instead. Alexander MacRae was hired to supervise construction of the new road, which was 18 miles long and from 12 to 14 feet wide. The new road was named the Yonahlossee Turnpike, supposedly an Indian word meaning "passing bear" or "bear trail." Many locals were hired to construct the road. Joe Hartley recalled, "It was really something to build. Through as rough and rugged a country as you'll ever find any place. All hand work. Mattocks and shovels, and axes and saws." The new road was a toll road, connecting Linville with the resort town of Blowing Rock on the Watauga-Caldwell County border.

In 1891, the Linville Improvement Company sponsored a contest to produce the best novel featuring Grandfather Mountain. The winner of the $1,000 cash prize was Maude Writtenhouse of Illinois. However, her book was never published. Another contestant was Shepherd Dugger, co-owner of the Grandfather Hotel. With a loan from the company, his manuscript, *The Balsam Groves of Grandfather Mountain*, was published.

A local rail connection did not arrive until 1915. In 1899, the Linville River Railway was incorporated. The narrow-gauge line ran from Cranberry to Pineola. The Cranberry Iron and Coal Company in 1913, a company that also owned the East Tennessee & Western North Carolina Railroad, acquired the Linville River Railway. Once the acquisition was complete, work began to extend the line through Montezuma, Linville, and Linville Gap and on into the Shull's Mill area of Watauga County. On reaching the Linville area, the Linville Improvement Company operated its own logging line to its property. The massive trees that had found refuge under the watchful eye of Grandfather Mountain for centuries were quickly harvested and shipped out via the railroad. Most of the lumber left the area. A few pieces were turned into furniture at a shop operated by Columbus "Lum" Hughes in Linville, while the bark of many of the harvested chestnut trees was used for siding in the Linville community.

A Congressional act created the Pisgah National Forest in 1916. In June 1917, there was talk of Hugh MacRae donating the Grandfather Mountain property to become the 18th national park. The idea was eventually rejected when National Park Service director Steve Mather judged the acreage, some 1,400 acres, not enough to protect from adjacent development by the Linville Improvement Company.

Discussion again came in 1924 regarding Grandfather Mountain as a potential national park. While there was much public support over the proposal, the Smoky Mountains were selected instead. As in the Smokies, widespread logging had denuded much of the forest in the area. The loggers left the tops and limbs of the trees behind, creating fire hazards. Just such a fire broke out in the summer of 1925. An estimated $1 million of timber was lost. By the mid-1930s, the area was barren of trees.

In the early 1930s, the Linville Improvement Company widened a horse path up the mountain and constructed Cliffsides, a wooden observation platform. Visitors could pay a small toll to drive up and park to enjoy the view.

Talks continued about the state or the federal government acquiring Grandfather Mountain. In the mid-1930s, work began on the Blue Ridge Parkway, a 469-mile road that connected the Shenandoah National Park in Virginia with the Great Smoky Mountains National Park in North Carolina. In 1939, the Linville Improvement Company worked out a deal, selling a large portion of property bordering the Yonahlossee Road. In 1941, the National Park Service drew up a plan for an 8,000-acre recreation area at Grandfather Mountain, and in 1942, Nelson MacRae put the property up for sale. But the deal never happened. In 1952, the Linville Improvement Company dissolved, and Hugh Morton became the sole owner of Grandfather Mountain.

Morton was a World War II veteran and avid photographer. Quickly, he widened the road to the top of the mountain and constructed the Mile-High Swinging Bridge. Over the next six decades, Morton worked tirelessly to promote and protect the mountain, building a visitor center in 1961 and an animal habitat facility in 1973. In 1989, Morton began working with the North Carolina Chapter of The Nature Conservancy to preserve 1,460 acres of wilderness backcountry. In 1992, the United Nations Educational, Scientific, and Cultural Organization (UNESCO) selected Grandfather Mountain as an international biosphere reserve. Morton also wrangled for decades with the National Park Service regarding the route of the Blue Ridge Parkway. The National Park Service wanted a route higher up on Grandfather Mountain. Eventually, they agreed to the middle route advocated by Morton, and in 1984, an engineering marvel, the Linn Cove Viaduct, completed the Blue Ridge Parkway. Hugh Morton, the "guardian of Grandfather Mountain," passed away in 2006, leaving behind a legacy born of his passion for the mountain.

In September 2008, the heirs of Morton announced that they were selling a large portion of the backcountry of Grandfather Mountain, some 2,456 acres, to the State of North Carolina, while at the same time, establishing the Grandfather Mountain Stewardship Foundation to manage the ever-popular attraction. The general assembly authorized the Grandfather Mountain State Park in 2009. With property already under the care of The Nature Conservancy, this brought the total area to almost 4,000 acres. Walter Lenoir's dream was finally realized—Grandfather Mountain was preserved as a park.

Today, tourists can still visit the Mile-High Swinging Bridge and the Mildred the Bear Animal Habitat, while hikers and naturalists have access to some of the most rugged and beautiful trails in Western North Carolina. Many of these visitors have chosen to commemorate their visits with photographs, including those that tell the story of Grandfather Mountain.

One

First Photographs

For the better part of a millennium, Grandfather Mountain has captivated the attention of travelers. Hundreds of years ago, those travelers were Native Americans, who left artifacts in the Indian House Cave. Then came the long hunters, like Daniel Boone. These men were followed by settlers, who, in turn, led naturalists, botanists, and conservationists, like André Michaux, Asa Gray, and John Muir, up the rocky slopes of the old mountain. The identity of the first person to set up a camera to capture the majestic and stately Grandfather Mountain is unknown. Frank W. Bicknel took some of the earliest known photographs in 1909, a little over a century ago. Some of his photographs are included in this chapter. Other photographers followed in Bicknel's footsteps, planting the legs of their camera tripods on some of the oldest rocks in the western hemisphere. Some of these old photographs were turned into early linen postcards, which were then sold to members of the public visiting one of the great wonders of North Carolina. These postcards could be used to show others what they were missing. Of course, continual improvements in technology brought cameras into the hands of the general public, and today, thousands of people take thousands of photographs of Grandfather Mountain. Yet one photographer stands above the others. Grandfather Mountain owner Hugh Morton was a passionate photographer during his life, taking hundreds of thousands of photographs, not only of his beloved Grandfather Mountain, but also of sporting events, politicians, battleships, and the events of everyday life. His photographs were donated to the North Carolina Collection at the University of North Carolina at Chapel Hill. There are an estimated 500,000 transparencies, photographs, and negatives, along with 60,000 linear feet of motion picture films. People continue to visit Grandfather Mountain with cameras in hand, and as their lives intertwine with the ancient rocks, wind-worn trees, and native animals, those pieces of time are captured at just 1/60th of a second.

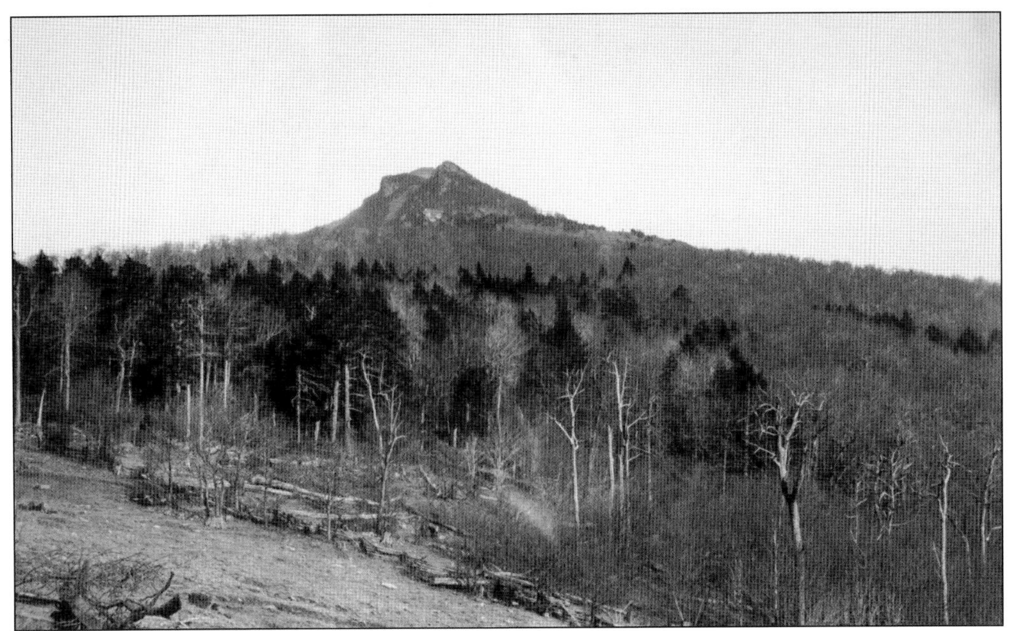

The following note was paired with this Frank Bicknell photograph: "Grandfather Mountain from road beyond Linville Jan 27, 1909." Bicknell lived in a cabin in the Linville Falls area and took numerous photographs of the high country of Western North Carolina. This early photograph shows Grandfather Mountain before it was clear-cut of its virgin timber. (Courtesy of North Carolina State Archives.)

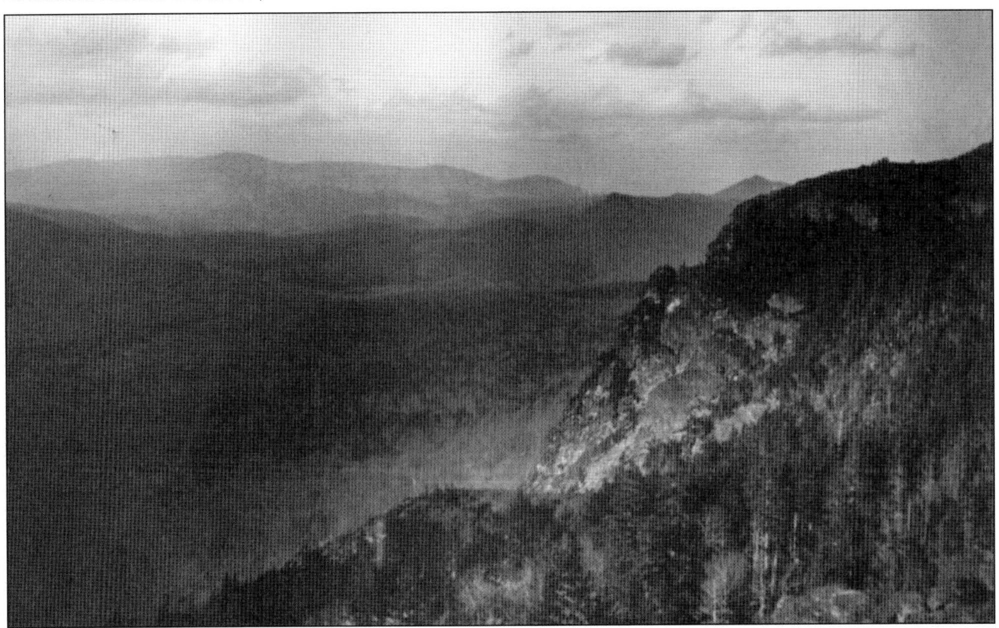

According to his notes, Frank Bicknell scaled the rocky precipice of Grandfather Mountain on January 27, 1909, to capture this image looking back into Watauga County, which was no mean feat considering the terrain and the time of year. The Bicknell family is one of the oldest families in the United States; Frank was born in Iowa in 1866 and moved to Linville Falls in 1908. (Courtesy of North Carolina State Archives.)

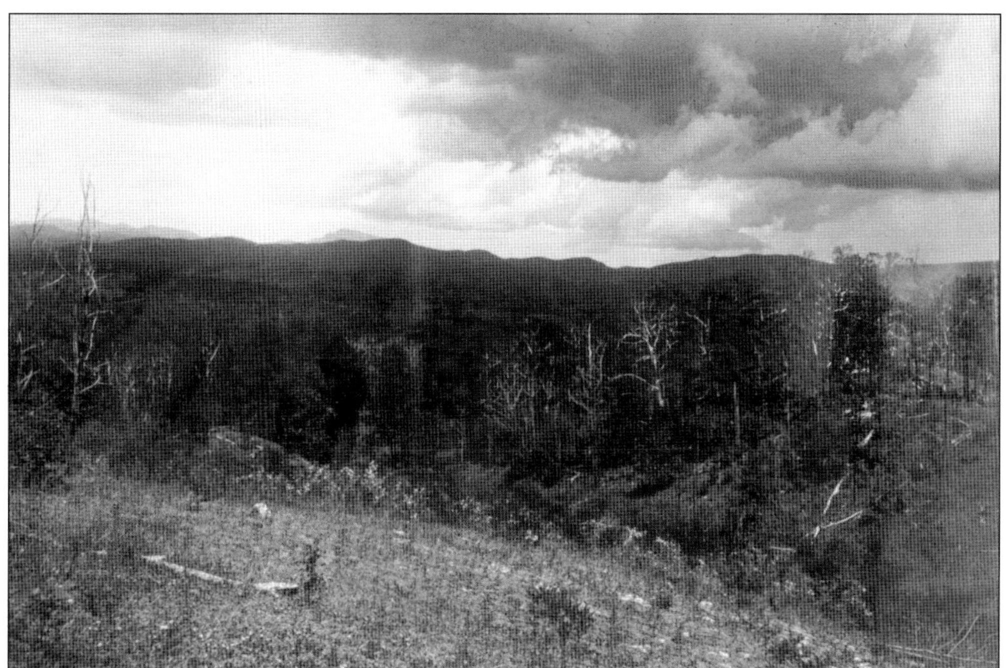

Frank Bicknell's wife, Jessie Vaupel, had an older sister, Katie, who married Frederick Hossfeld, a German immigrant who purchased Linville Falls. The visiting Bicknells fell in love with the mountains and moved to the area. Frank Bicknell took this photograph "from above Burleson's" on May 15, 1908, and the photograph's title is "The Blue Ridge Just Before a Storm." Grandfather Mountain is in the center of the photograph. (Courtesy of North Carolina State Archives.)

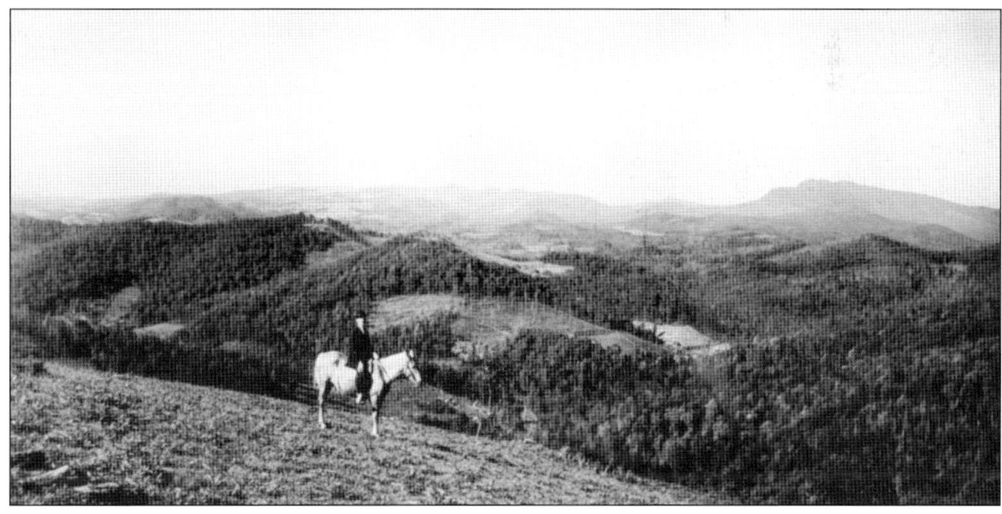

F.W. "Frank" Bicknell's caption for this photograph reads, "From the Jonas Ridge bald ground above Salem Franklin's 4,400 Ft., looking toward Grandfather Mu. 5964 ft., Sept 24, 1916 A. D. E." Appalachian balds are mountain summits or crests devoid of trees and often covered by native grasses or shrubs. Their unusual deforestation often led to legends among native tribes like the Cherokee. (Courtesy of North Carolina State Archives.)

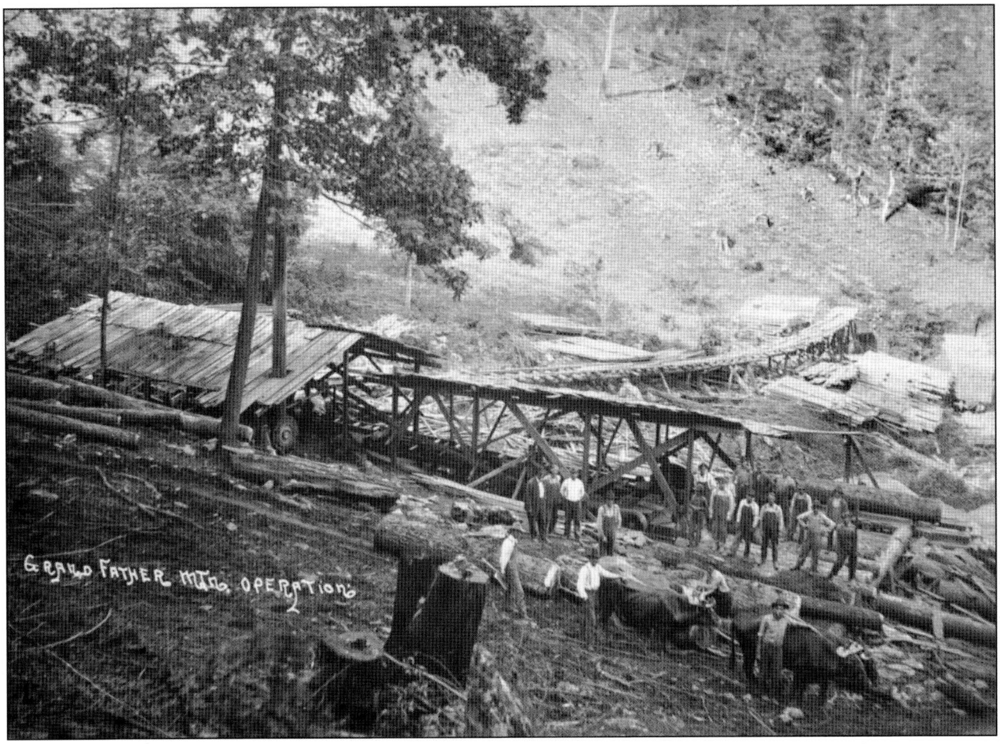

Lumber was a booming business around Grandfather Mountain during the early 20th century. Prior to the arrival of the railroad, the cut lumber was transported via wagon. One of the improvements Hugh MacRae made was his own narrow-gauge line connecting with the Linville River Railway in Linville. Once this was in place, large-scale clear-cutting stripped the mountain of much of its old-growth timber. (Courtesy of Historic Boone Collection.)

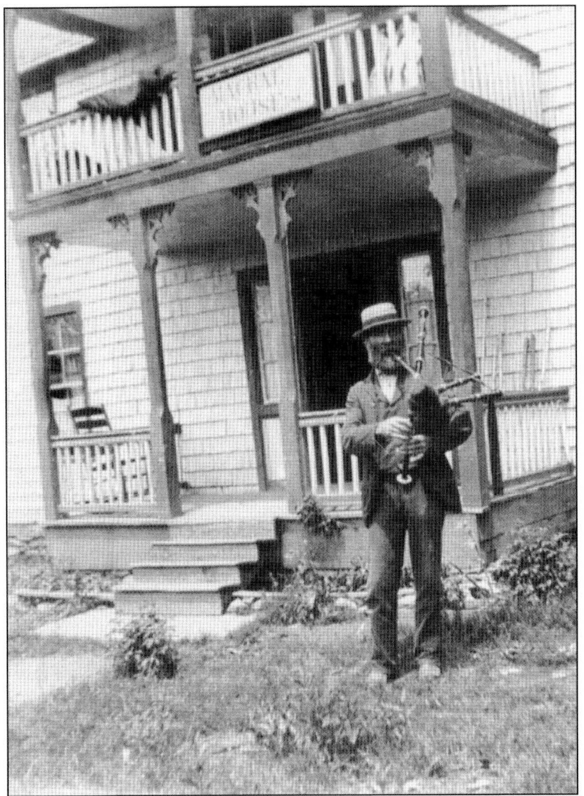

Alexander MacRae could often be heard playing his bagpipes for people passing along the Yonahlossee Road. MacRae had originally come from Scotland to work as a shepherd for Capt. Walter W. Lenoir. He later supervised the construction of the road and also ran a boardinghouse at the edge of the field that now bears his name, MacRae Meadows. (Courtesy of Grandfather Mountain Highland Games.)

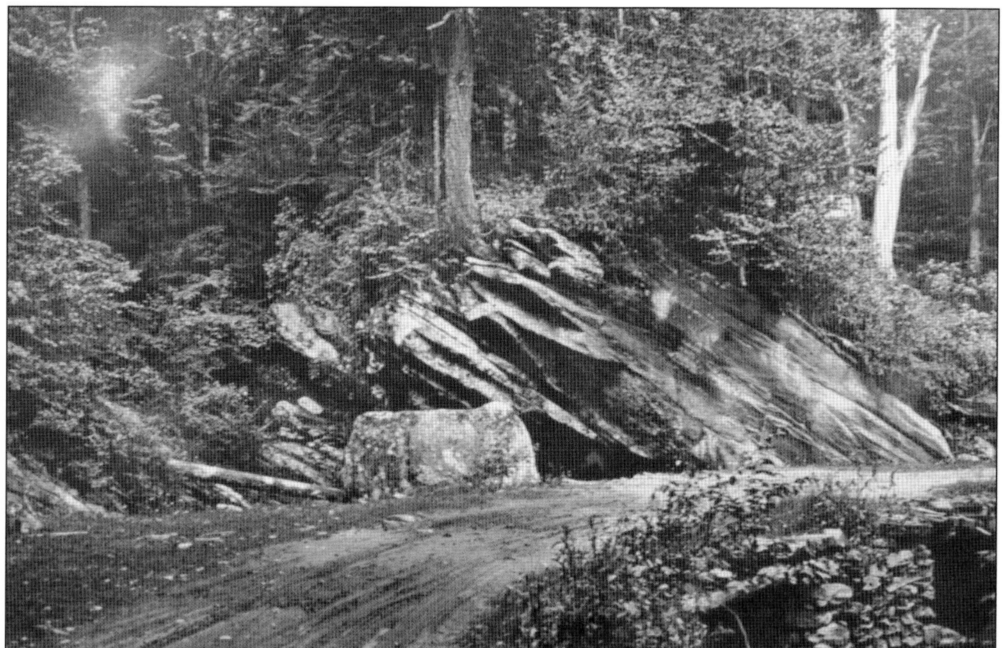

Workmen constructed the bridge over Wilson Creek on the Yonahlossee Road; they first laid down wooden beams and then installed stone supports. The Yonahlossee Road was a toll road between Blowing Rock and Linville. Supervised by Alexander MacRae, the project employed a workforce of local citizens and was completed in 1891. (Courtesy of Lees-McRae College.)

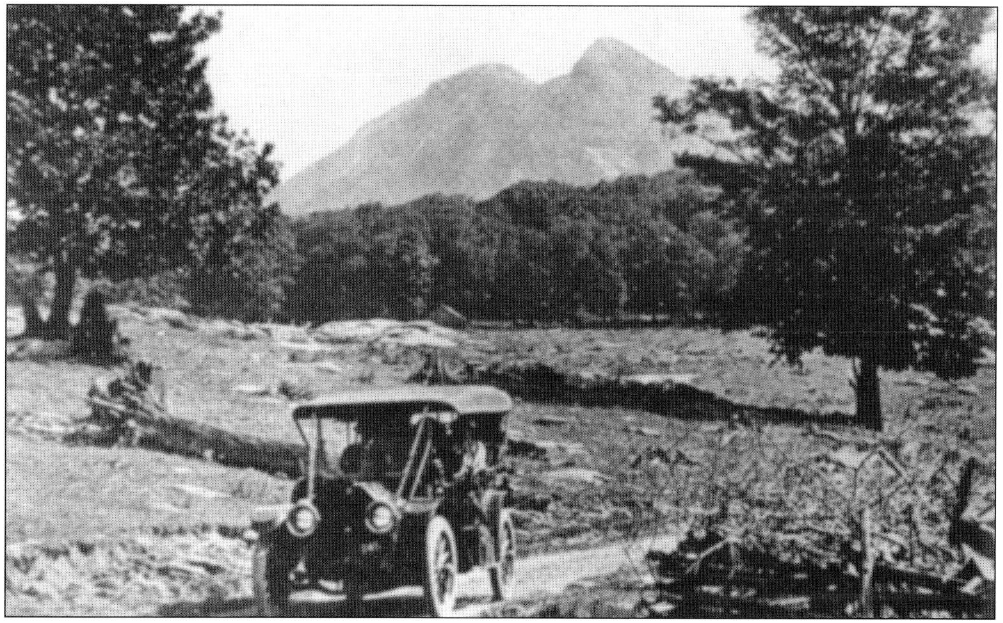

As soon as roads were passable, automobiles started to make their way up the Yonahlossee Road, often coming by way of Lenoir in Caldwell County and Blowing Rock in Watauga County. The road was originally constructed as a carriage road, moving tourists from the resorts in Blowing Rock to the new Eseeola resort in Linville. As people traveled along the route, they could visit Grandfather Mountain. (Courtesy of Library of Congress.)

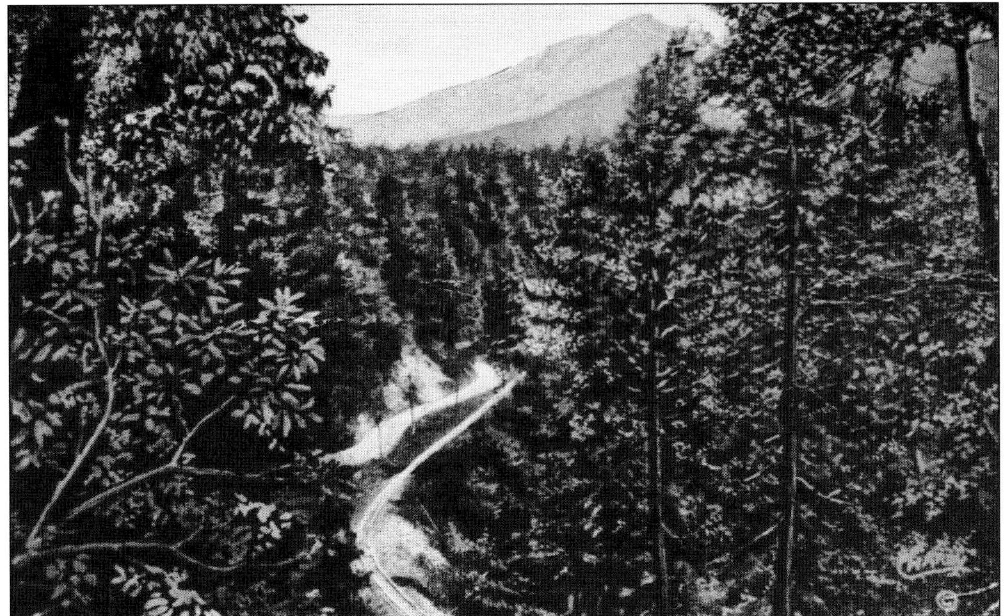

Upon leaving the depot in the community of Linville, the train chugged up the mountain to Linville Gap, now known as Tynecastle. Linville Gap, at 4,100 feet above sea level, was the highest point east of the Mississippi River to be served by a railroad. There was only a shelter, but the stop was the closest rail access for students attending present-day Lees-McRae College. (Courtesy of the Baird family.)

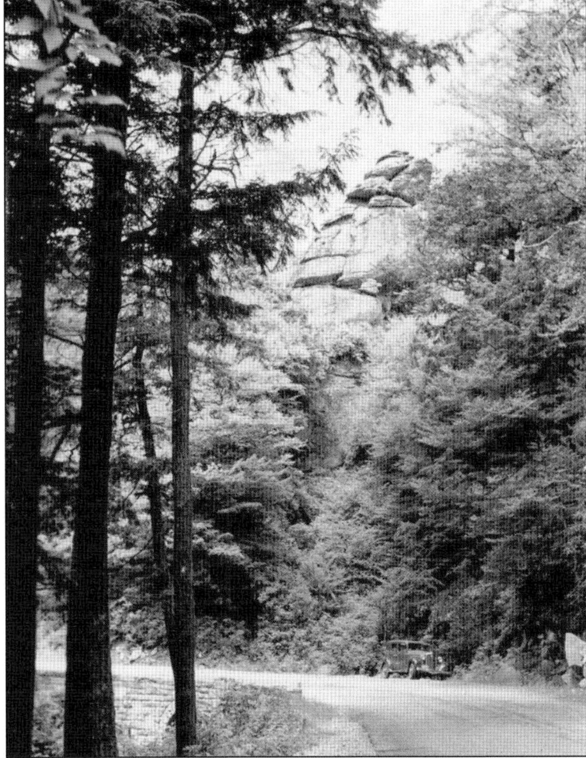

Often, rock formations were named for places or objects that they somewhat resembled, like Grandfather Mountain or the Sphinx Rock. Chimney Rock, along the Yonahlossee Road, brings to mind an old stone chimney of one of the many simple cabins that once were the primary local residences. (Courtesy of Blue Ridge Parkway.)

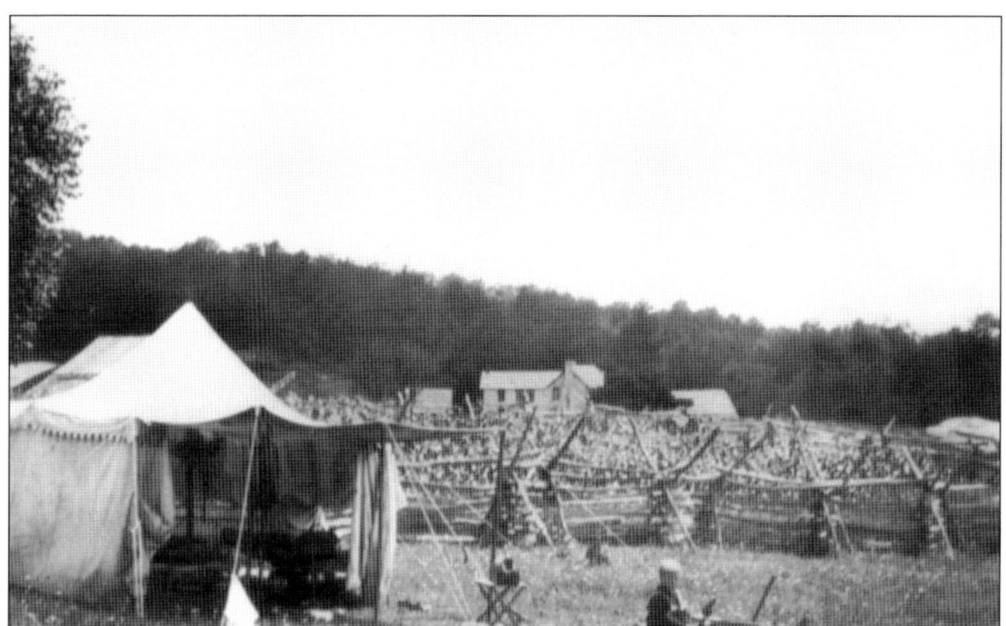

There has always been some controversy regarding the exact location of the home of Alexander MacRae. In this early photograph, MacRae's home, which also served as a popular inn for visitors, can be seen in the center of the image; a large rock outcropping is on the right. MacRae, a native of Scotland, often entertained his guests by playing the bagpipes. (Courtesy of Don MacRae.)

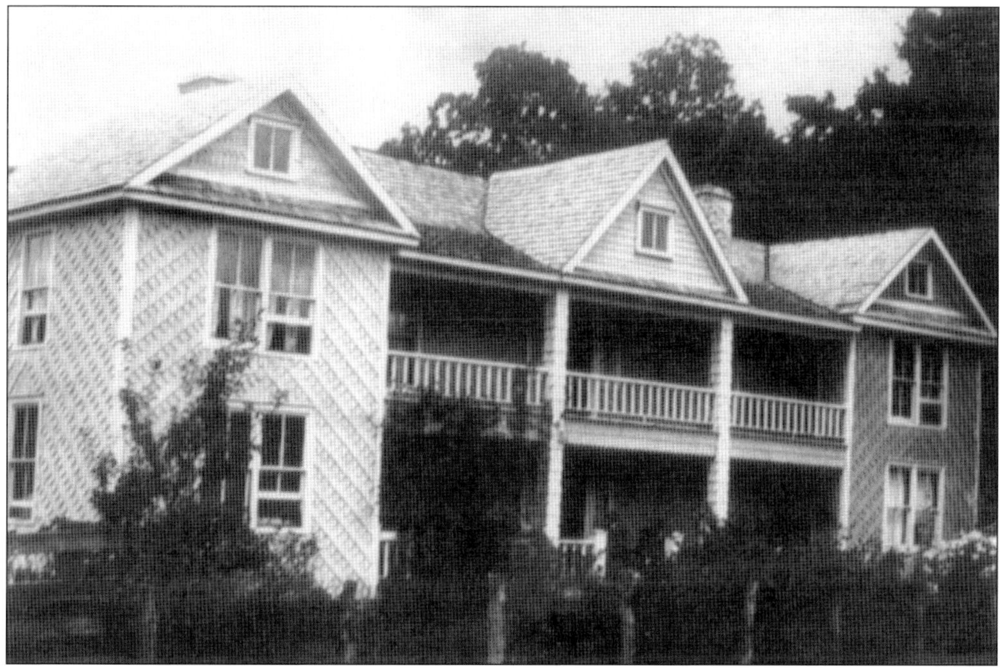

The MacRae House sat in what is today MacRae Meadows. The large inn accommodated travelers. Shepherd Dugger wrote that a visit to the McRae House was "the best substitute for a visit to Scotland." The house burned in 1932. (Courtesy of Don MacRae.)

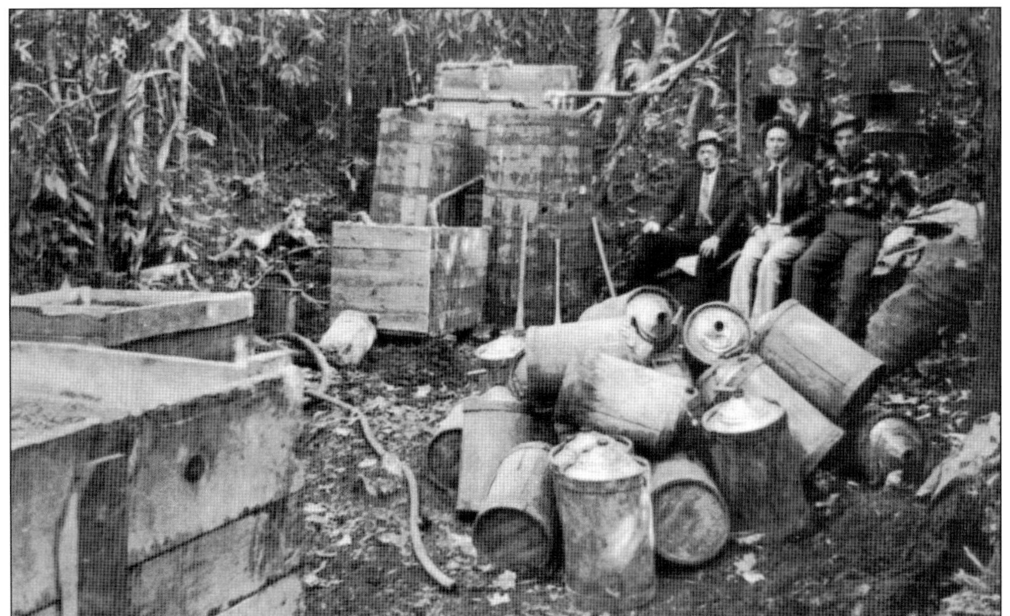

In the first half of the 20th century, raids on illegally manufactured and distributed liquor were frequent in the Western North Carolina mountains This 500-gallon capacity still was found on the eastern slopes of Grandfather Mountain in the mid-1950s. Pictured with the elaborate moonshining equipment are, from left to right, Sheriff Wilburn Hughes, Chief Deputy Stuart Buchanan, and Newland police chief Julian Greene. (Courtesy of Avery County Historical Museum.)

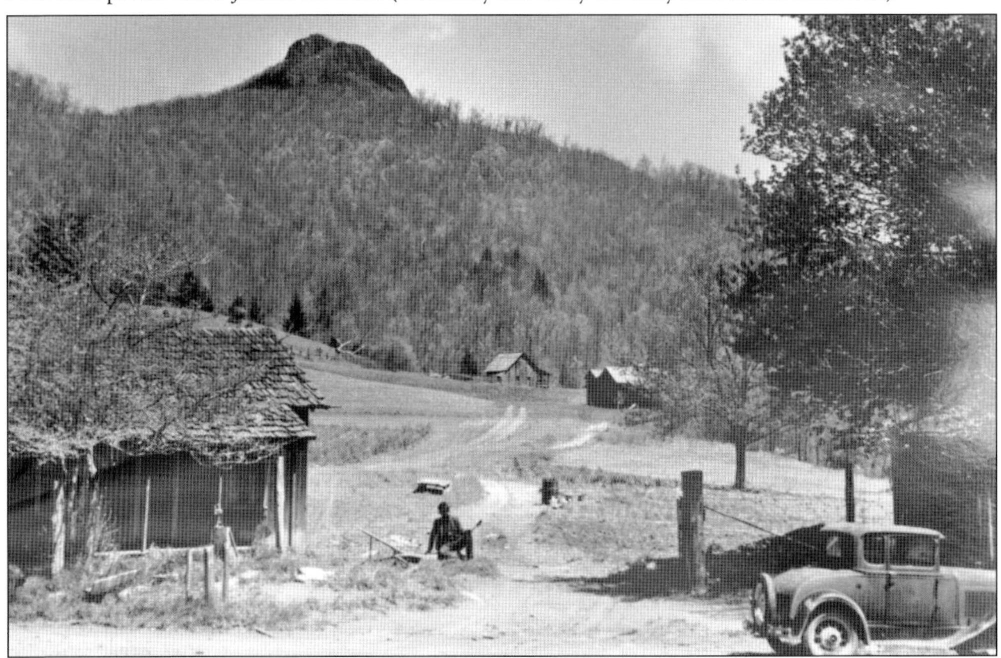

Before Grandfather Mountain State Park and before the Grandfather Mountain attraction, much of the property in and around Grandfather Mountain was farmland, like this simple mountain farm. Peak Mountain, located across Linville Gap from Grandfather Mountain, can be seen rising above the trees. (Courtesy of Lees-McRae College/Grandfather Mountain.)

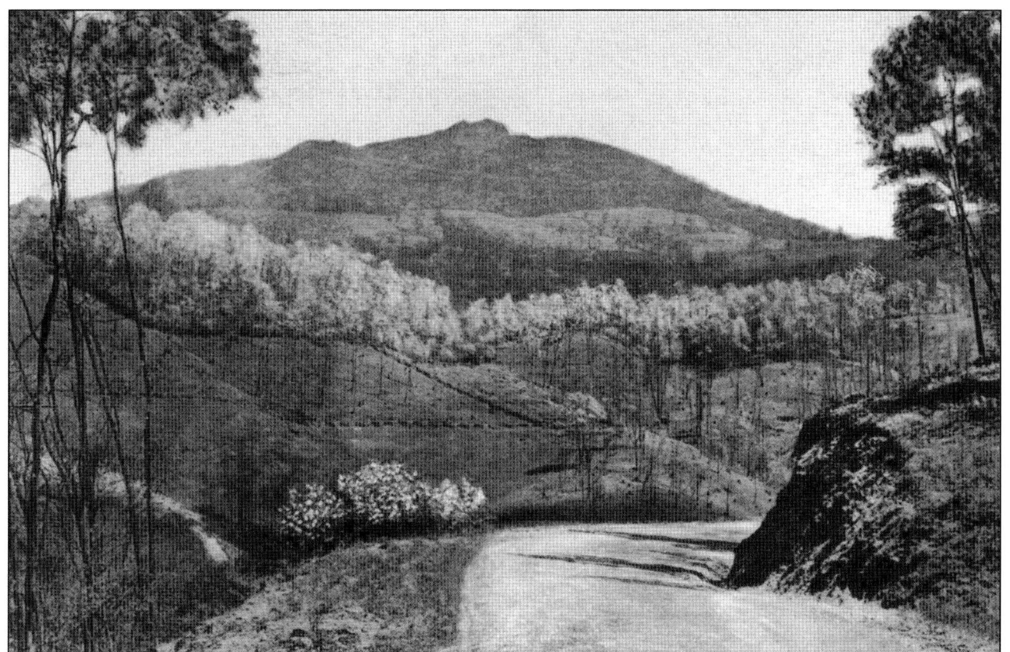

"No words can paint this first born of the southern mountains. To gaze upon him is to feel an awe that is new . . . about as far as the eye can reach, is a brilliant, vivid green but he has been tanned by the suns of a million years and all his tones are dark and gloomy," reported a visitor in the *Daily Journal* of Knoxville, Tennessee, on June 26, 1892. (Courtesy of Michael Hardy.)

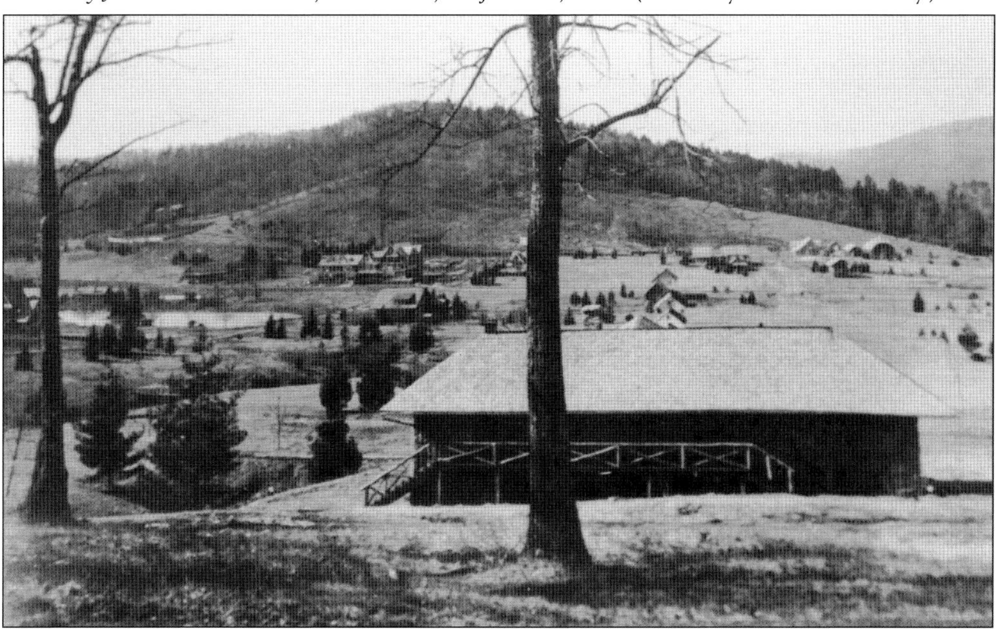

The town of Linville was first called Clay in 1883, then Porcelain in 1885, and finally Linville in 1888. Locally, it was known as Stumptown, testimony to the effects of logging. The offices for the Linville Improvement Company were located in the town. Representatives of Wedgewood once came to mine a train carload of clay from the area to be shipped to their factory in London. (Courtesy of Tense Banks.)

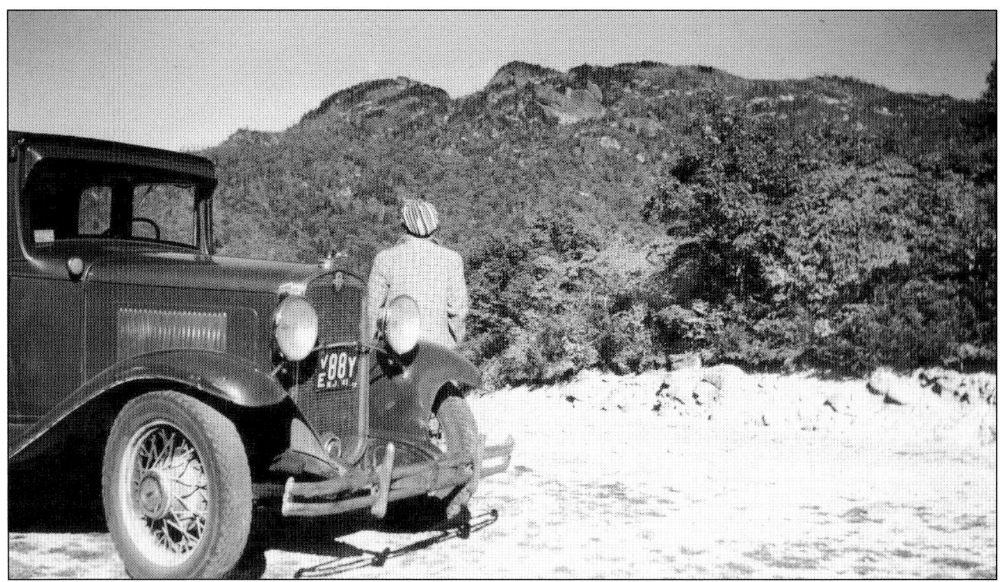

The advent of cheap automobiles provided travel opportunities to the masses. Prior to this point, only locals, or those wealthy enough to afford travel, visited Grandfather Mountain. Cheaper, mass-produced cars, along with better roads, opened the area to most Americans and began the long tradition of Grandfather as a popular tourist attraction. (Courtesy of Blue Ridge National Heritage Area.)

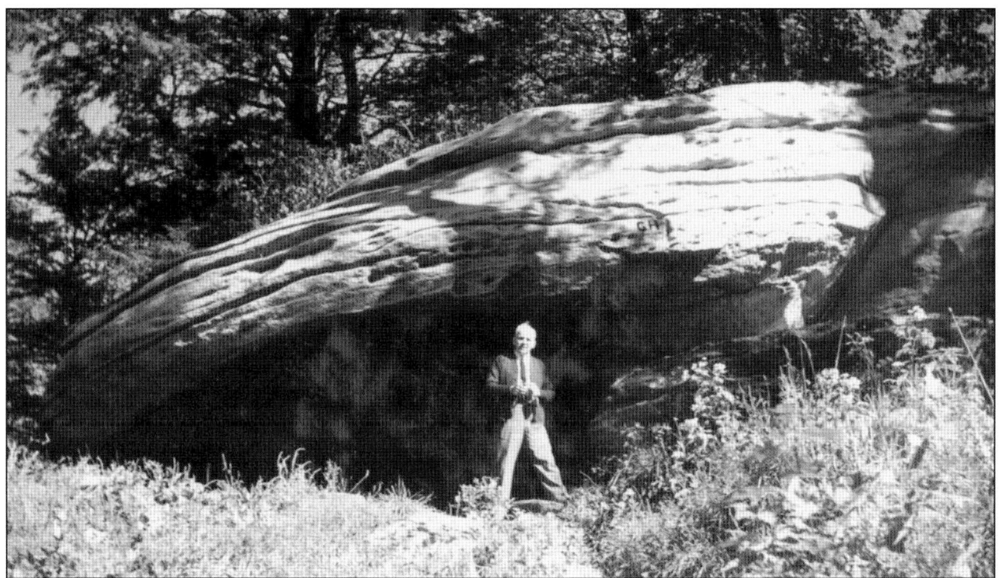

Paul Allen visited the Grandfather Mountain area in the early 1940s, and in this photograph, on the rock behind him, the initials of early visitors are visible. Though graffiti and other acts of vandalism are forbidden, one can still see evidence of visitors who have damaged the rocks and trees of Grandfather Mountain to "leave their mark." (Courtesy of Blue Ridge National Heritage Area.)

Two

Famous Faces of Grandfather Mountain

Numerous people have left their imprint upon Grandfather Mountain. Native Americans were first, followed by long hunters, settlers, and explorers. Some people have had a truly profound impact on the mountain's history. William B. Lenoir acquired larger portions of Grandfather Mountain prior to the Civil War. He died in 1861, and eventually, his brother Walter W. Lenoir purchased the property from his siblings. It was from Lenoir that Samuel T. Kelsey acquired the property prior to Lenoir's death. Kelsey formed a partnership with the MacRae family of Wilmington, North Carolina. When it dissolved, the property went to Hugh MacRae Morton, who owned Grandfather Mountain until his death in 2006. His heirs divided the property, selling a portion to the State of North Carolina for the creation of a state park, while the attraction that Morton created became a not-for-profit managed by the Grandfather Mountain Stewardship Foundation. Part of a much larger story are the many celebrities who have visited Grandfather Mountain, including North Carolina governors Melville Broughton, William Umstead, Luther Hodges, James Holshouser, Dan K. Moore, and Jim Hunt; US generals William Westmoreland and Matthew Ridgway; musicians Doc Watson, Roy Clark, Johnny Cash and June Carter Cash, Bascom Lamar Lunsford, Arthur Smith, George Hamilton IV, David Holt, and Scotty and Lulu Belle Wiseman; journalists Charles Kuralt and Aberlardo Raidi; politicians Newt Gingrich, Sam Ervin, Terry Sanford, Elizabeth Dole, James T. Broyhill, B. Everett Jordan, and John Edwards; athletes Tommy Burleson, Charlie "Choo Choo" Justice, Dale Earnhardt, and Mickey Mantle; pastors Billy Graham, Franklin Graham, Will Graham, Jerry Falwell, and Oral Roberts; and actors Bob Hope, Darby Hinton, and Fess Parker. Of course, tens of thousands visit the park every year. Though their names may not be household words, they are the people who have woven their lives into the fabric of Grandfather Mountain.

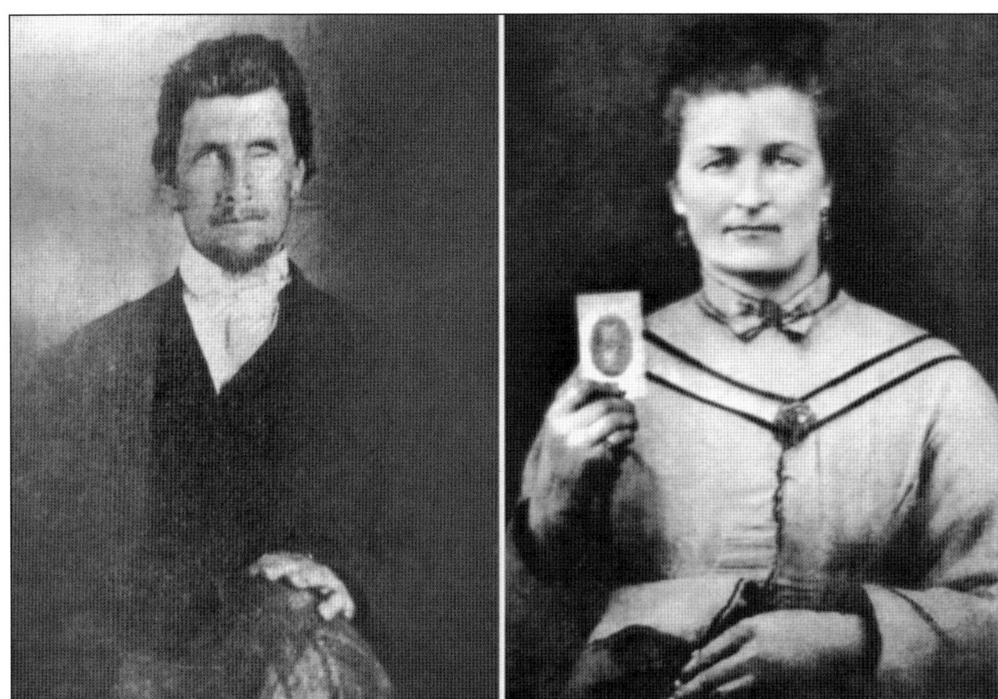

The notorious William M. "Keith" Blalock and his wife, Sara Malinda Pritchard Blalock, lived just north of Grandfather Mountain in 1860 in the Coffey Gap area of Watauga County. They were chased up Grandfather Mountain by Confederate conscription officers and were forced to hide in a hog pen on the mountain. Later, they guided escaped Federal prisoners of war through the area and to safety in east Tennessee. (Courtesy of Avery County Historical Museum.)

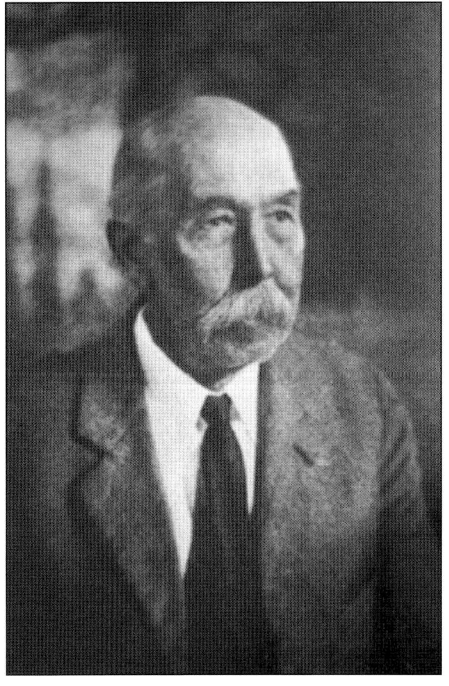

Shepherd Monroe Dugger not only operated a hotel on the side of Grandfather Mountain in the late 19th century, but he also wrote the first book about the mountain, *The Balsam Groves of the Grandfather Mountain* (1892). The book was the runner-up in a publicity contest sponsored by the Linville Improvement Company and has gone through five editions. (Courtesy of Avery County Historical Museum.)

On September 26, 1952, North Carolina gubernatorial nominee William B. Umstead spoke to the gathered crowd on the opening of the recently completed Mile-High Swinging Bridge. Umstead praised Hugh Morton on his many accomplishments, which included turning Grandfather Mountain into a successful business and his becoming a leader in the tourism industry in the Tar Heel State. (Courtesy of Patricia Combs.)

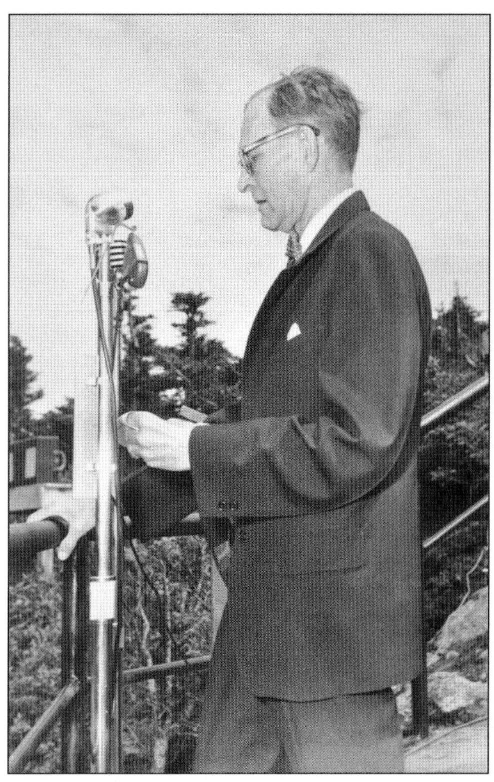

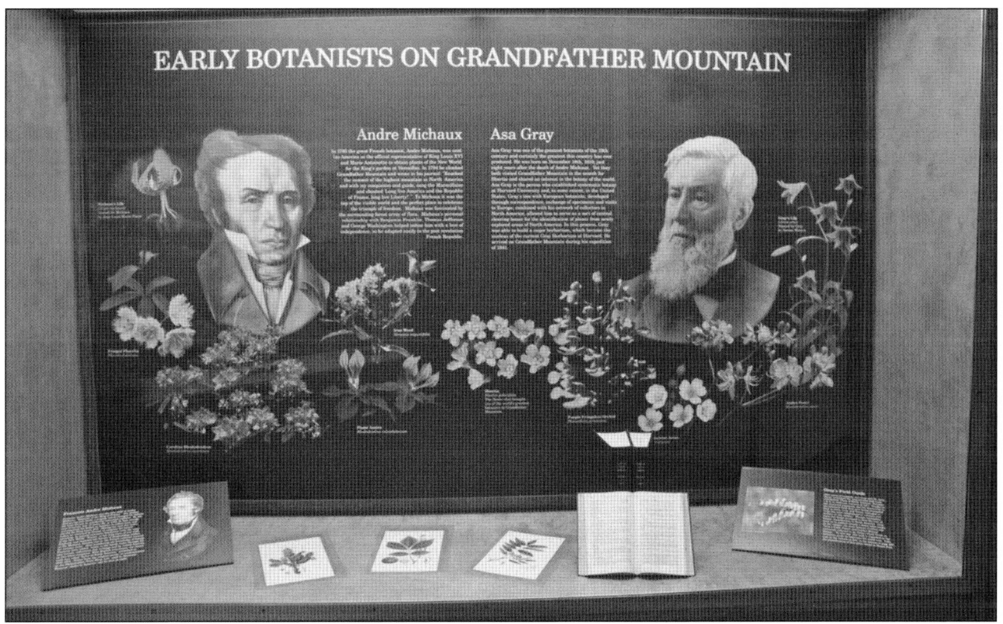

Asa Gray and André Michaux were just two of the many early naturalists and scientists who came to explore the diverse ecosystem of the Grandfather Mountain area. Countless professional and amateur botanists have since come to see Grandfather Mountain's unique plant life. The Nature Museum at the Grandfather Mountain attraction has an exhibit featuring Gray and Michaux. (Courtesy of Michael Hardy.)

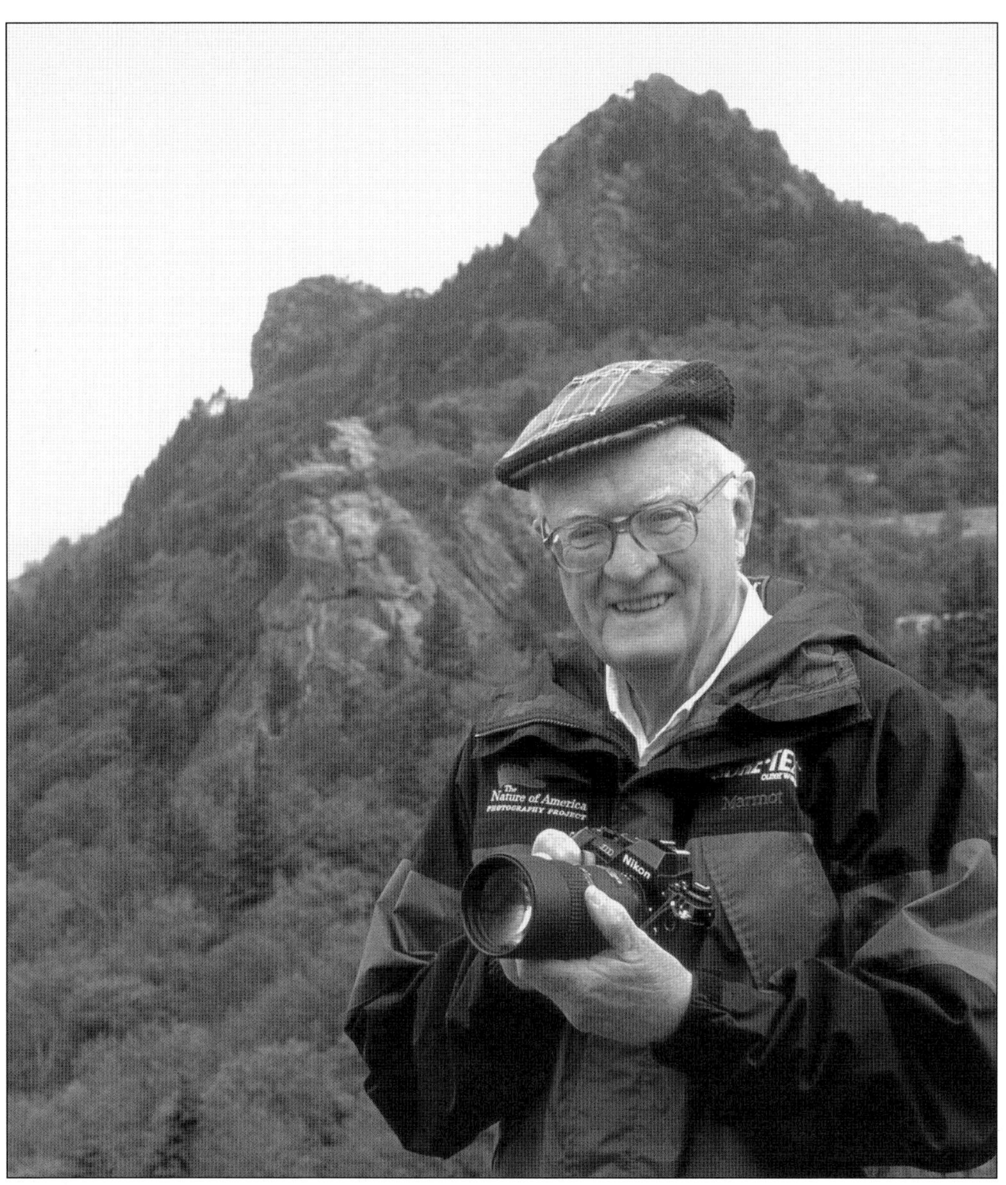

In 1968, the *Greensboro Record* referred to Hugh Morton as "Mr. Grandfather Mountain." It was just one of the many well-earned honorifics Hugh Morton proudly wore. Born in Wilmington in 1921, he was a University of North Carolina at Chapel Hill graduate and World War II veteran before inheriting the mountain in 1952 from his grandfather, Hugh McRae. Morton quickly extended the road to the top of the mountain and constructed the Mile-High Swinging Bridge. He went on to further develop seven native wildlife habitats, a nature museum, and a theater; he also donated conservation easements for over 3,000 acres of Grandfather Mountain to The Nature Conservancy. However, there was far more to Morton's distinguished life and career—he took over 500,000 photographs in his lifetime; saved a battleship, the USS *North Carolina*; and received seven honorary doctorates. Hugh Morton passed away in 2006. (Courtesy of Grandfather Mountain.)

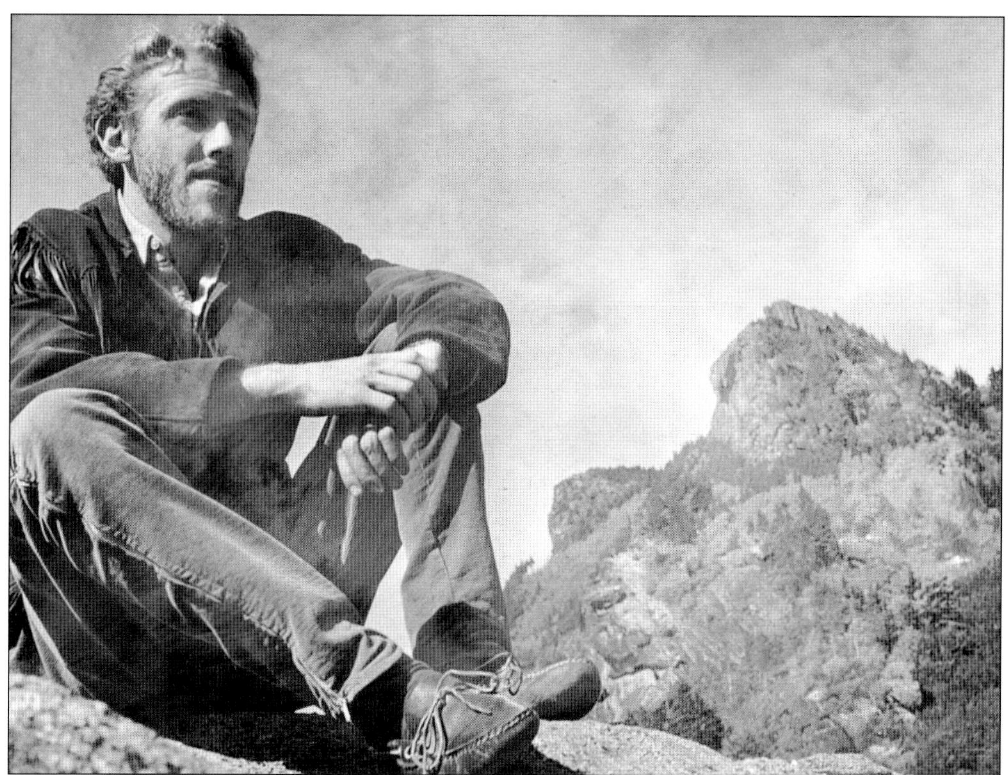

Ned Austin was the very first actor to play the role of Daniel Boone in the long-running *Horn in the West* outdoor stage production in Boone. He is pictured here with the towering peaks of Grandfather Mountain behind him. Tradition holds that the actual Daniel Boone explored Grandfather Mountain on one of his many hunting trips to the area. (Courtesy of Historic Boone Collection.)

The famed conservationist John Muir visited Grandfather Mountain and the surrounding area in September 1898. "I couldn't hold it in, and began to jump about and sing and glory in it all," stated Muir in an article in the *American Museum Journal* about his visit. Muir established the Sierra Club in 1892 for other environmentally minded citizens and outdoor enthusiasts. (Courtesy of Library of Congress.)

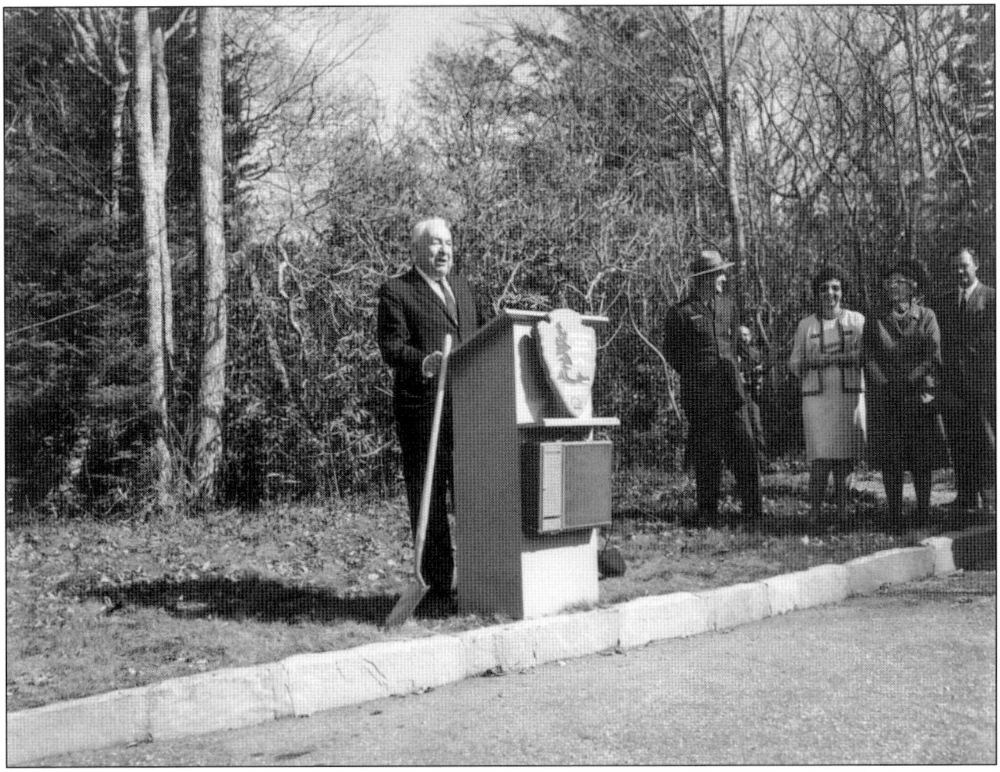

Sam Ervin spoke at Beacon Heights on October 22, 1968, in a ceremony marking the end of a heated debate regarding the completion of the Blue Ridge Parkway around Grandfather Mountain. Ervin, a World War I veteran, University of North Carolina at Chapel Hill graduate, lawyer, and judge, was serving as a US senator at the time of his speech. (Courtesy of Blue Ridge Parkway.)

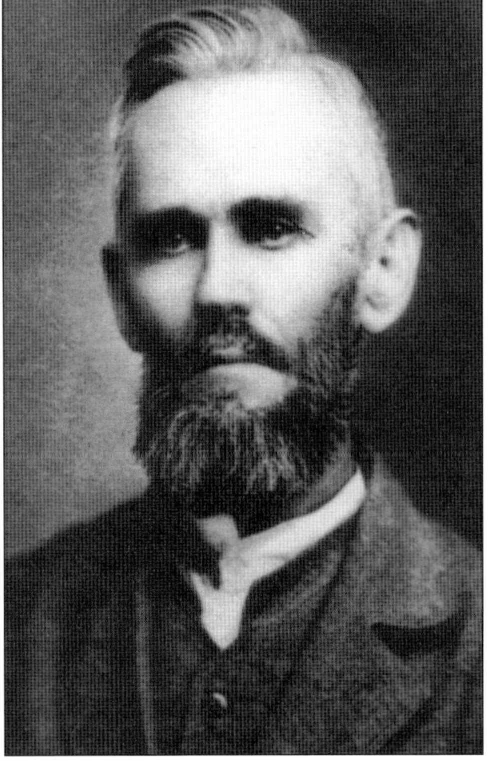

Caldwell County native Walter W. Lenoir had served in the Confederate army during the Civil War. In the 1860s, he began acquiring land on and around Grandfather Mountain. It was his desire to see the mountain become a park for others to enjoy. Lenoir sold his property to developer Samuel Kelsey in 1887. (Courtesy of Avery County Historical Museum.)

Legendary journalist Charles Kuralt once considered Mildred the Bear the second of three wonders of the world located in Avery County. The other two were also part of Grandfather Mountain: Hugh Morton and the Mile-High Swinging Bridge. Kuralt spoke on September 2, 1992, at the 40th anniversary of the opening of the Mile-High Swinging Bridge. (Courtesy of *Mountain Times*.)

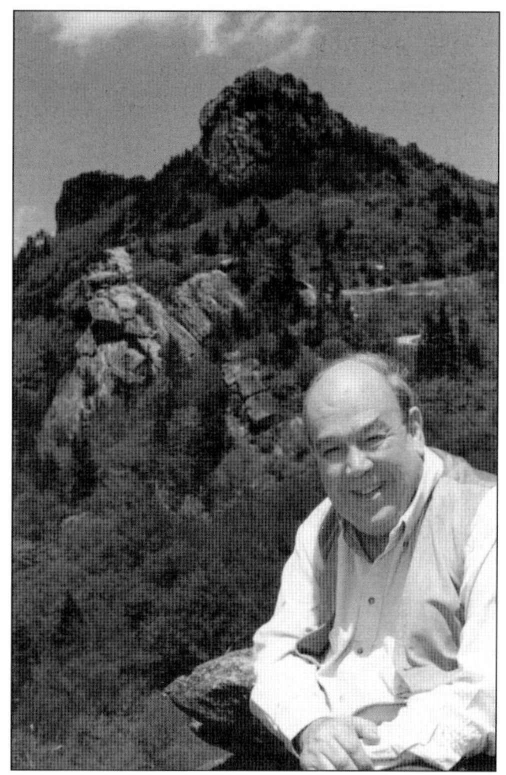

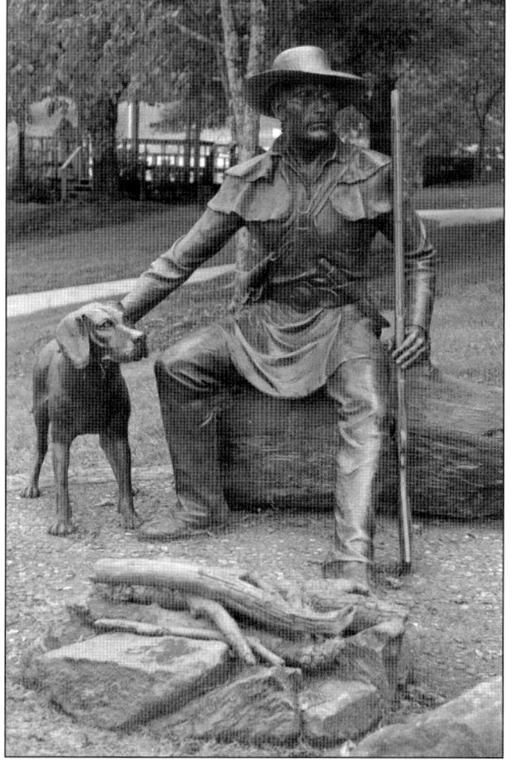

While Daniel Boone was not the first white man to explore the area in the 1700s, he was the most famous. He roamed the high country of Western North Carolina in the 1760s. Local tradition claims that he sometimes stayed in a cabin on Grandfather Mountain. This statue is in Boone, North Carolina, on the campus of Appalachian State University. (Courtesy of Michael Hardy.)

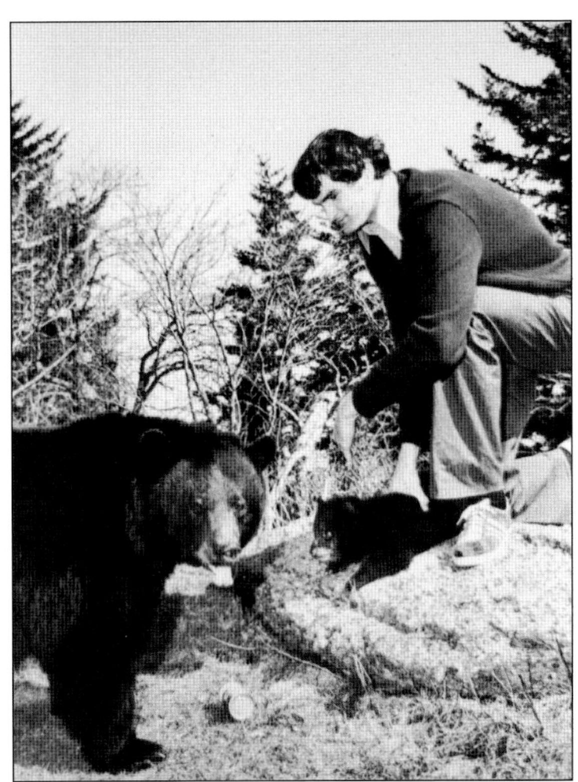

In 1973, basketball great Tommy Burleson returned to Avery County for Tommy Burleson Day. Growing up in Avery County, Burleson worked at Grandfather Mountain in the summers. He was an All-American center for North Carolina State University and went on to play for the United States in the 1972 Olympics. He was drafted in 1973 to play for the Seattle SuperSonics and played professionally until 1981. (Courtesy of Grandfather Mountain.)

On more than one occasion, nationally recognized music legends Lulu Belle and Scotty, the Hayloft Sweethearts, performed at events on Grandfather Mountain. Scotty had grown up in the area, and the couple met while performing on WLS in Chicago. After appearing on stage for many years and starring in several Hollywood movies, the couple retired to Avery County. (Courtesy of Avery County Historical Museum.)

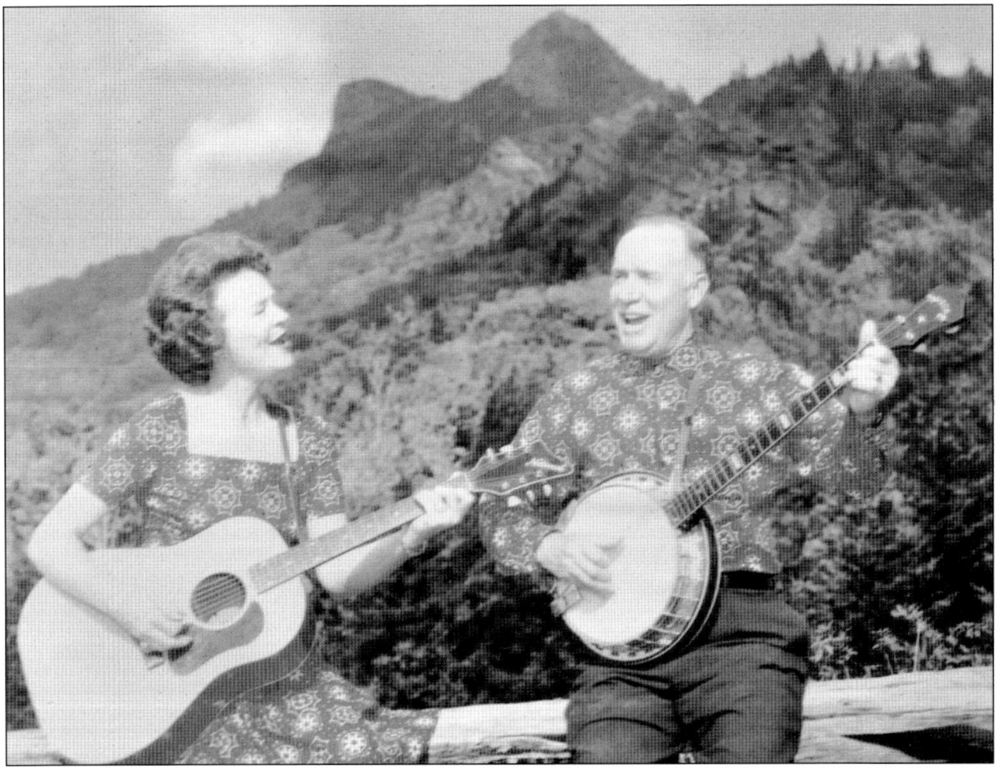

Three

Grandfather Mountain from Afar

Standing on the top of Linville Peak or hiking along the Grandfather Trail, visitors cannot see the profile of the sleeping grandfather from which the mountain draws its name. That view is only visible from Watauga County, looking toward the south. All other views of Grandfather Mountain show the rocky and otherwise inhospitable slopes of the mountain, with numerous peaks. Over the past 100 years, many people, both visitors and locals alike, have scouted numerous advantageous sites to photograph Grandfather Mountain. The Foscoe community in Watauga County and along the Profile Trail in Avery County are some of the best places to observe and photograph the profile. Other places to view the profile are from the parking lot of the Watauga campus of Caldwell Community College in Boone or from the top of Howard's Knob. The Blowing Rock community has several locations conducive to photographing the mountain. Visitors on Sugar or Beech Mountains in Avery County can photograph the entire mountain ridge, including all of the peaks that make up Grandfather Mountain area. Toward the south, the playground area located in front of the Cannon Memorial Hospital offers some great vantage points. And there are several other useful locations to the east, particularly coming up through the Pisgah National Forest from the Globe Community in Caldwell County. Most visitors can be found capturing images of Grandfather Mountain along the Blue Ridge Parkway. There are many sites from which to shoot snapshots or set up a tripod for more serious photographic work. These include along Old Johns River Road, the Flat Top Mountain Carriage Road at the Moses H. Cone Memorial Park, the Green Knob Trail, Price Lake Loop Trail, several places along the Tanawha Trail, Beacon Heights, and a mile farther south at the aptly named Grandfather Mountain overlook.

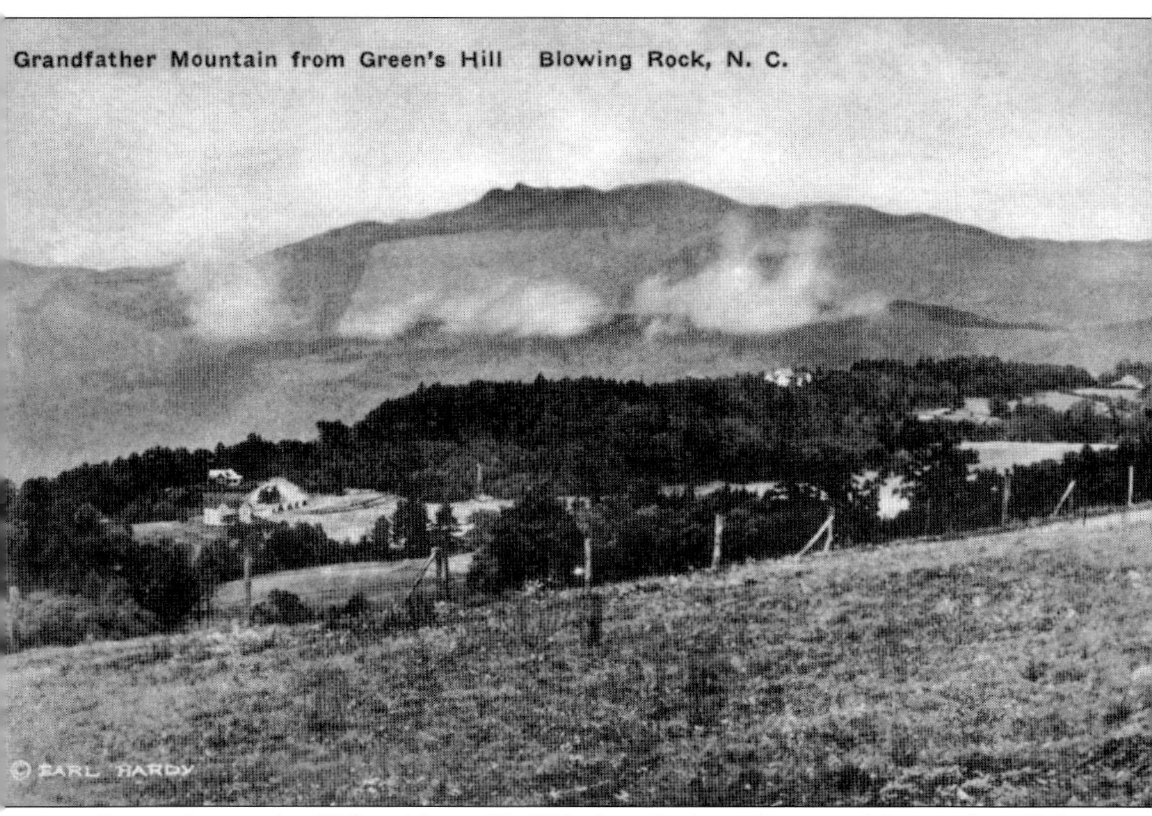

Lenoir photographer William Marion "Earl" Hardy made this early postcard showing Grandfather Mountain from Green's Hill, near Blowing Rock. Local people often photographed the mountain and surrounding countryside in order to sell the images to the numerous visitors who came to spend spring, summer, and fall in the high country of Western North Carolina. (Courtesy of Michael Hardy.)

The fodder shocks and pumpkins in this linen postcard serve as a reminder that the property around Grandfather Mountain was for many generations used as agricultural land. People farmed the valleys and riversides, trying to eke out a living with a short growing season and long winters. (Courtesy of Carl Dykes.)

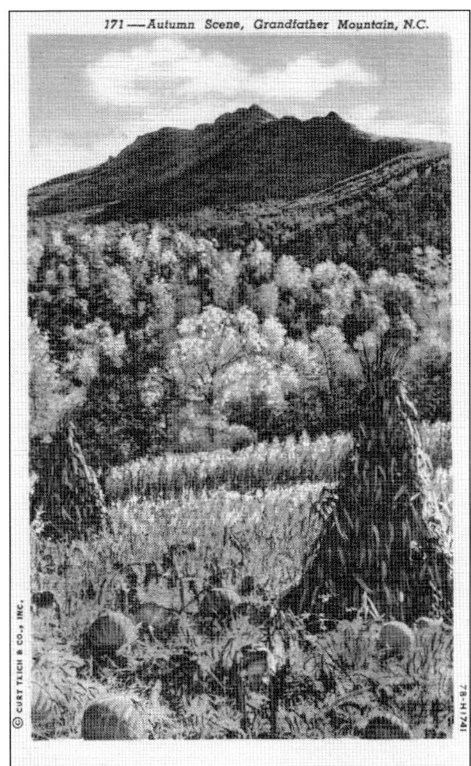

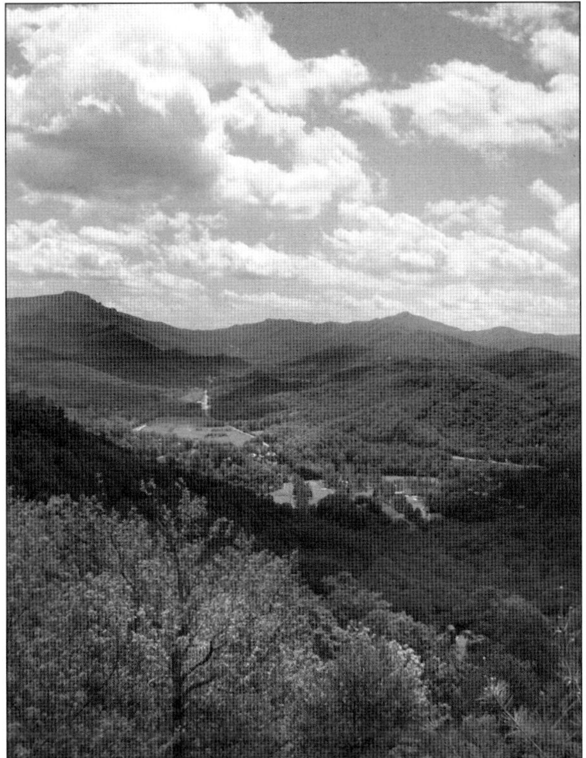

In 1964, the Hound Ears Golf and Ski Resort opened in the Shulls Mill area of Watauga County. George Cobb designed the golf course. The whole development was the brainchild of Harry and Grover Robbins, whose family had owned a hotel in Shulls Mill and was responsible for bringing Tweetsie Railroad to the area. This image was taken from Hound Ears Rock. (Courtesy of Kyle Grove.)

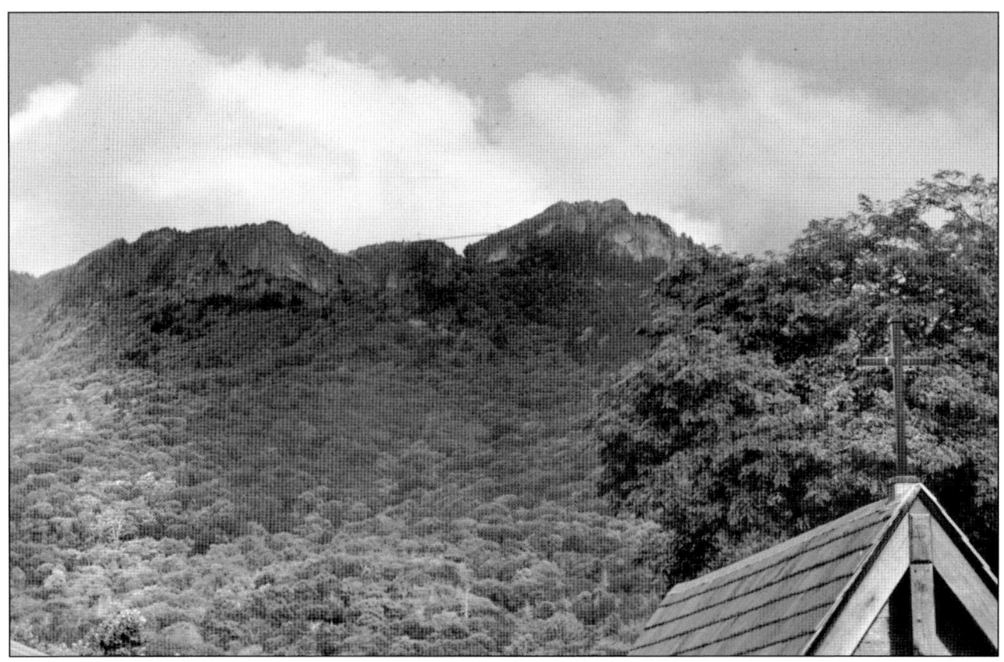

This photograph, taken from the St. Bernadette Roman Catholic Church in Linville, shows the Mile-High Swinging Bridge and several of the Grandfather Mountain peaks. A mission parish was established in 1940 in Linville, and St. Bernadette, which celebrated its first Mass on December 31, 1988, was an outgrowth of this mission. (Courtesy of Michael Hardy.)

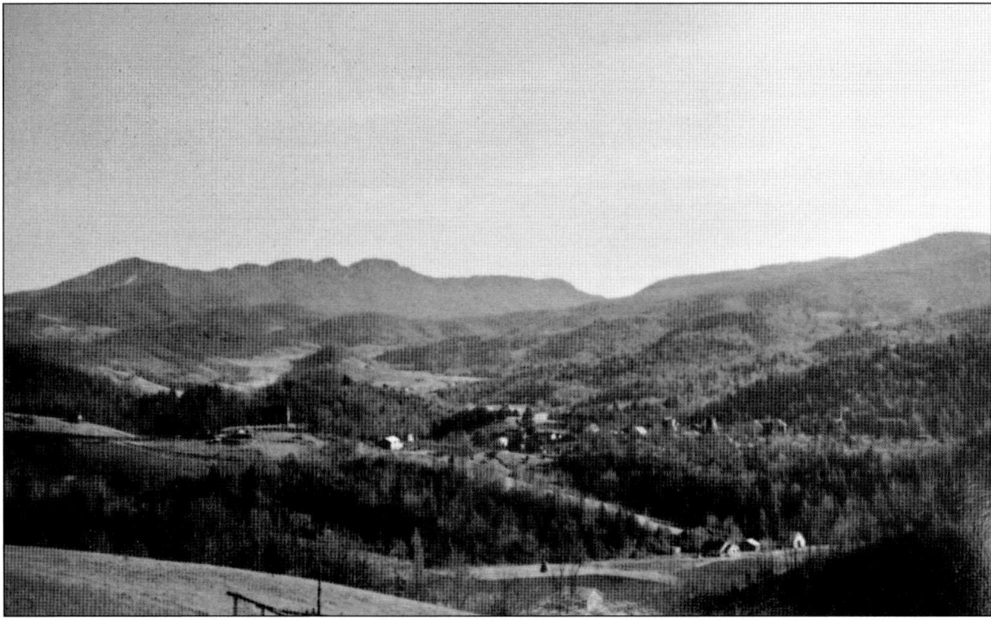

Grandfather Mountain is seen here as viewed from nearby Beech Mountain. None of the mountain's more distinctive features, like the face or the twin peaks, can be discerned from this perspective. Beech Mountain's elevation is 5,506 feet, while Grandfather Mountain is 5,945 feet above sea level. The ski slopes on Beech Mountain are a recent tourist attraction. (Courtesy of Lees-McRae College.)

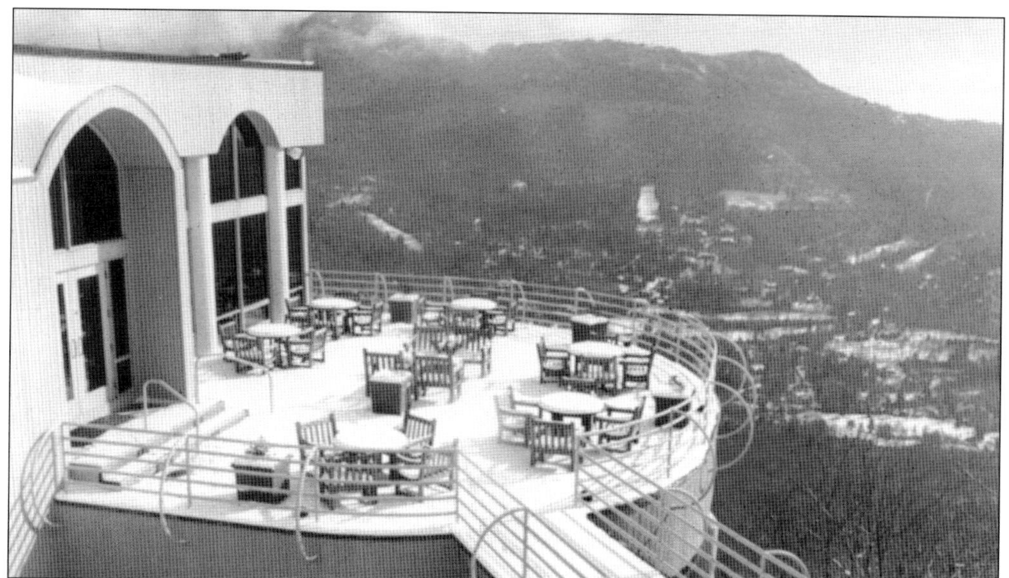

There are many spots in Western North Carolina from which one can obtain an excellent view of Grandfather Mountain. Some are secluded and remote while others offer grand, sweeping views of the entire mountain. One view can be found from the clubhouse at the Linville Ridge Development, opened in 1982. (Courtesy of Historic Boone Collection.)

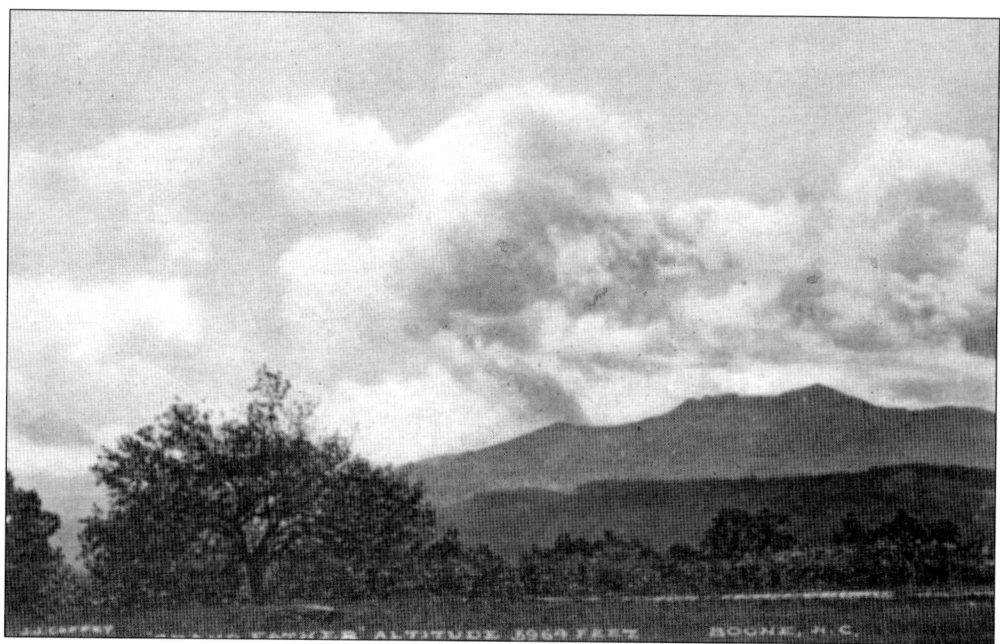

Many local photographers made Grandfather Mountain postcards. J.J. Coffey provided this photograph of Grandfather Mountain. Coffey also took photographs of Boone, the Appalachian Training School, and Blowing Rock. (Courtesy of Historic Boone Collection.)

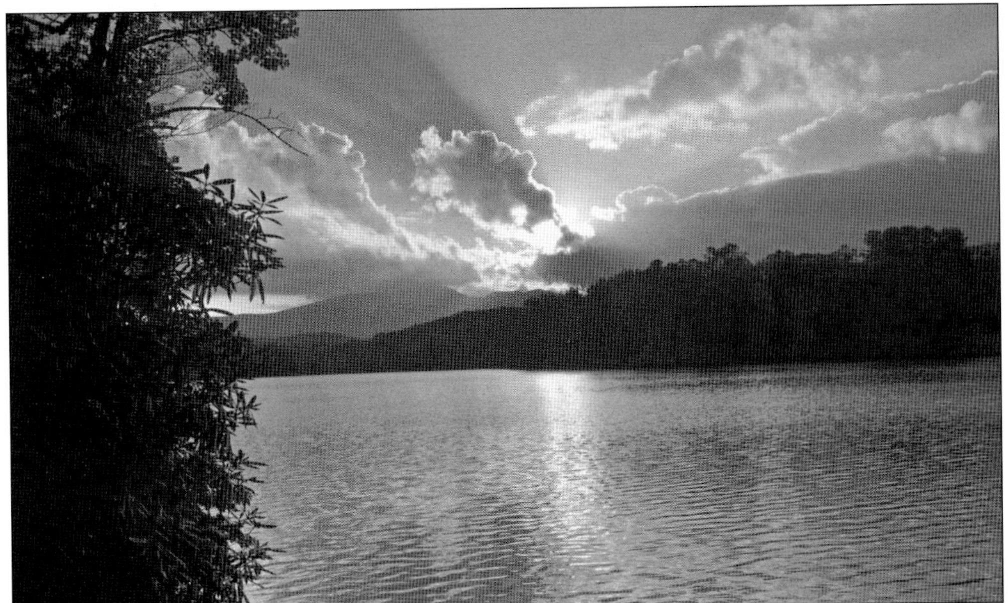

A great view of Grandfather Mountain can be found by looking across Price Lake. The lake is named in honor of Julian Price, an insurance executive who purchased the 4,300-acre area in the 1930s and 1940s to be used as a retreat for his employees. After Price's death, the property was donated to the Blue Ridge Parkway. (Courtesy of Michael Hardy.)

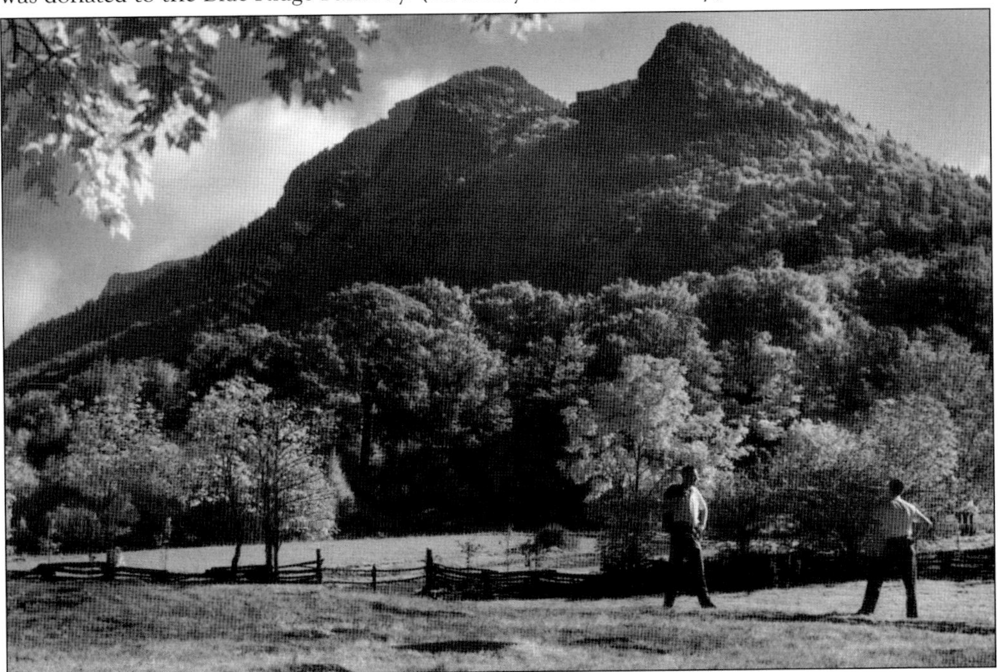

The peak on the right is Linville Peak. In 1766, William Linville, his son, and another man were hunting in the area when they were ambushed by a party of Indians. The two Linvilles were killed, but the other man, though wounded, escaped. A party from the Yadkin River valley came searching for their bodies, which supposedly lie buried near Linville Falls. (Courtesy of *Mountain Times*/Hugh Morton.)

Golfers at the Linville Golf Course had a fine view of Grandfather Mountain in this 1939 image. The first golf course in present-day Avery County opened in Linville in 1895. This original 14-hole course was replaced by a championship 18-hole course, designed by Donald Ross, in the 1920s. (Courtesy of North Carolina Department of Archives and History.)

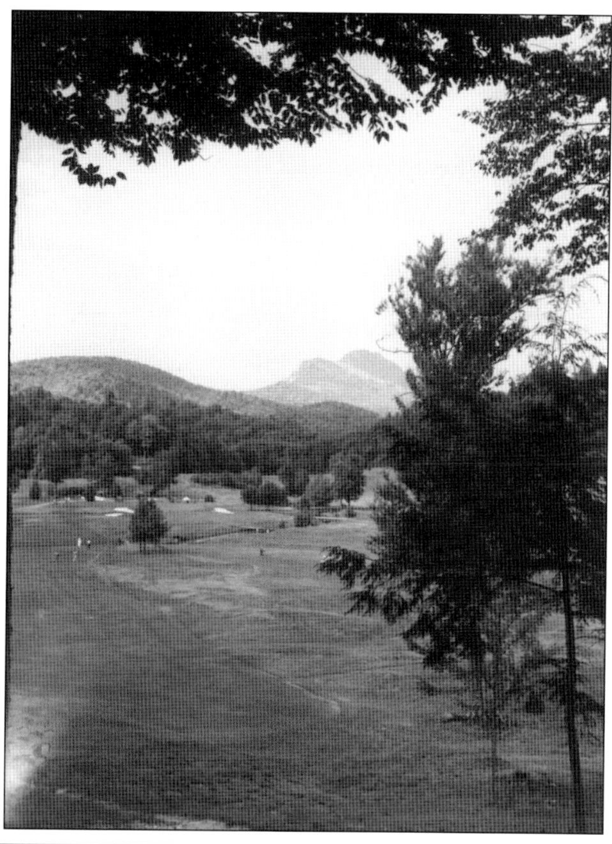

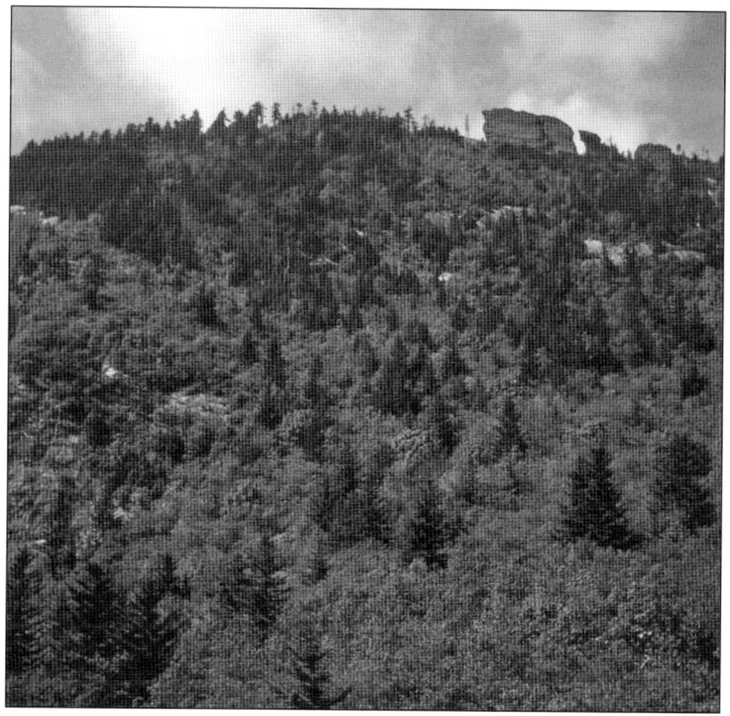

Many of the large rocks on Grandfather Mountain were pushed into place during the last ice age. However, when two geologists claimed that they had found grooves on Grandfather that supported claims of local ice age glacial movement, it was discovered that 20th-century logging chains had left the marks. (Courtesy of Floyd Hayes Photograph Collection.)

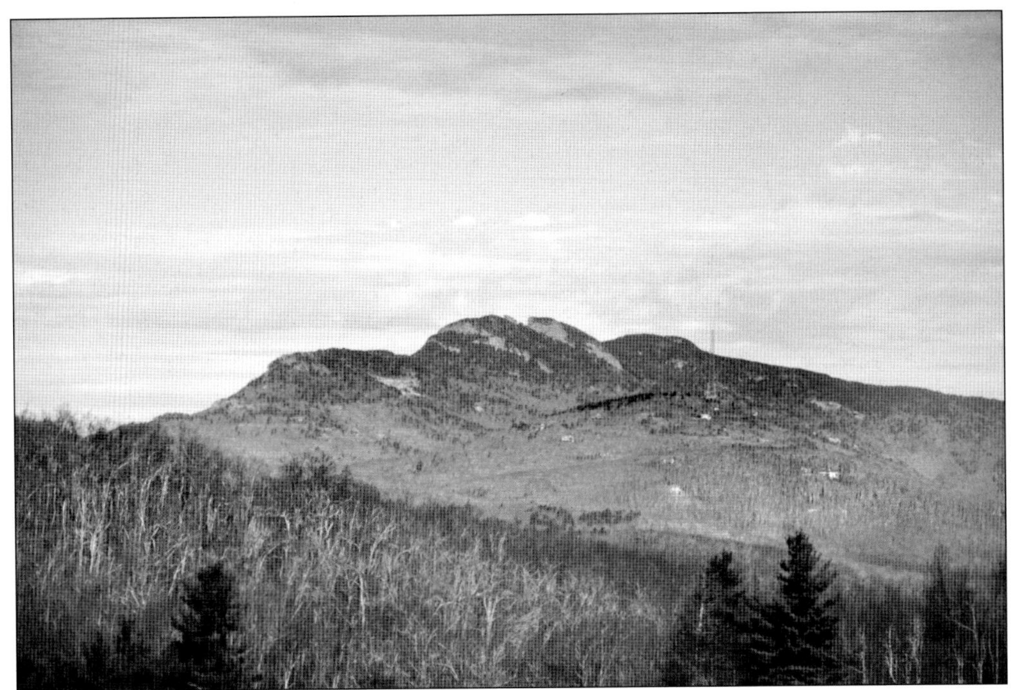

Grandmother Mountain, in the foreground, has an elevation of 4,603 above sea level, and several streams originating on it feed into the Linville River. The tower is a broadcasting antenna for the University of North Carolina Public Television. (Courtesy of Michael Hardy.)

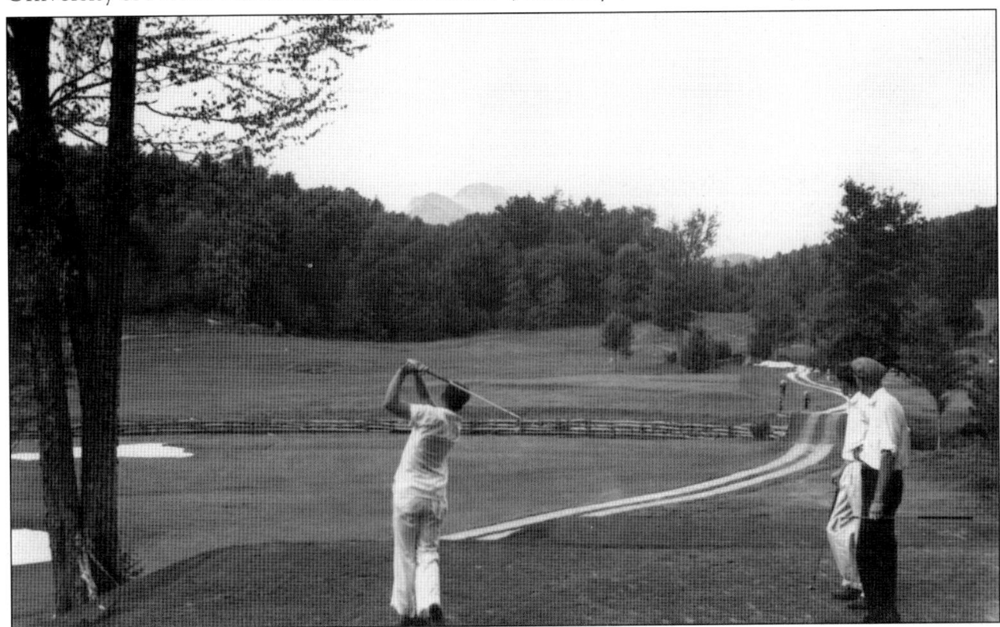

Grandfather Mountain appears just over the tops of the trees as this golfer tees off in a 1939 photograph. Scottish-born Donald Ross, who designed or redesigned around 400 golf courses between 1900 and 1948, designed the Linville Golf Course. Most famous were Pinehurst No. 2, Aronimink Golf Club, Oakland Hills, Inverness Club, Oak Hill, and the Seminole Golf Club. (Courtesy of North Carolina Department of Archives and History.)

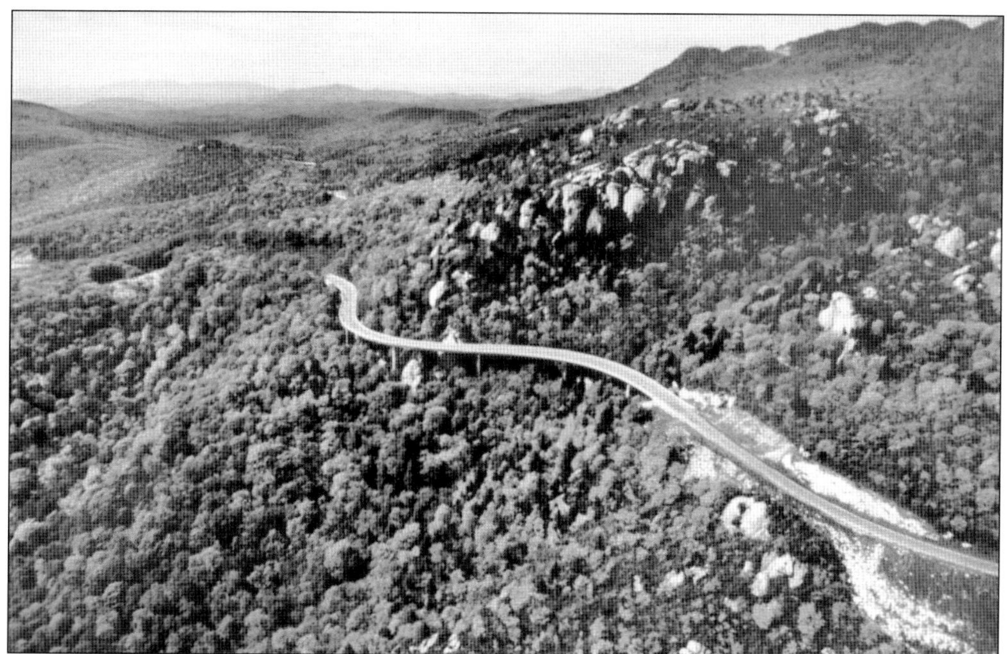

The Linn Cove Viaduct, part of the Blue Ridge Parkway, snakes around the side of Grandfather Mountain. This bridge over sensitive portions of the mountain was the last link of the 469-mile road to be finished. The Blue Ridge Parkway is the most visited unit of 401 parks in the National Park System. (Courtesy of Lees-McRae College.)

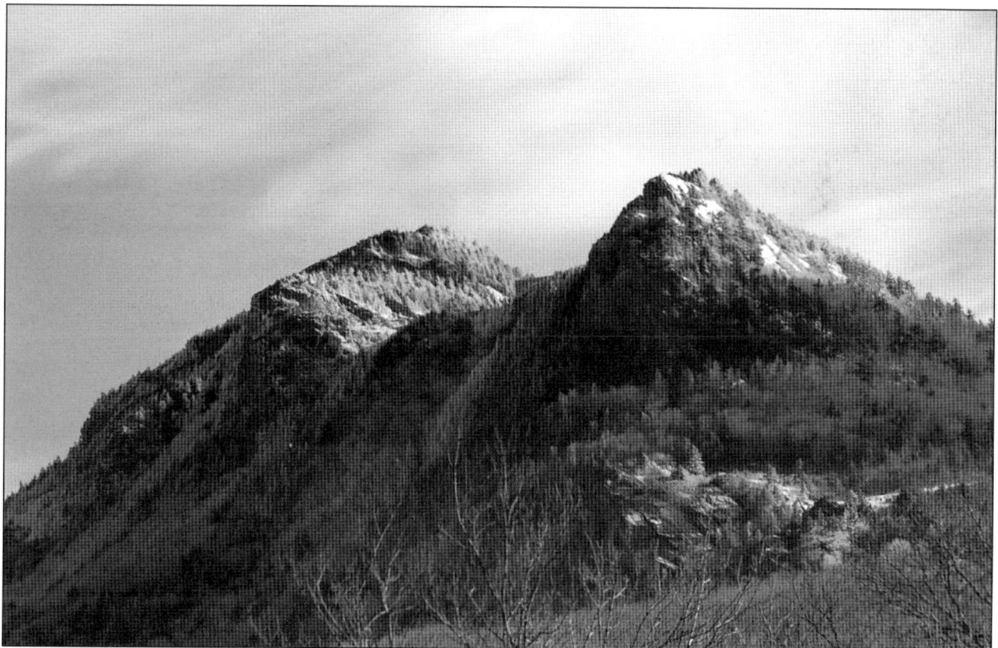

The peaks of Grandfather Mountain are often covered in snow during winter. The coldest temperature ever recorded was -32 degrees on January 21, 1985. The most snow recorded in one day was 24 inches on March 16, 1993, while the snowiest winter was when 129 inches fell in 1959–1960. (Courtesy of Michael Hardy.)

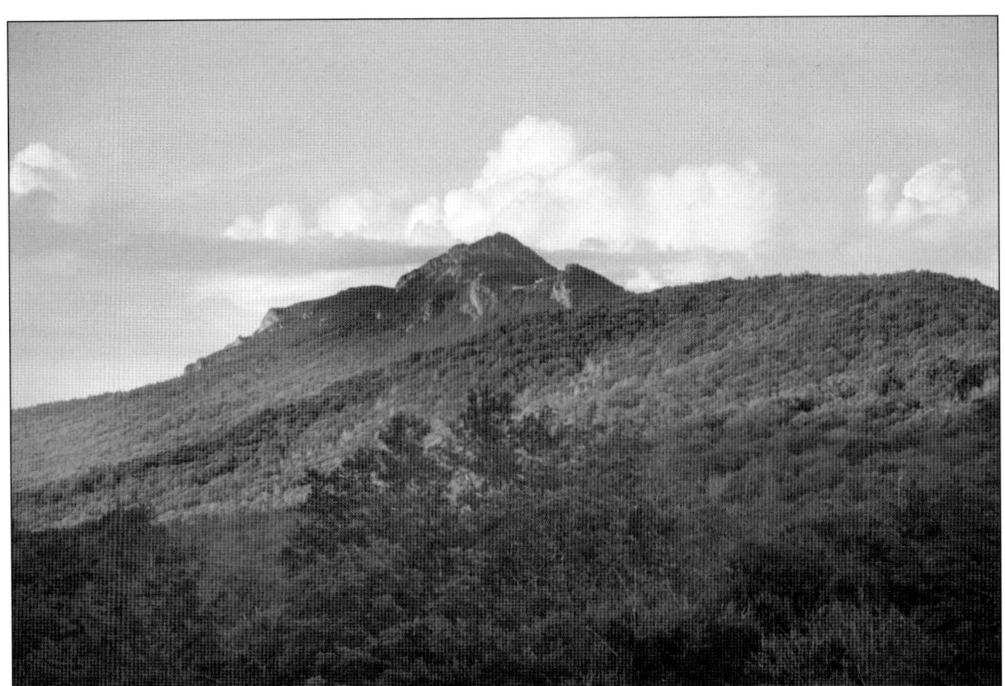

Linville Peak is the first mountain on the right, followed by MacRae Peak, with an elevation of 5,844 feet, and Attic Window Peak, elevation 5,880 feet. MacRae Peak is named for Alexander MacRae, who tended sheep for Capt. Walter W. Lenoir in the 1880s. (Courtesy of Michael Hardy.)

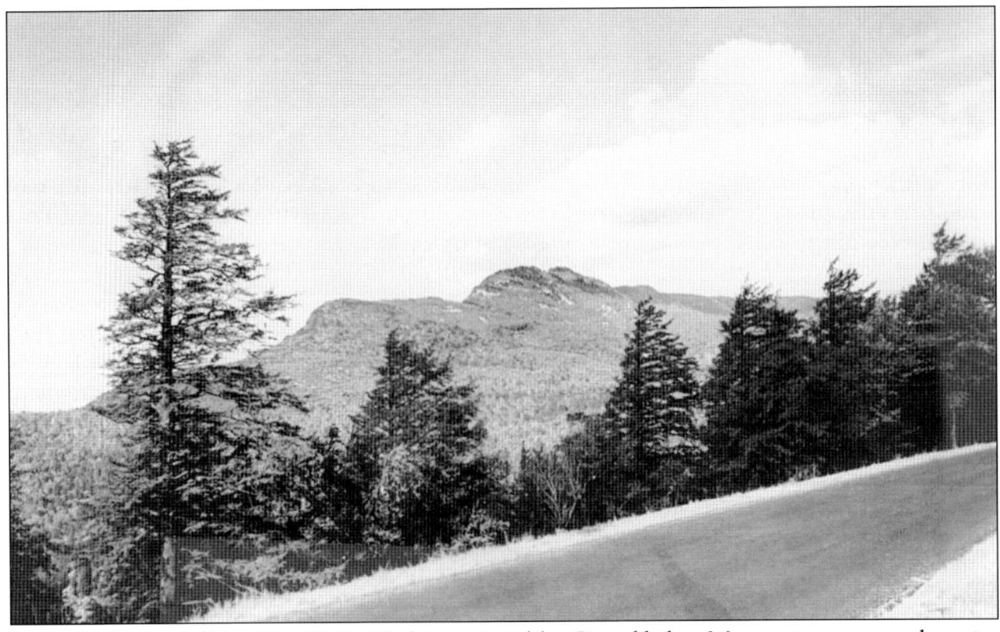

In the early days of the Blue Ridge Parkway, sites like Grandfather Mountain were much easier to photograph. Many of the trees in the area had been logged. One of the jobs of the Civilian Conservation Corps, a part of the New Deal directives from US president Franklin D. Roosevelt, was to replant trees in areas that had been clear-cut, hence the thick foliage today. (Courtesy of Blue Ridge Parkway.)

Four

Grandfather Mountain's Winding Roads

The first explorers to reach the Blue Ridge Mountains found a wilderness. Roads were simply paths worn down by native animals as they migrated or looked for food. Native Americans might have also used a few paths as they traveled, also looking for food, or possibly for a route to ambush another local tribe. These early paths were expanded to accommodate the settlers who attempted to carve out a living in the area in the 1770s and 1780s. The Linville Improvement Company created the first real road in the region between 1890 and 1891, and it was called the Yonahlossee Turnpike. The road connected Linville with Blowing Rock and passed along the eastern side of Grandfather Mountain. Later, the state assumed ownership and maintenance of the road, which today is known as US 221. In 1915, the Linville River Railway passed along the western side of Grandfather Mountain, connecting Linville with Boone. The flood of 1940 washed out the tracks, and the line was abandoned. The old train right-of-way was used in 1956 to construct North Carolina Highway 105, which opened the Watauga River area, along with Linville Gap, to development. Construction began on the Blue Ridge Parkway, running between the Shenandoah National Park in Virginia and the Great Smoky Mountains National Park in North Carolina, in the 1930s. The last section, which runs along the eastern side of Grandfather Mountain, was not finished until 1987. Linking the two sections was the Linn Cove Viaduct, a bridge hailed as an architectural wonder. Today, a large network of hiking trails crosses much of Grandfather Mountain. The National Park Service, the Grandfather Mountain State Park, and the Grandfather Mountain Stewardship Foundation manage these trails.

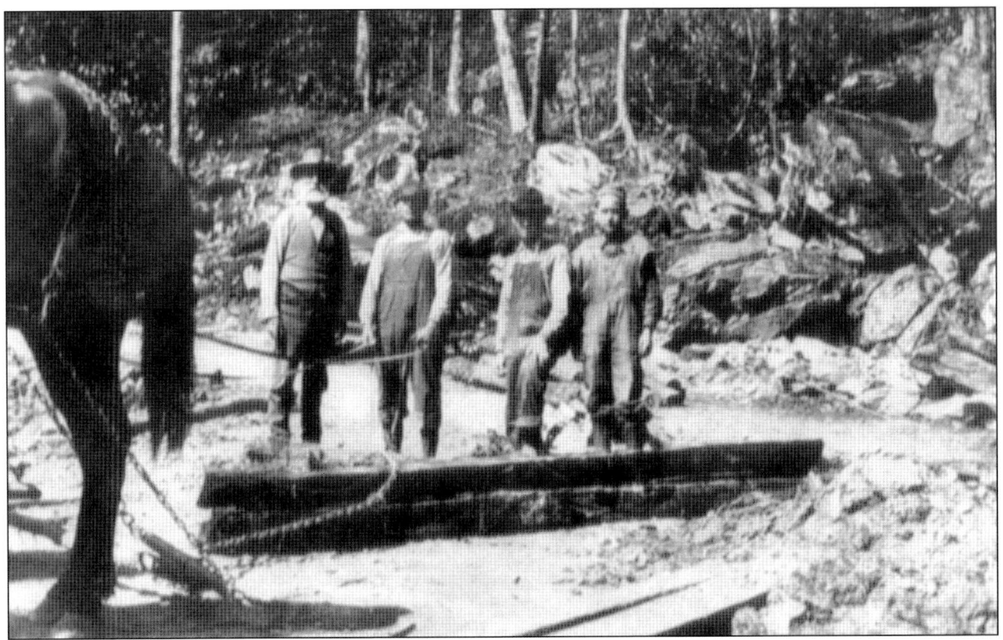

In an effort to bring both tourists and investors to the area, Samuel Kelsey laid out plans for a new road, the Yonahlossee Turnpike, to connect Linville with Blowing Rock. Alex MacRae, who was originally hired by Capt. Walter W. Lenoir as a shepherd, was hired to oversee the work crews grading the new road. MacRae is on the left, and the other men are unidentified. (Courtesy of Don MacRae.)

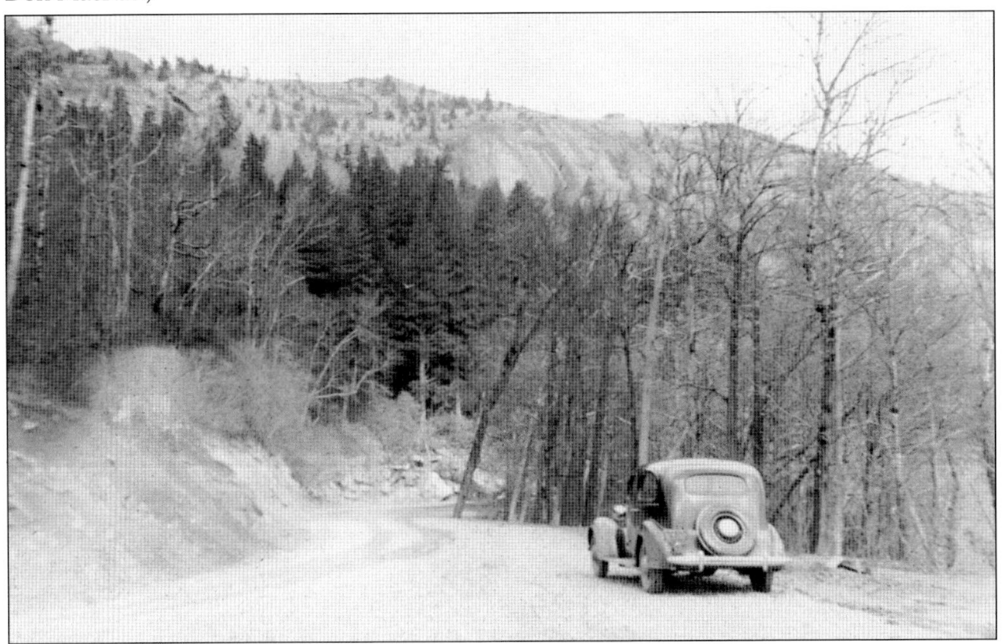

As a young man, local Joe Hartley worked on the Yonahlossee Turnpike. He later wrote that, despite the backbreaking work, "it was a marvel to behold. There'd never been anything like it in these parts. It was the first road that could be called by that name." This photograph comes from the James P. Dodge Jr. Collection. (Courtesy of North Carolina Archives.)

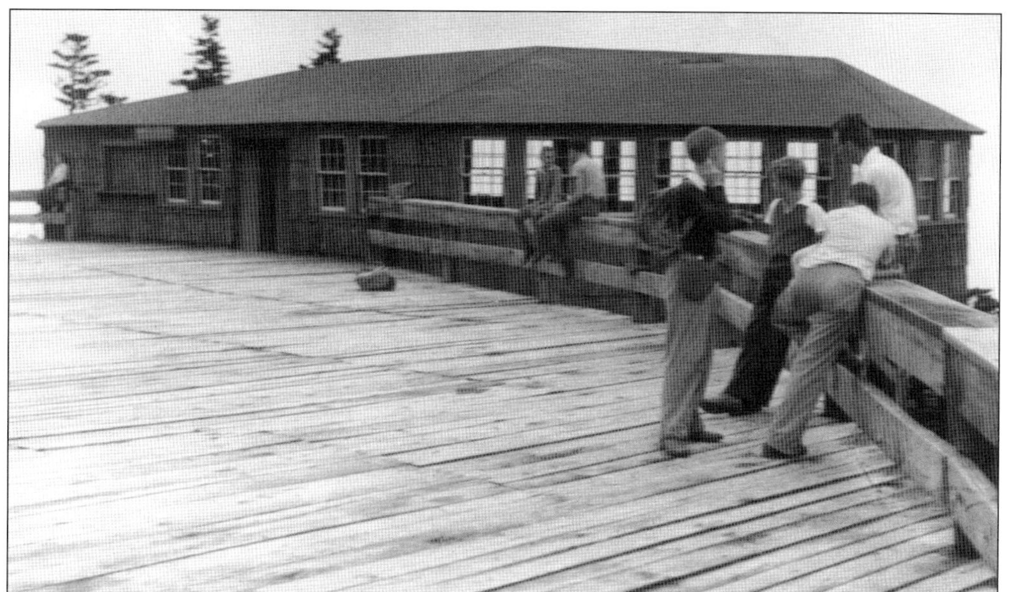

Early in the 1900s, the Linville Improvement Company constructed on Grandfather Mountain a wooden observation platform known as Cliffsides. In the 1930s, the company widened the horse path leading to Cliffsides into a one-lane gravel road to accommodate automobiles, which were charged a small toll to access the site. (Courtesy of Avery County Historical Museum.)

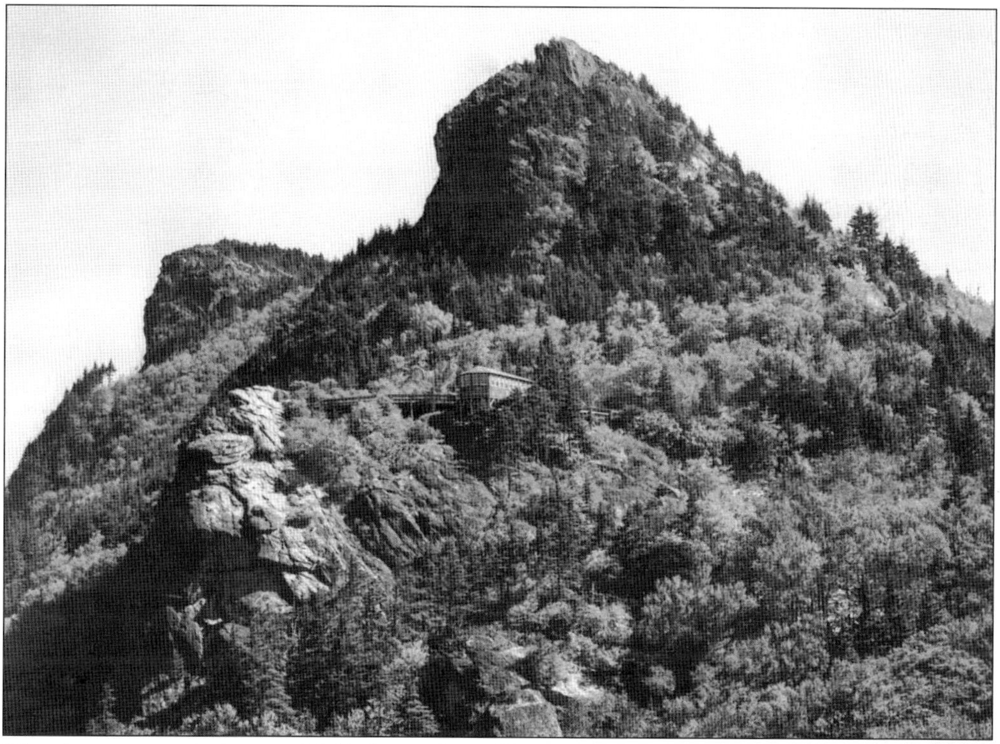

The observation platform at Cliffsides on Grandfather Mountain was expanded over a couple of decades. Its wooden deck could even hold automobiles. The platform was dismantled after the road was extended to the Mile-High Swinging Bridge. (Courtesy of Appalachian Collection.)

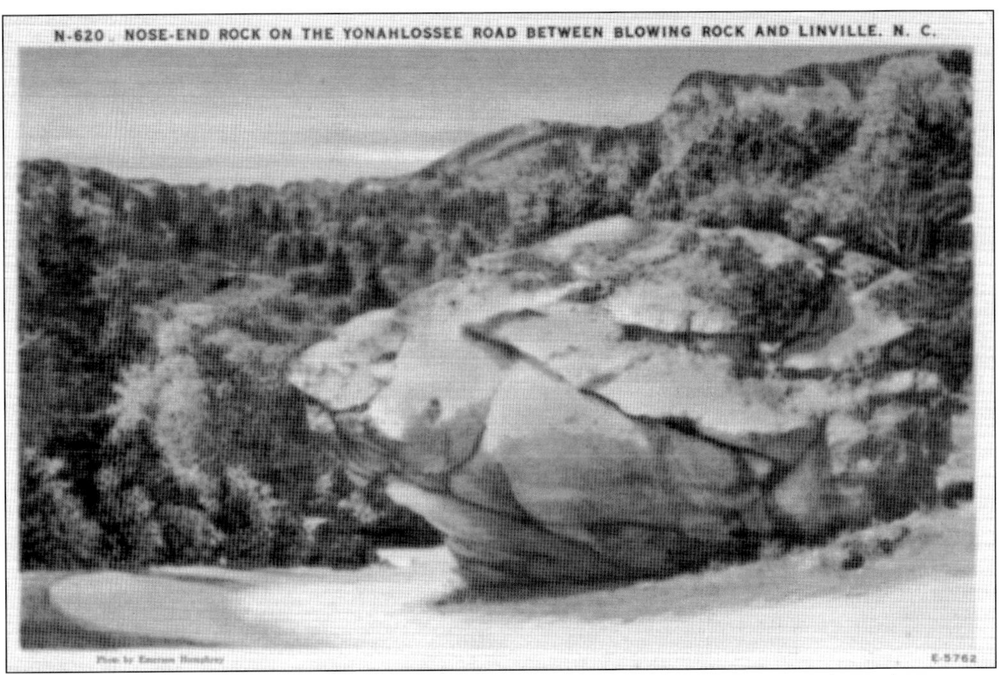

Nose End Rock, along the Yonahlossee Road, is just one of many scenic spots along the eastern flank of Grandfather Mountain. The rock, which seemingly juts out into the road, was the background for many photographs and more than one postcard. (Courtesy of Michael Hardy.)

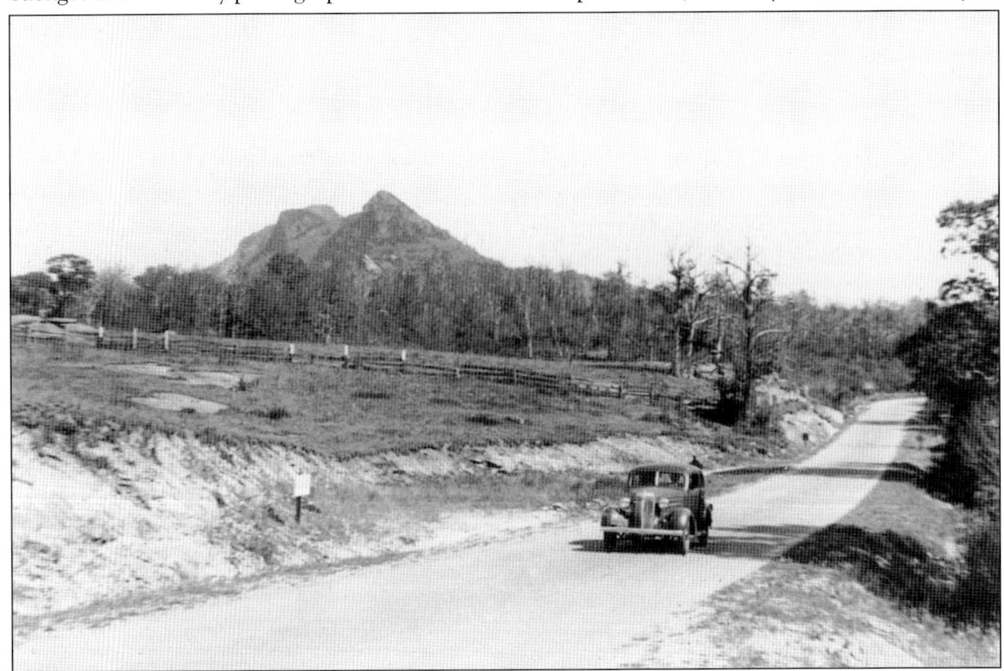

With the automobile came new travel opportunities and the desire to give roads memorable names. Hugh MacRae helped create the Black Bear Trail in December 1924. The trail began in Quebec, Canada, and ran south into the United States, passing through the Adirondacks, the Catskills, and the Allegheny Mountains. (Courtesy of North Carolina Archives.)

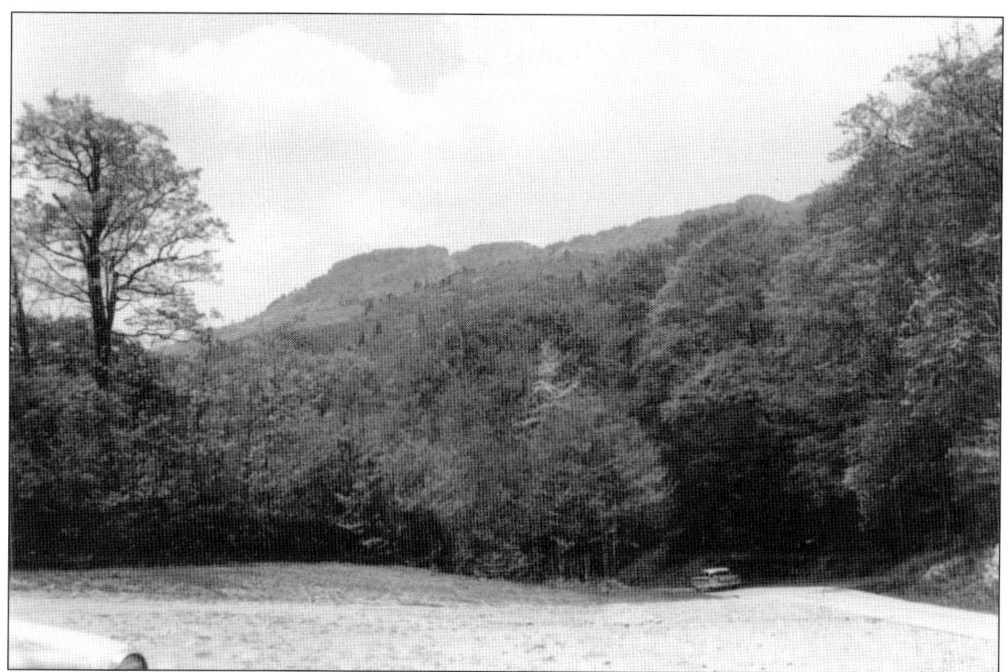

Upon reaching North Carolina, the Black Bear Trail passed through Sparta, Jefferson, Boone, and Blowing, continuing south along the Yonahlossee Road into Linville. From there, the route continued through South Carolina, Georgia, and Florida, eventually ending in Miami. "To travel this route with intelligent interest," wrote one journalist, "is to know the history of the United States." (Courtesy of Blue Ridge Parkway.)

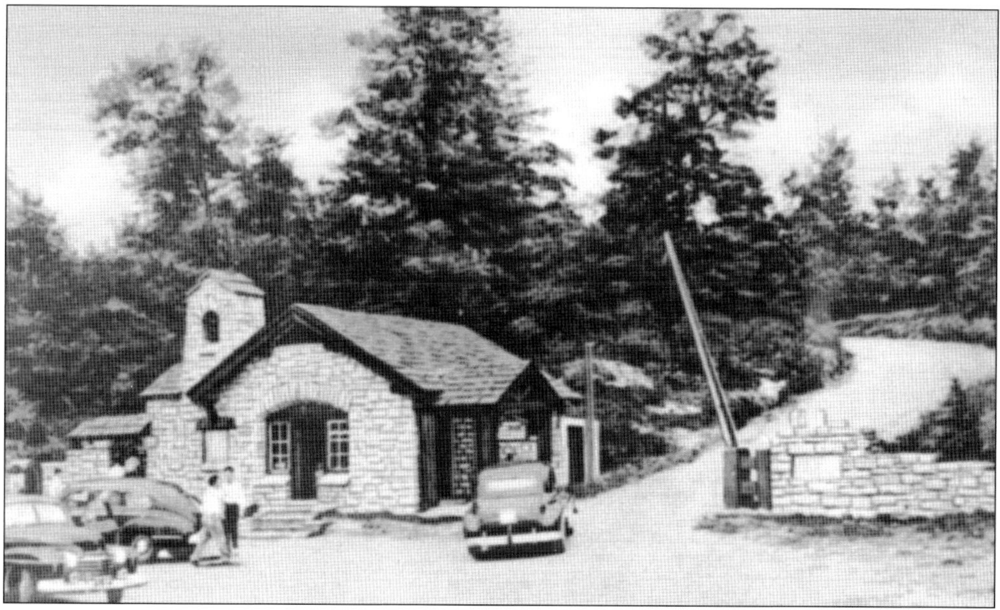

Visitors once had to pass through a tollgate and pay a small fee off US 221 to have access to the incredible views that Grandfather Mountain provided. The building not only served as a tollgate, but also as a service station and convenience store. The building still stands today, and while gas is not available, visitors can get more information about the area. (Courtesy of Michael Hardy.)

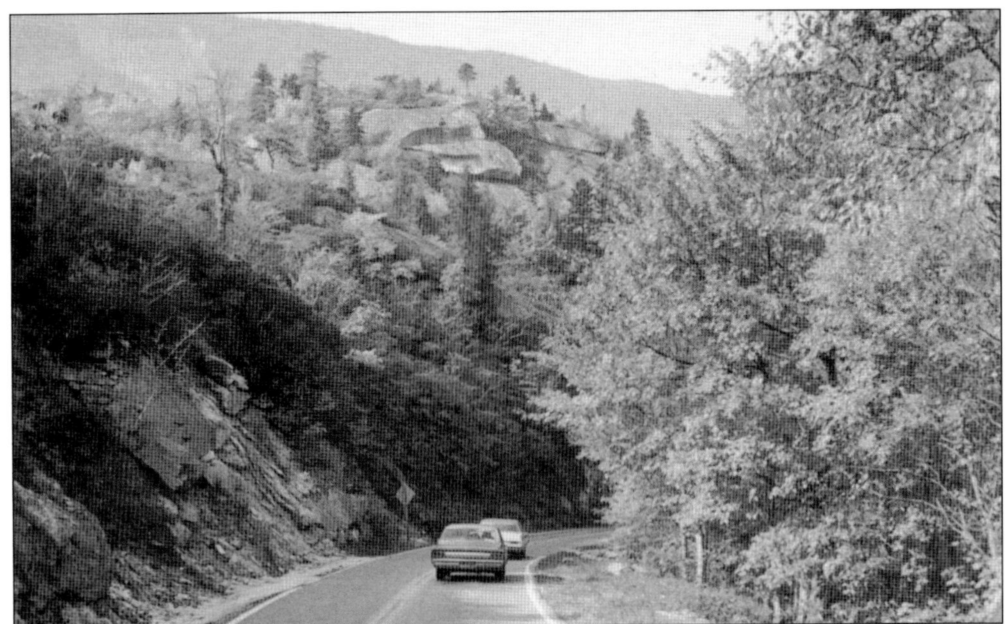

Construction on the Blue Ridge Parkway started in September 1935. The National Park Service laid out the route, while the states were responsible for acquiring the property. Originally, the route followed the Yonahlossee Road. But the National Park Service deemed the road too narrow and curvy. So they proposed two other routes, one halfway between the Yonahlossee Road and the top of the mountain and another nearer the crest. (Courtesy of Blue Ridge Parkway.)

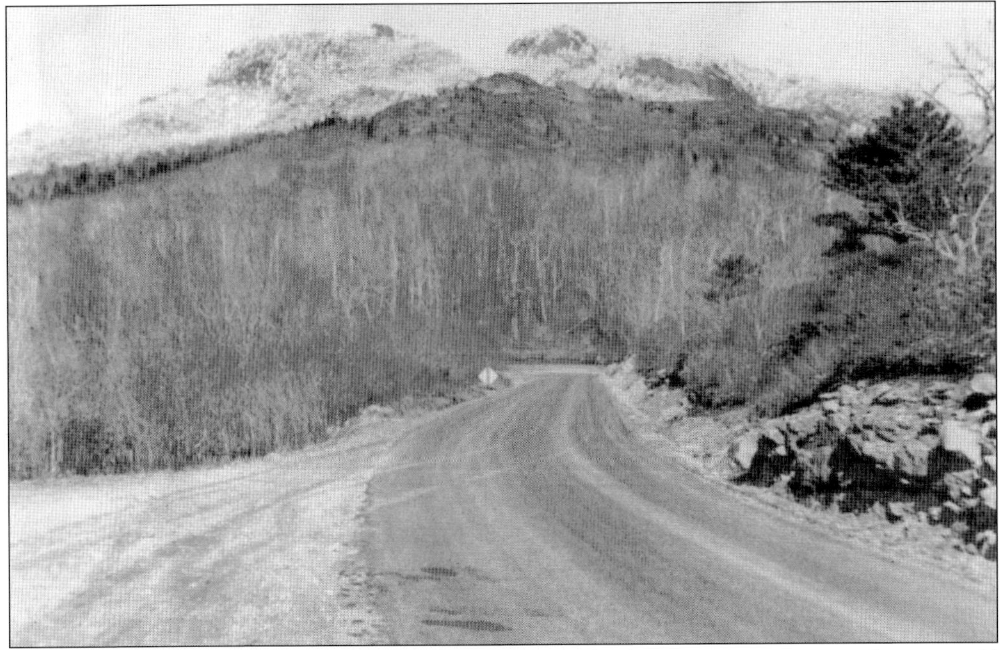

Hugh Morton was opposed to the high route over Grandfather Mountain, stating that it would be expensive, impractical, foolish, and would produce an unsightly gash. The road would "be like taking a switchblade to the Mona Lisa." Critics argued that Morton had already cut that gash, building the road to the Mile-High Swinging Bridge. (Courtesy of Blue Ridge Parkway.)

Upon taking ownership of Grandfather Mountain, Hugh Morton extended the road farther toward the top. Now, instead of stopping near the present-day nature museum, visitors could go all the way to the top of the mountain, where they find a parking lot, the Top Shop, and the Mile-High Swinging Bridge. (Courtesy of Suzanne Tucker.)

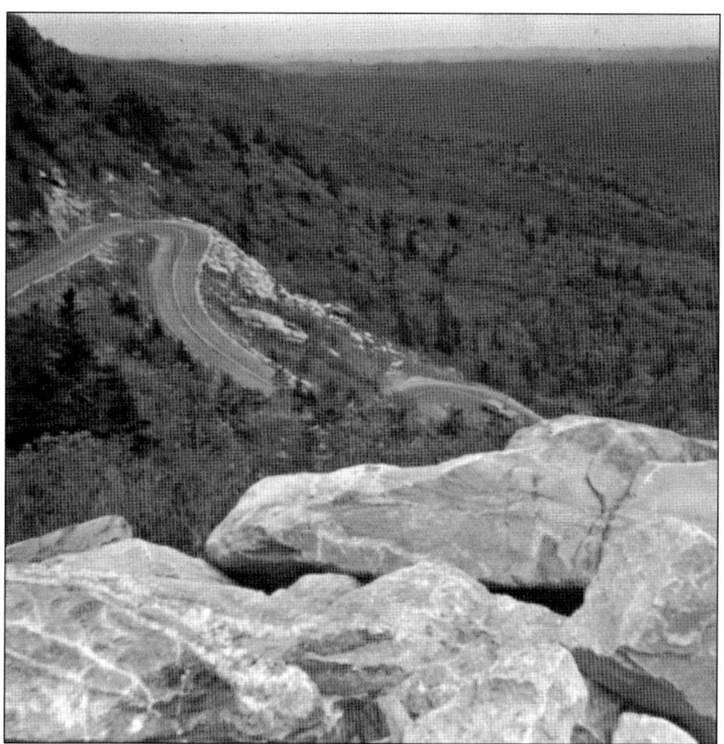

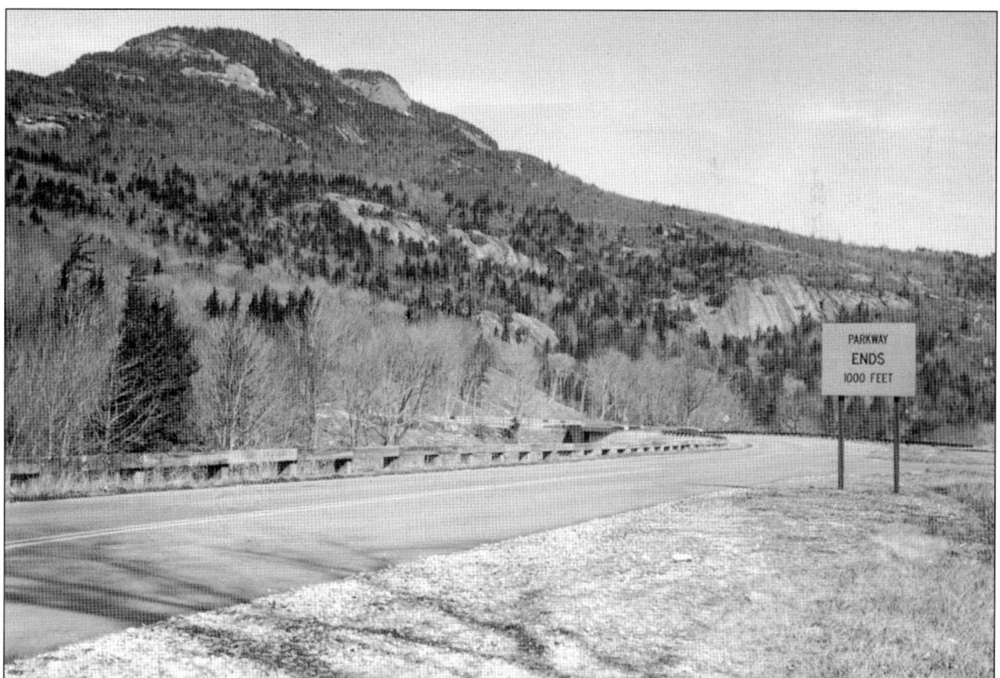

For several decades, the Blue Ridge Parkway was incomplete. Visitors found signs such as this one at the Beacon Heights parking area. Motorists had to exit the parkway and drive along the Yonahlossee Road, taking them past the entrance to Grandfather Mountain, before getting back on the parkway to continue their journey. (Courtesy of Blue Ridge Parkway.)

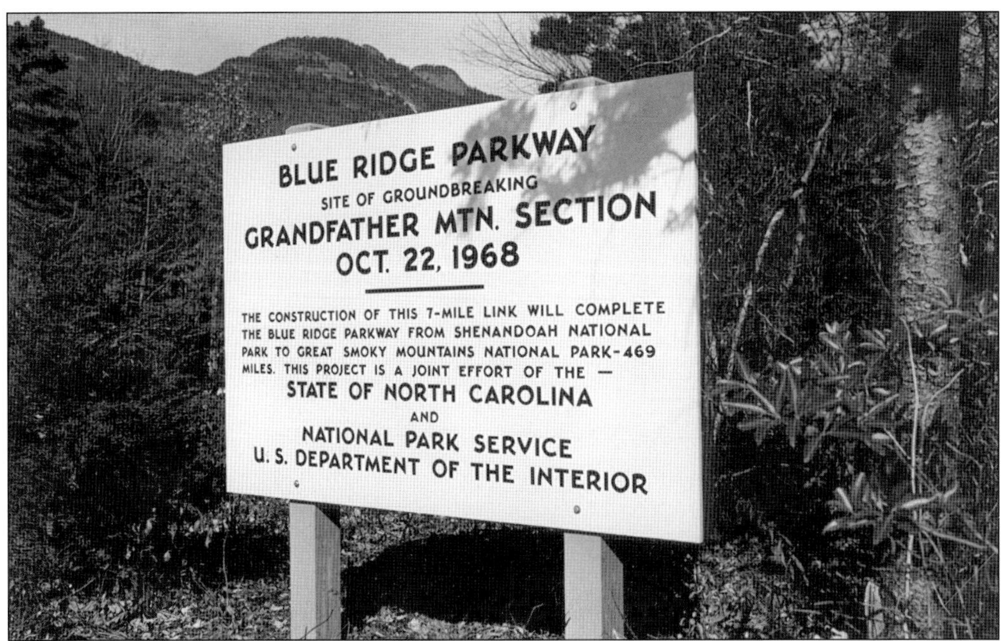

Hugh Morton and the National Park Service sparred for years, even once appearing on a televised debate. Morton was seen as a private landowner defending wilderness property against Washington bureaucrats. Finally, in 1965, he agreed to swap lands along the Yonahlossee Road for the middle route property. In 1968, the deal was considered finished. (Courtesy of Blue Ridge Parkway.)

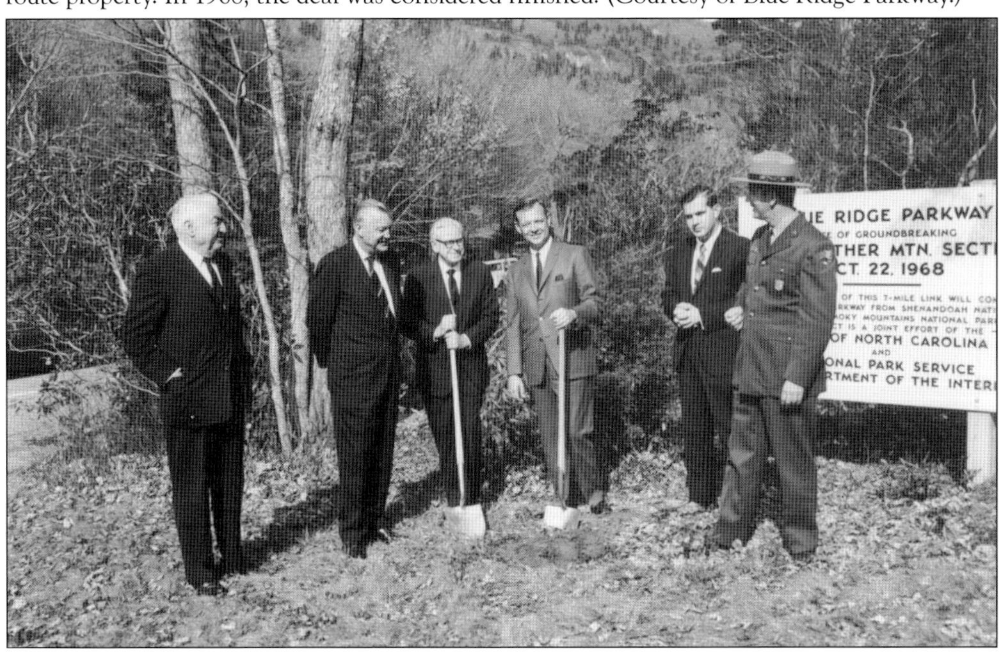

"Today's event marks the end of toil, the end of waiting and the beginning of the end of the Parkway as we know it—incomplete and unfinished," stated North Carolina governor Dan Moore in an article in the *Greensboro Daily News*. Moore gathered with other dignitaries, including Harthon Bill, acting director of the National Park Service, to turn a shovel full of earth at Beacon Heights. (Courtesy of Blue Ridge Parkway.)

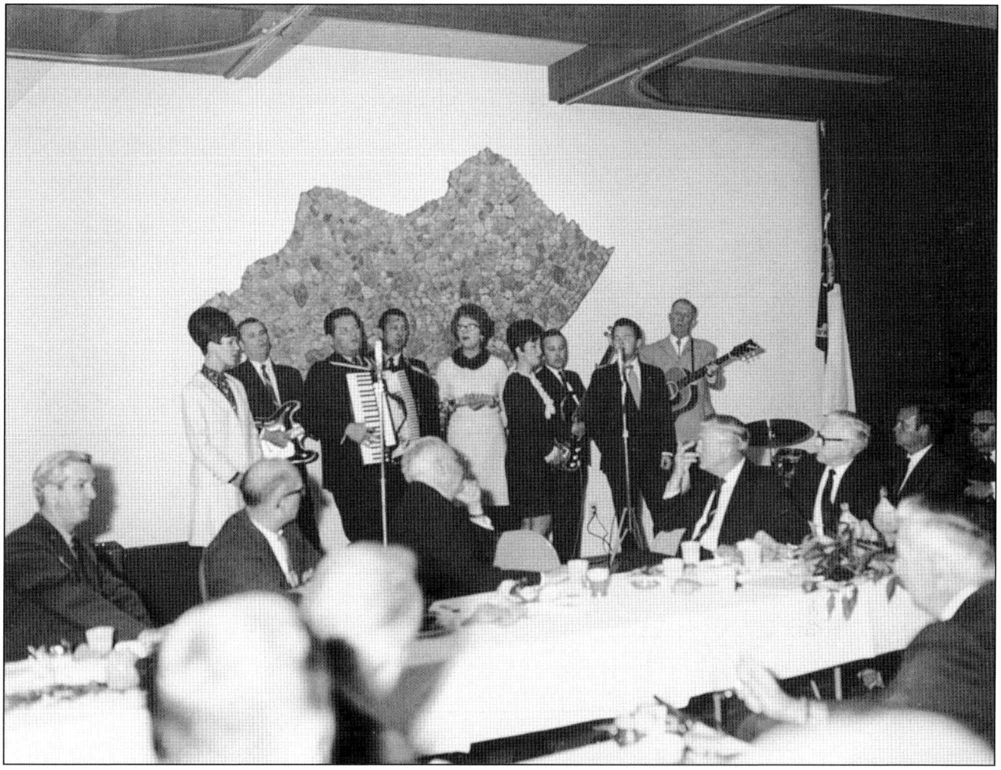

Following the symbolic ground breaking with golden shovels, 200 invited guests gathered for a barbecued chicken luncheon in the visitor center at Grandfather Mountain. There was entertainment, and Governor Moore delivered an address, thanking Hugh Morton on behalf of the state and the National Park Service for facilitating the completion of the Blue Ridge Parkway. (Courtesy of Blue Ridge Parkway.)

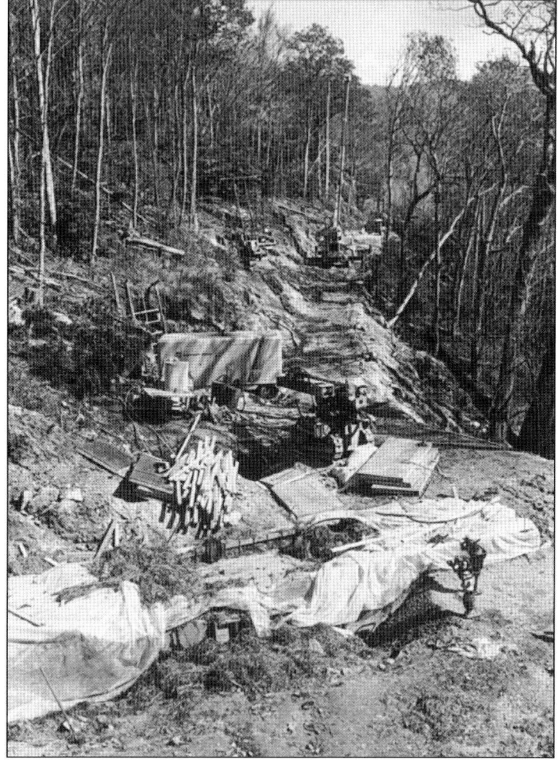

The *Greensboro Daily News*, on reporting the events of the National Park Service's acquisition of the property around Grandfather Mountain in October 1968, believed that the entire project would be completed by 1972. However, it took over 20 years to finish the short seven-mile section of the incomplete Blue Ridge Parkway. (Courtesy of Blue Ridge Parkway.)

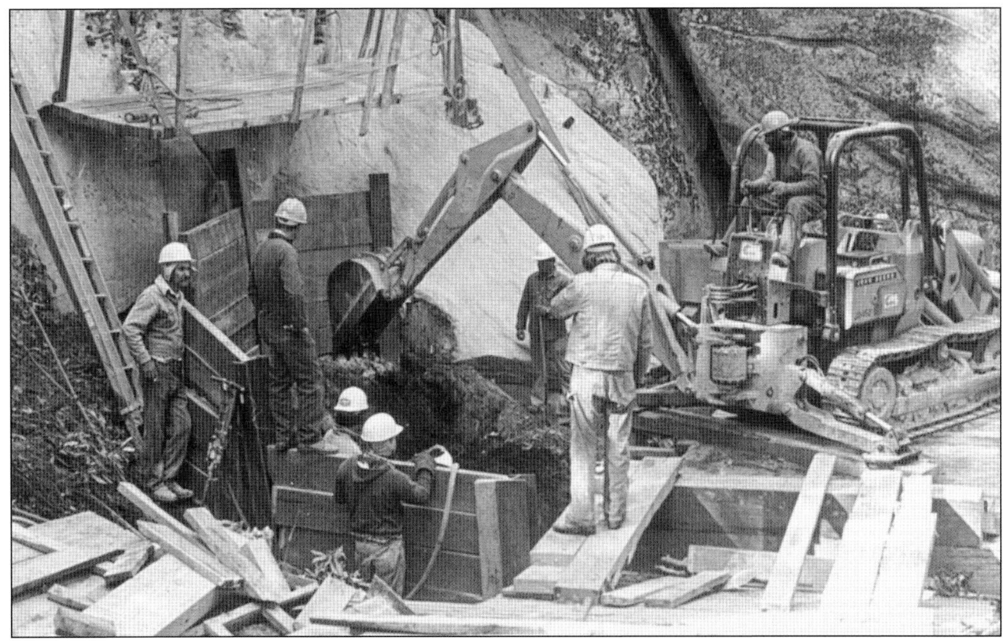

One of the challenges was how to negotiate a boulder field along the proposed route. The land was very unstable, and architects chose to construct a bridge, or viaduct, around the side of the mountain. In this photograph, workers pour concrete for one of the supports for the viaduct. (Courtesy of Blue Ridge Parkway.)

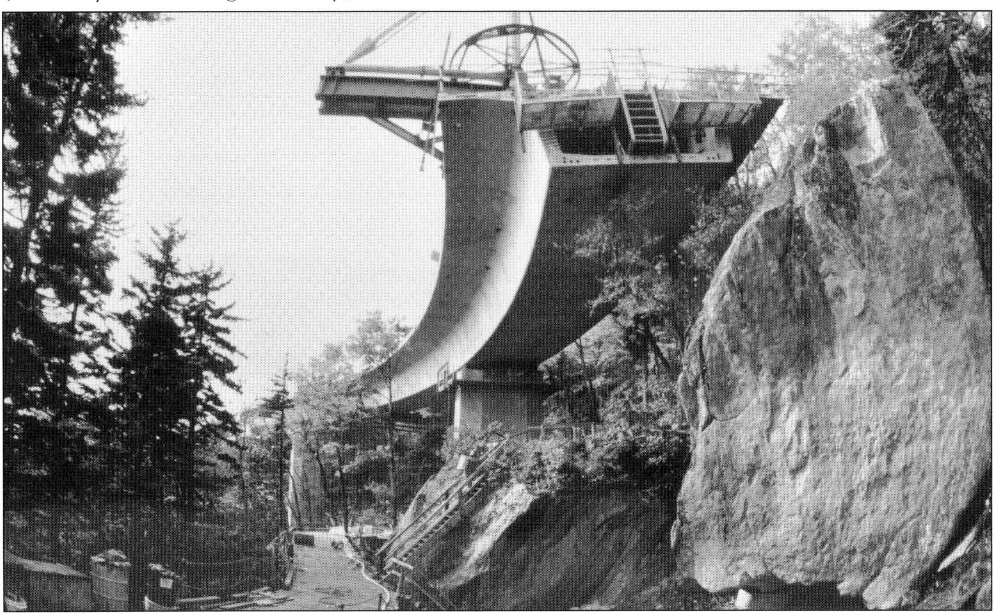

To navigate the boulder field, the Florida architectural firm of Figg and Miller Engineers, Inc., was employed. The viaduct is considered the most complicated bridge ever built and the crowning architectural achievement of the Blue Ridge Parkway. It is a prime example of a precast concrete cantilever bridge girder construction, meaning that a precast concrete section adjoins a segment already completed, eliminating the need for scaffolding. (Courtesy of Lees-McRae College/ Grandfather Mountain.)

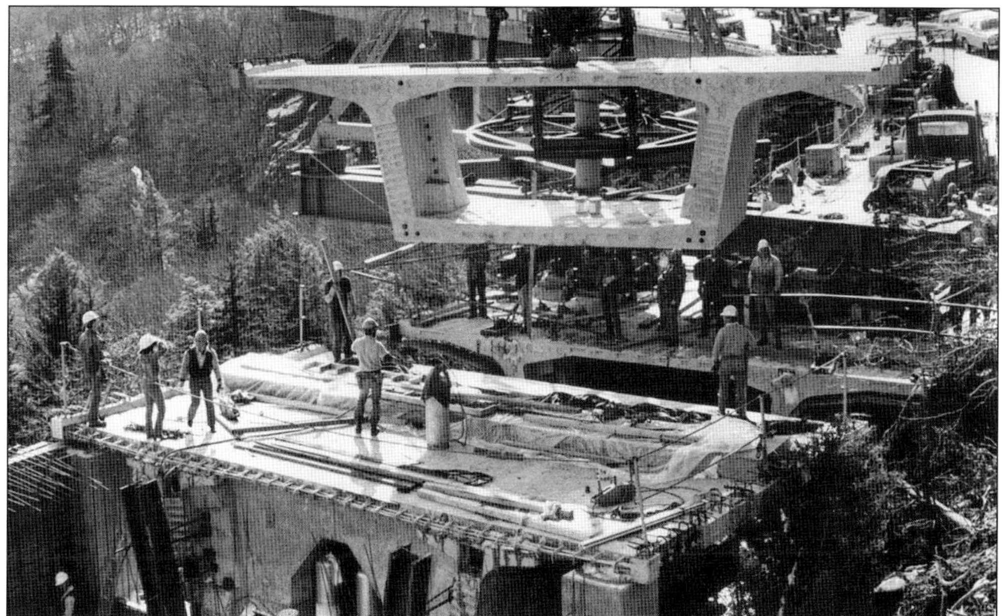

The Linn Cove Viaduct is composed of 153 fifty-ton concrete segments. Each piece of the bridge was built on a curve and had to be designed to fit in its own individual part of the bridge. When a section was installed, epoxy and massive steel post-tensioning tendons joined it. To help the bridge blend into the mountainside, the construction crews added black iron oxide to the concrete. (Courtesy of Grandfather Mountain.)

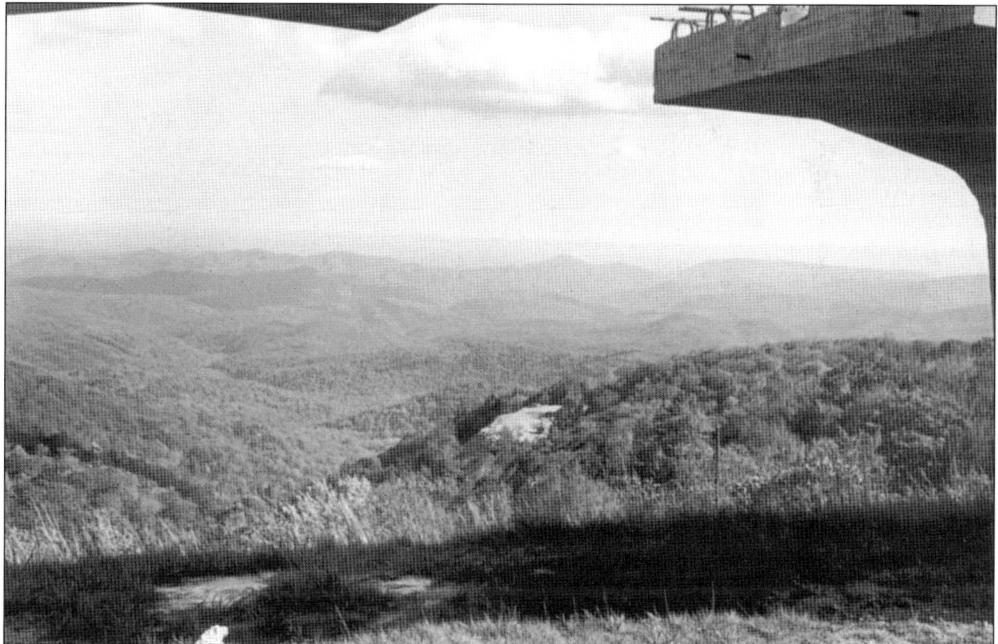

In an effort to make the work blend into the natural surroundings, stone used along the Blue Ridge Parkway was mined locally. Located between the unfinished sections of this bridge on Grandfather Mountain, one of the rock quarries can be seen in the distance. (Courtesy of Blue Ridge Parkway.)

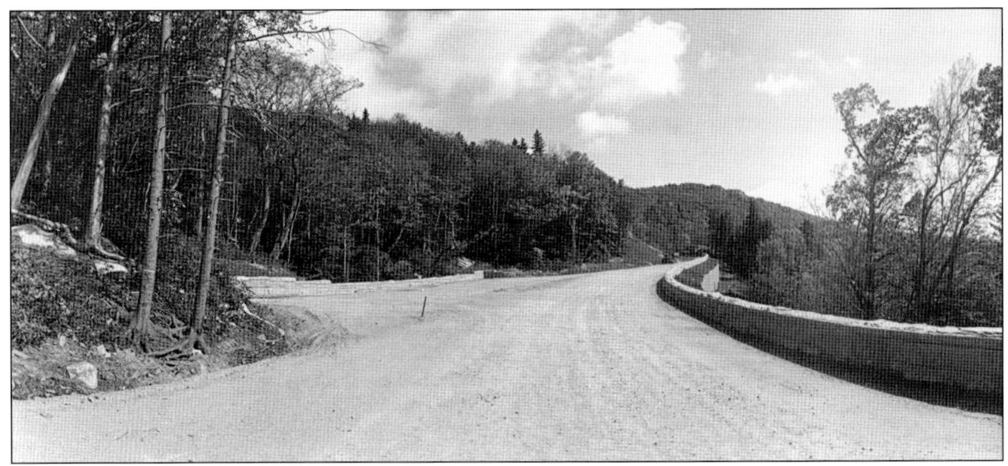

While also constructing the Linn Cove Viaduct, the National Park Service built a couple of overlooks along less sensitive areas of the Blue Ridge Parkway. This is the Rough Ridge Parking Area, not far from the viaduct. Local quarries provided the stone. These parking areas and overlooks provide access to the Tanawha Trail. (Courtesy of Blue Ridge Parkway.)

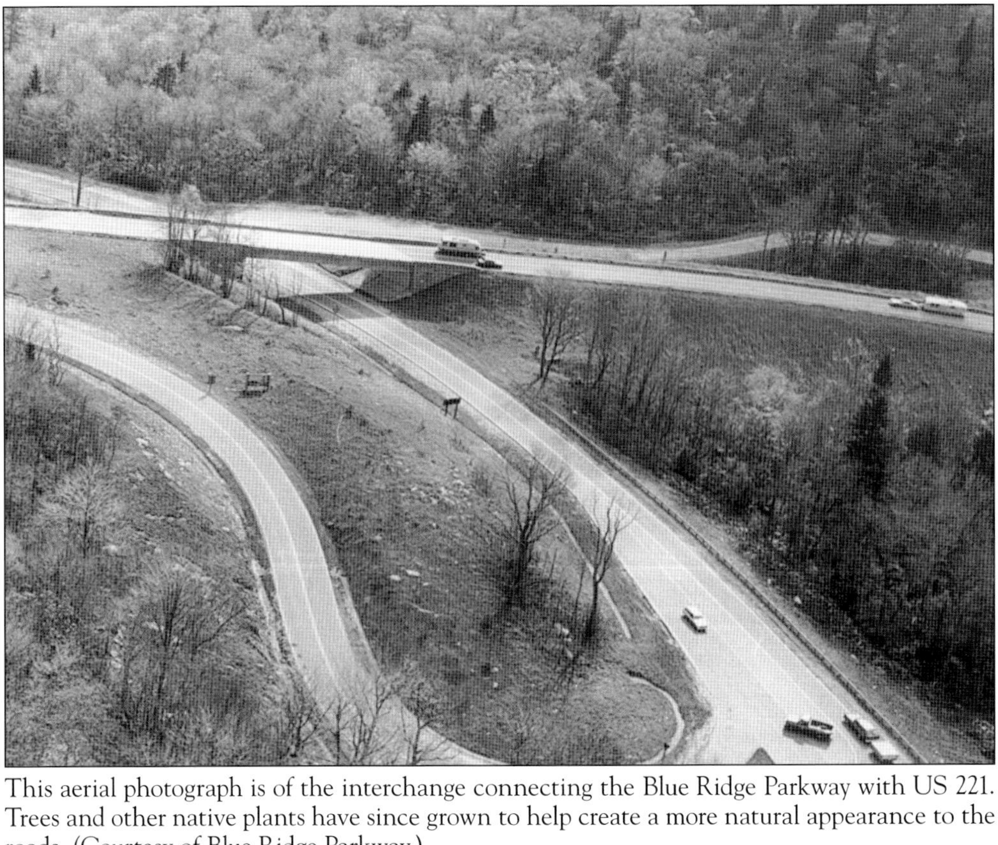

This aerial photograph is of the interchange connecting the Blue Ridge Parkway with US 221. Trees and other native plants have since grown to help create a more natural appearance to the roads. (Courtesy of Blue Ridge Parkway.)

Following the ribbon-cutting ceremonies at the Linn Cove Viaduct on September 11, 1987, a motorcade made its way across the famous S-shaped bridge; there was a car representing each year the Blue Ridge Parkway was under construction, led by a 1935 yellow Studebaker. North Carolina governor Jim Martin, pictured at right, participated in the parade of cars. (Courtesy of Grandfather Mountain/Hugh Morton.)

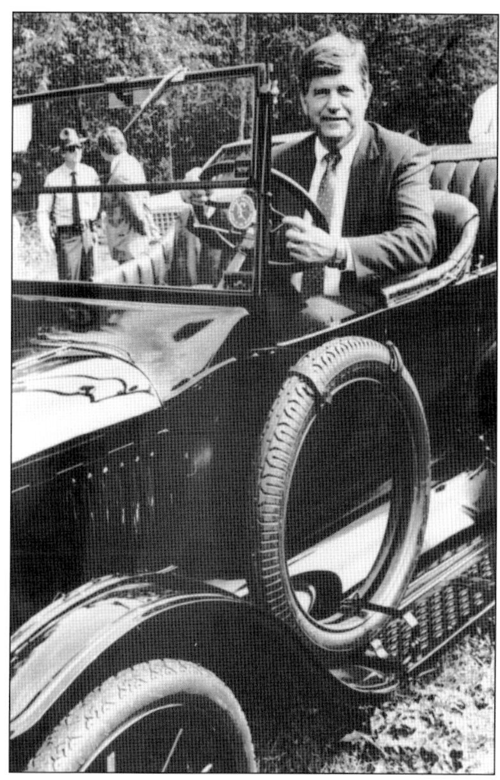

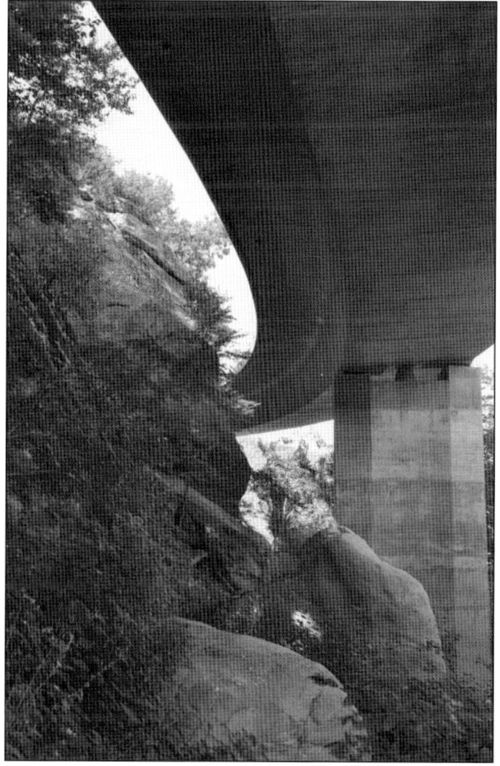

On leaving the Linn Cove Viaduct Visitor Center, travelers are encouraged to take the short .15-mile stroll along a paved path to view the underside of the Linn Cove Viaduct. From this vantage point, visitors can closely examine the preset individual concrete sections of the famous road. (Courtesy of Michael Hardy.)

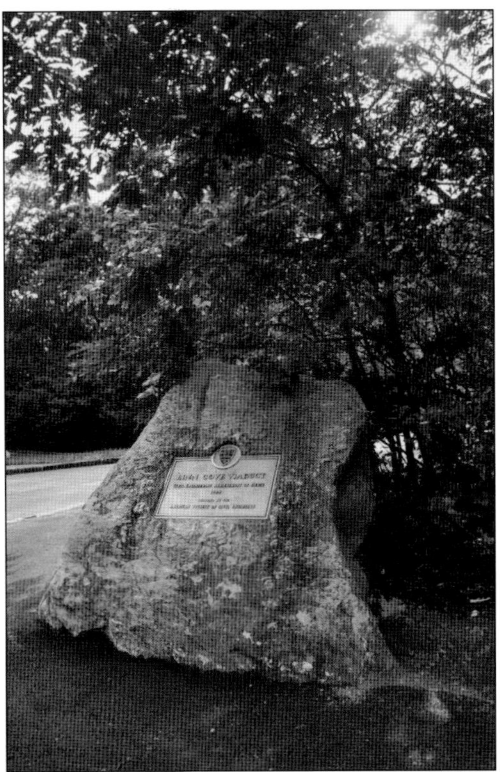

One of the monuments at the Linn Cove Viaduct Visitor Center is this boulder with a plaque telling how the American Society of Civil Engineers gave the Civil Engineering Achievement of Merit Award to the Linn Cove Viaduct in 1984. Other engineering marvels awarded the achievement of merit include the Living Seas at Epcot and the West Desert Pumping Project in Utah. (Courtesy of Michael Hardy.)

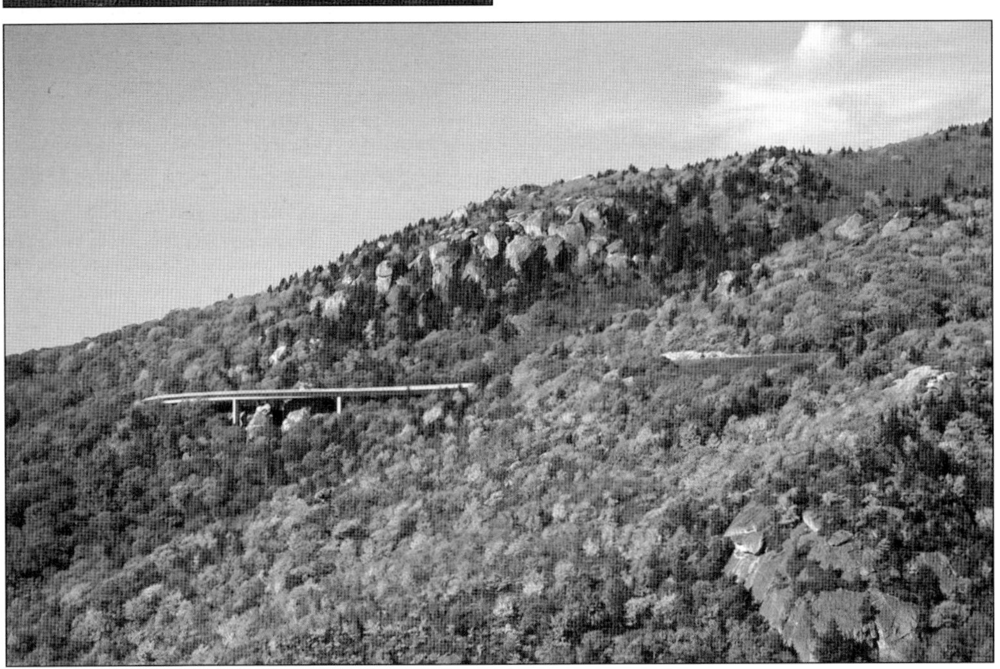

Once completed, the Linn Cove Viaduct was 1,243 feet in length. It is quite possibly the most photographed structure along the Blue Ridge Parkway. Not only do thousands of people stop to capture an image, but the viaduct can also be seen in countless brochures, pamphlets, and television commercials for everything from cars to motels. (Courtesy of Michael Hardy.)

Five

Singing on the Mountain

Singing on the Mountain began in June 1925, when Joe L. Hartley, fire warden and caretaker at Grandfather Mountain, convened a Sunday school picnic. About 150 people attended, with the first sermon preached by the Rev. L.W. Sudderth. Everyone who attended believed that the picnic should be an annual event, and the second Singing on the Mountain drew 500 people. Hartley, who was appointed chairman, reported that the fourth convention in 1928 had 4,000 people in attendance. The event continued to grow. In 1931, Hartley noted that there "was almost all denominations represented, Methodist, Baptist, Lutheran, Advent, Catholic, Presbyterian, Mormons, [and] Holiness," with an estimated 15,000 people in attendance. Hartley's slogan was "Whosoever Will May Come." The early Singing on the Mountain events did not have a set schedule, and church choirs and Sunday school classes were invited to participate. Events continued to be held throughout the World War II years, despite the rationing of gasoline. Hartley reported in his book *Walking for Health and Traveling to Eternity, Combined with Singing on the Mountain* that 40,000 people were on hand. In the late 1940s, Singing on the Mountain began to change, with the events becoming more structured. Also at that time, famous names started to headline the event. Lulu Belle and Scotty Wiseman performed in 1947, and North Carolina governor Luther Hodges spoke in 1953. Among frequent favorites were Arthur Smith and the Crossroads Quartet, George Hamilton IV, and the Chuck Wagon Gang. The largest Singing on the Mountain events were held when Billy Graham preached in 1962 and when Johnny and June Carter Cash and Carl Perkins sang and played in 1974. Also speaking that day were Bob Hope and Gov. Jim Holshouser. Oral Roberts preached in 1976, and in 2009, Rev. Freida Hartley Hobson became the first woman to preach at the annual event. In 2013, Will Graham, the grandson of Billy Graham, delivered the annual message. Will's father, Franklin Graham, had also preached at the event, making the Grahams the only family with three members who have delivered a message there.

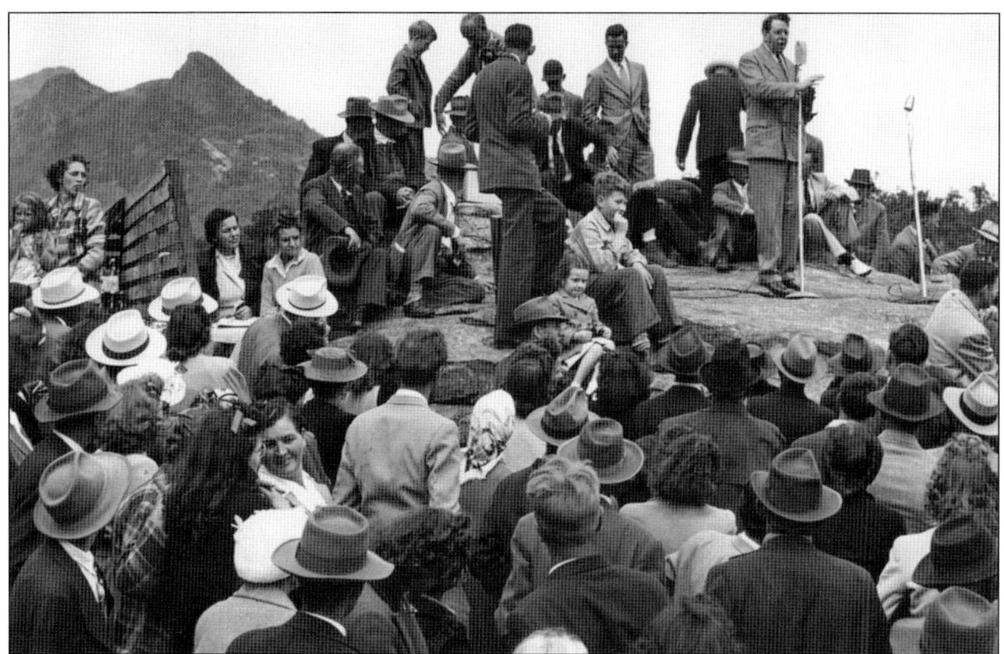

The annual Singing on the Mountain has brought numerous evangelists, preachers, entertainers, and politicians to preach, sing, and deliver remarks. Here, North Carolina governor J. Melville Broughton addresses the gathered crowd in McRae Meadow. Broughton was governor from 1941 to 1945 and was known for his reforms in education and health policy. (Courtesy of Grandfather Mountain.)

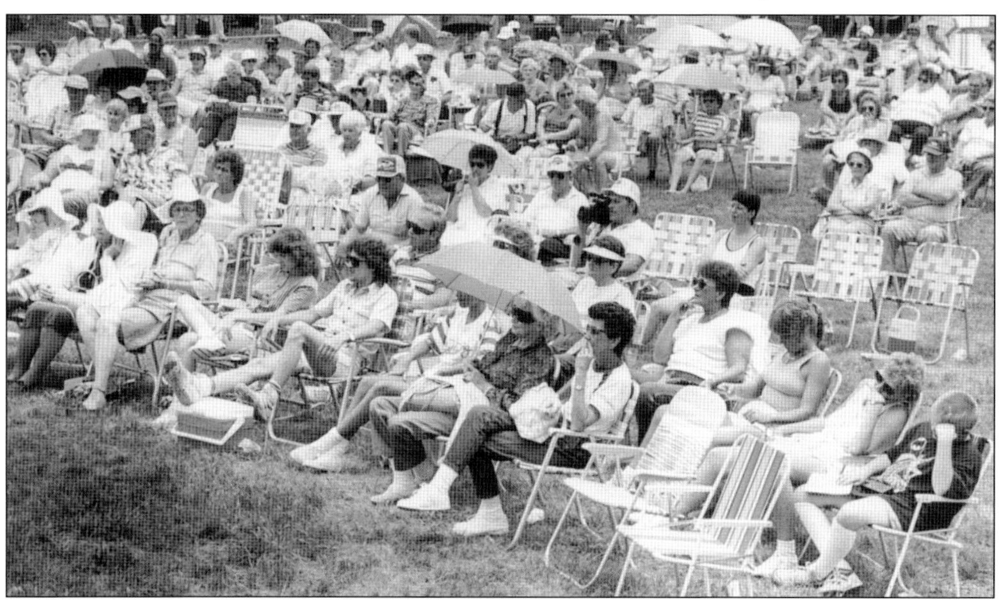

In the first several decades of the annual Singing on the Mountain event, people wore their Sunday best and everyone stood to hear the music and preaching. At some point, the attire became more relaxed, and people brought their coolers and lawn chairs. This photograph dates from the early 1990s. (Courtesy of Historic Boone Collection.)

For the first Singing on the Mountain convention, Joe Hartley selected as preacher his friend the Reverend Lloyd Sudderth, who was born in Caldwell County; his family had ventured to Washington State before returning to the area and settling in Montezuma. Sudderth was educated at the Appalachian State Teacher's College, taught school, sold insurance, was a Mason and justice of the peace, and was pastor at local Baptist churches. (Courtesy of the Sudderth family.)

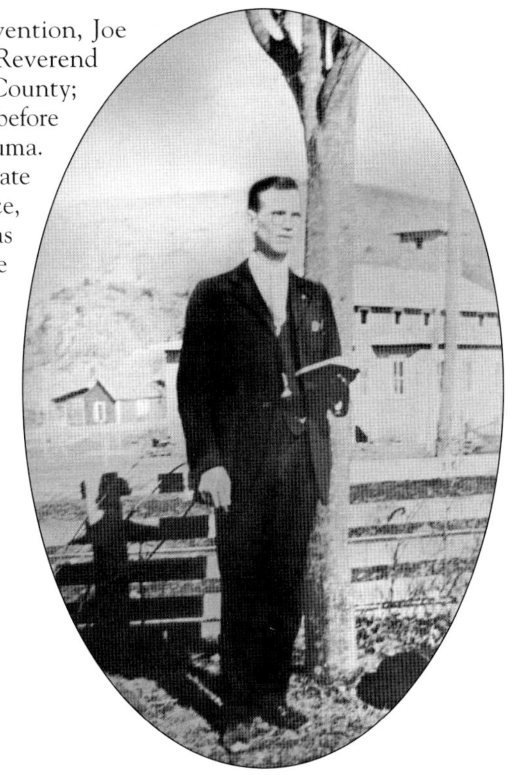

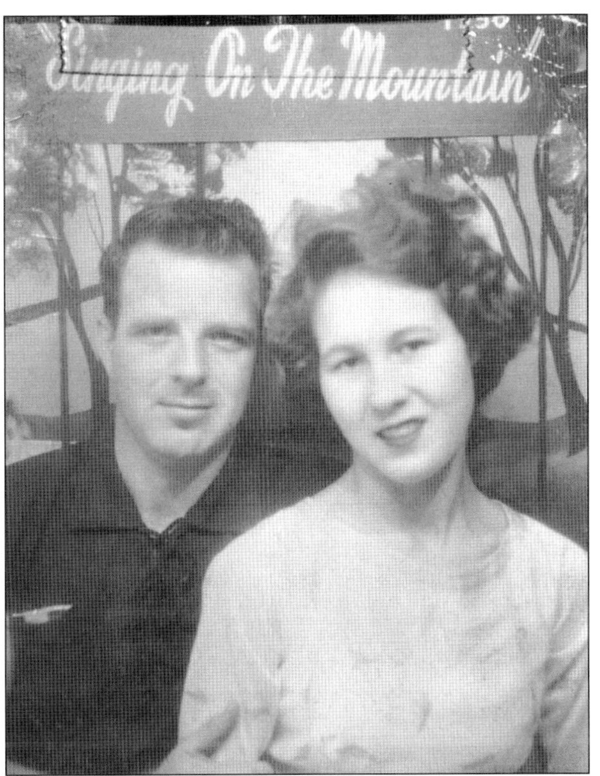

Before the advent of digital cameras, having a photograph made at the annual Singing on the Mountain event every June was a real treat. While the name of this Avery County couple appears to be lost, the photograph proves there was an official photo booth at the event. (Courtesy of Avery County Historical Museum.)

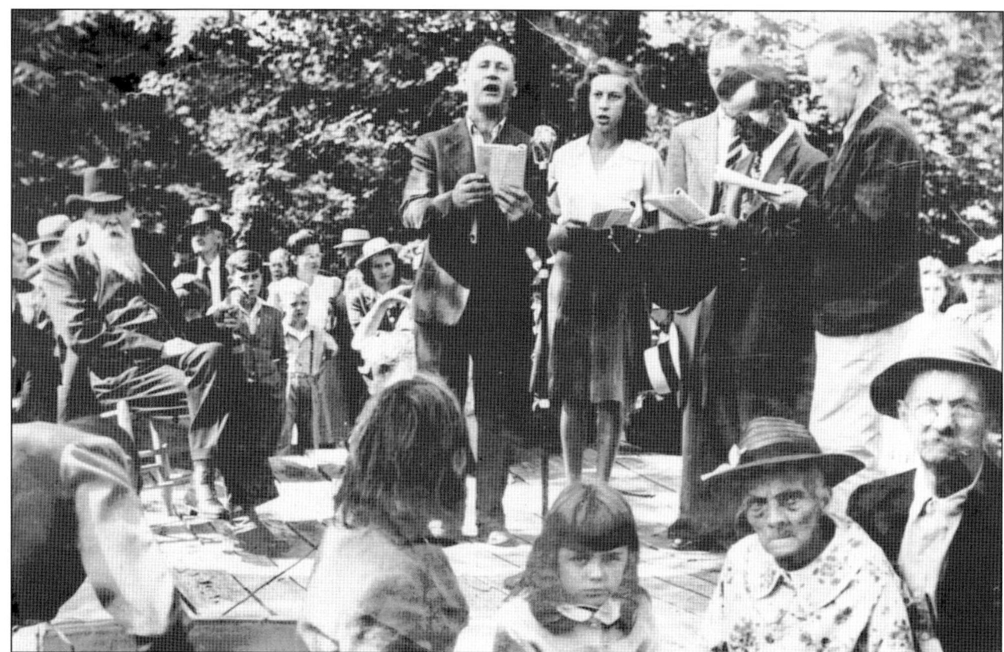

In the first couple of decades of the "Singing Convention at Grandfather Mountain," there was not a set agenda. Most of the singers were choirs and Sunday school classes from surrounding churches. No one actually knew who might show up to sing. This led organizer Joe Hartley to coin the logo, "Whosoever Will May Come." (Courtesy of Grandfather Mountain.)

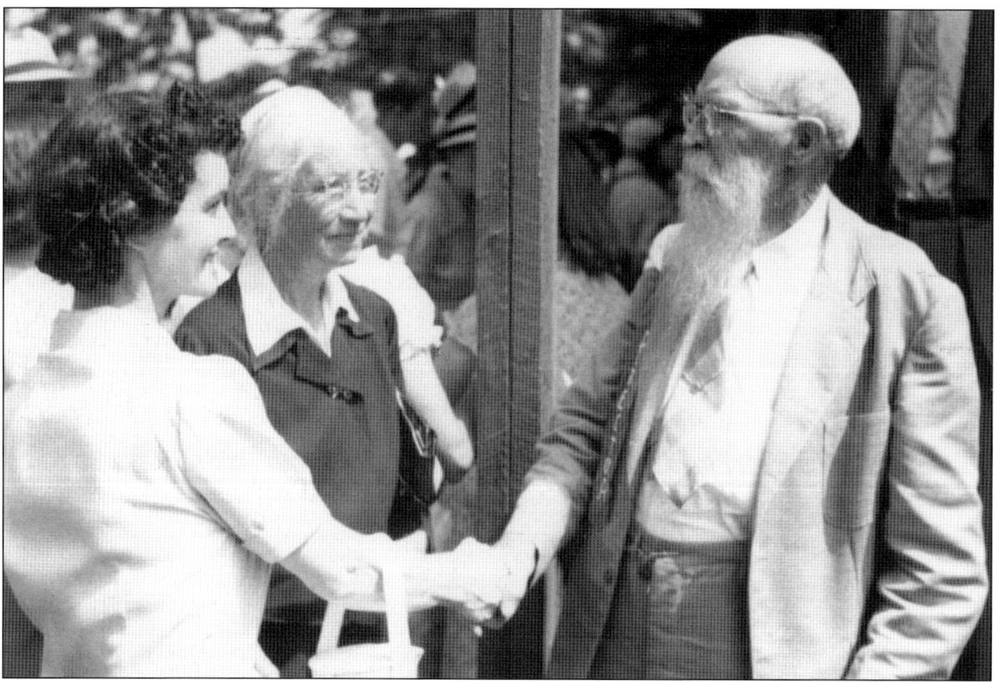

The Reverend Shelby E. Gragg, a Watauga County native, was 90 years old when this photograph was taken at Singing on the Mountain in 1951. He often preached at the annual event for over three decades. (Courtesy of North Carolina Archives.)

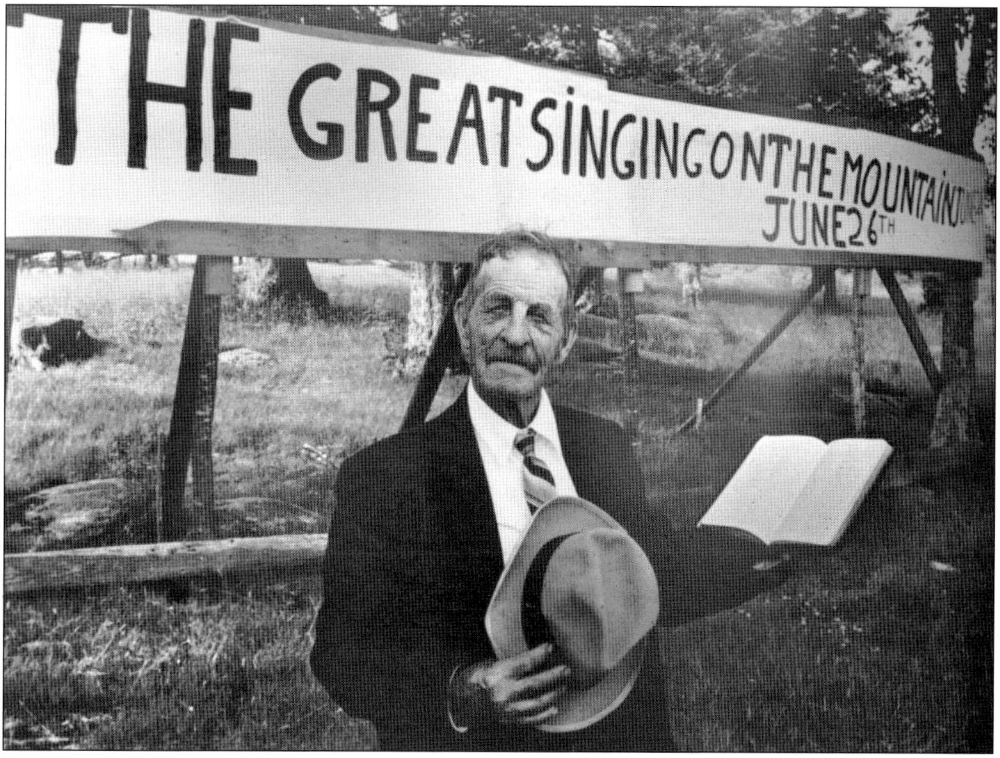

Joe Hartley is standing in front of a hand-lettered sign promoting the annual Singing on the Mountain event. Hartley was once quoted as saying, "The Almighty didn't make but one mistake. He didn't make a man who would last 200 years." Hartley died at the age of 95. (Courtesy of the Avery County Historical Museum.)

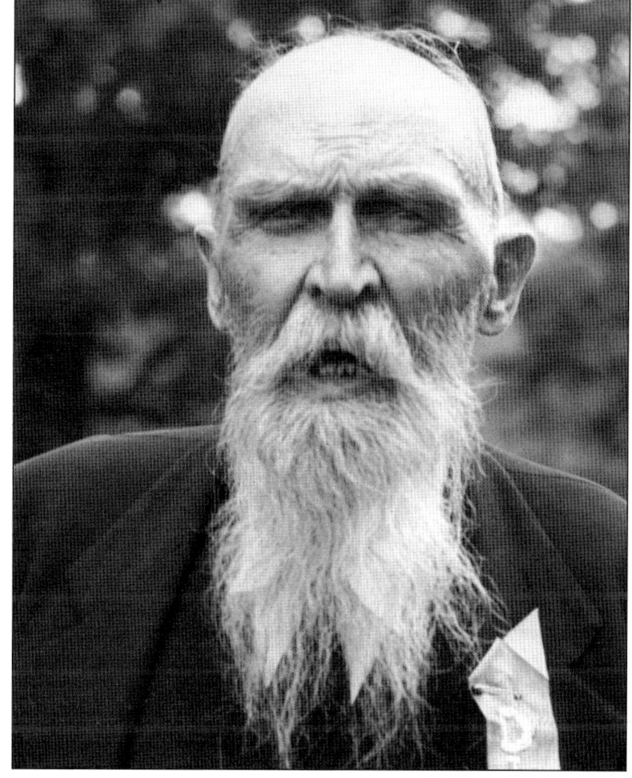

The Reverend Shelby Gragg, dubbed the "Patriarch of the Hills" by the press, was 94 years old when he passed away in 1956. Born in Watauga County, Gragg had participated in the Singing on the Mountain for 25 years. (Courtesy of Avery County Historical Museum.)

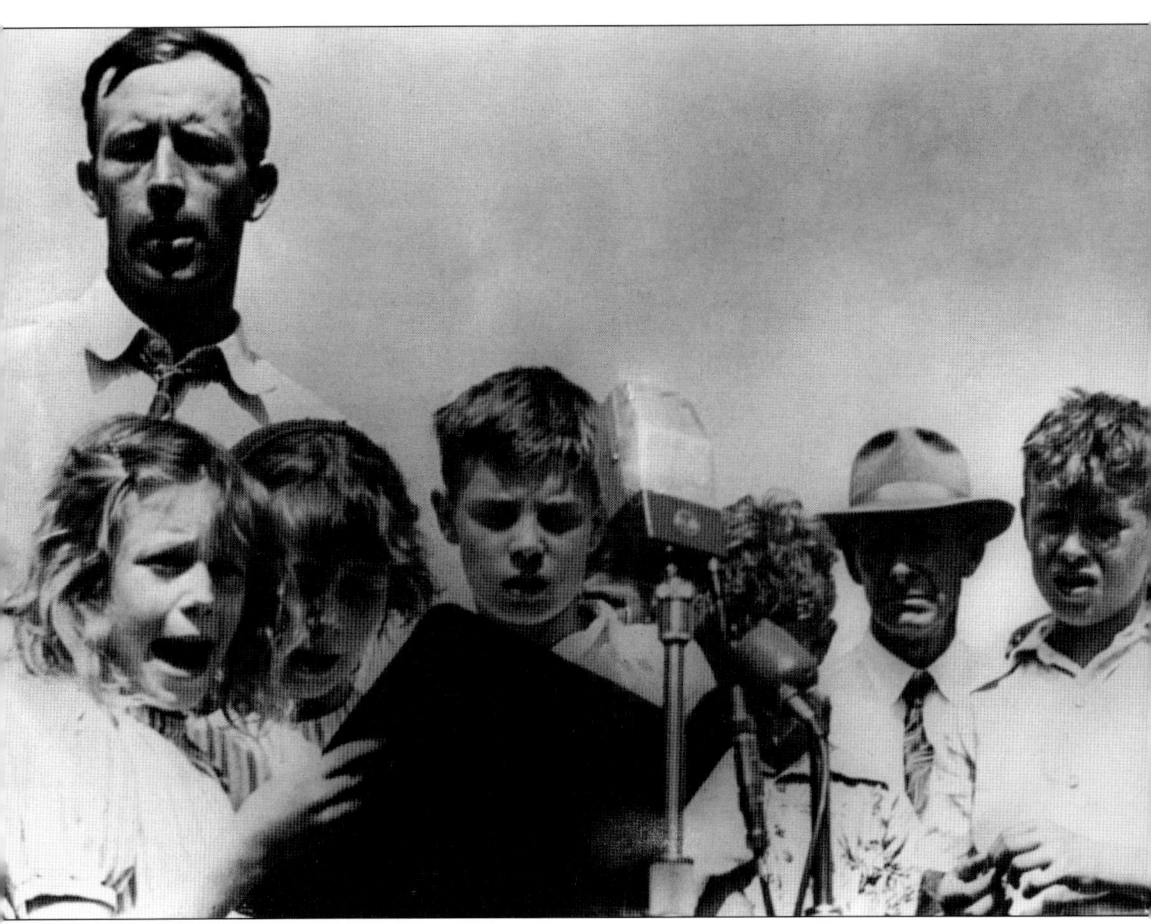

The early Singing on the Mountain events, like this one in the late 1940s, allowed anyone to sing. The two young ladies on the left are sisters Jean (left) and Betty Crawford, while their father, Cecil Crawford, stands behind them. The other gentleman in the photograph is the grandfather of the girls, Elmer Crawford. The other youngsters are unidentified. (Courtesy of Dana Crawford.)

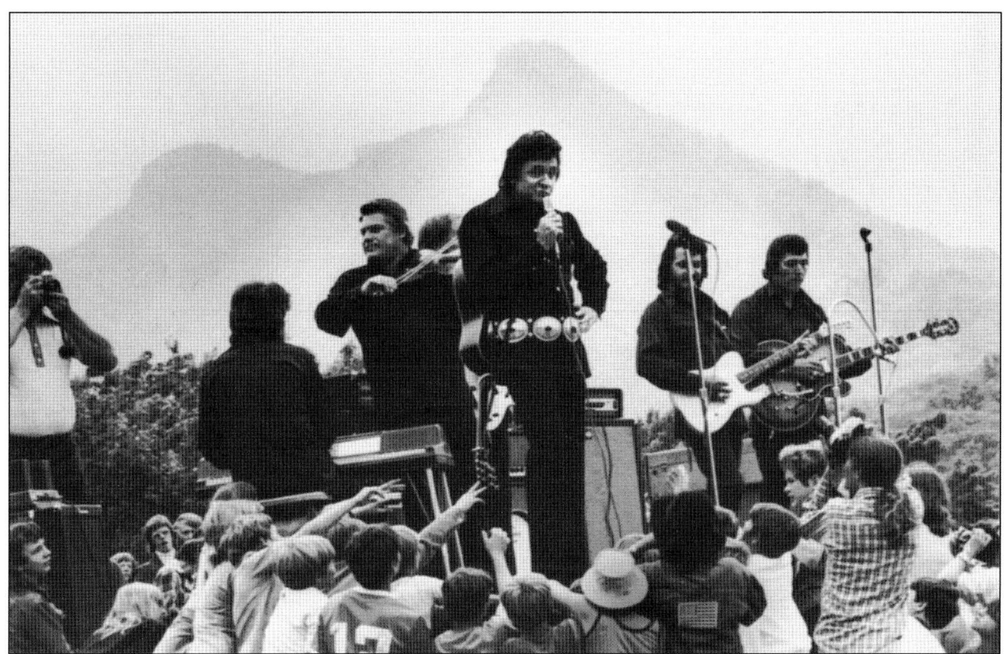

One of the biggest turnouts for a Singing on the Mountain event came in 1974, when country music superstar Johnny Cash sang to a crowd of thousands. Also on the bill that day with Johnny were June Carter Cash, Arthur Smith, Carl Perkins, and George Hamilton IV. Among the speakers was North Carolina governor Jim Holshouser. (Courtesy of Grandfather Mountain.)

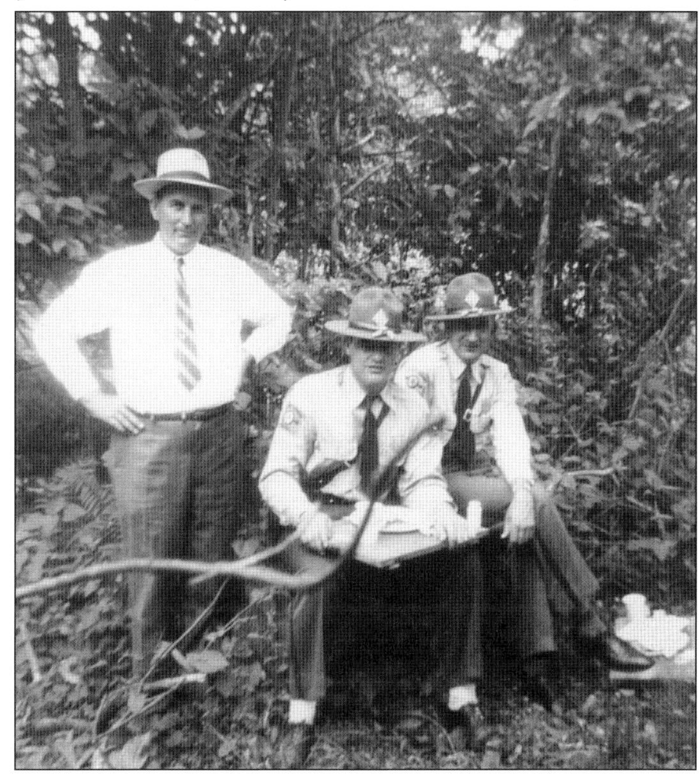

From left to right, Floyd Hayes is pictured with North Carolina Highway Patrol troopers Bolin and Pipes. For many years, the annual Singing on the Mountain event was a strain on law enforcement officers. On the Friday night before the celebration, a small carnival-type event was held, and numerous people, moved by the wrong "spirit," found themselves in the Avery County Jail. (Courtesy of Floyd Hayes Photograph Collection.)

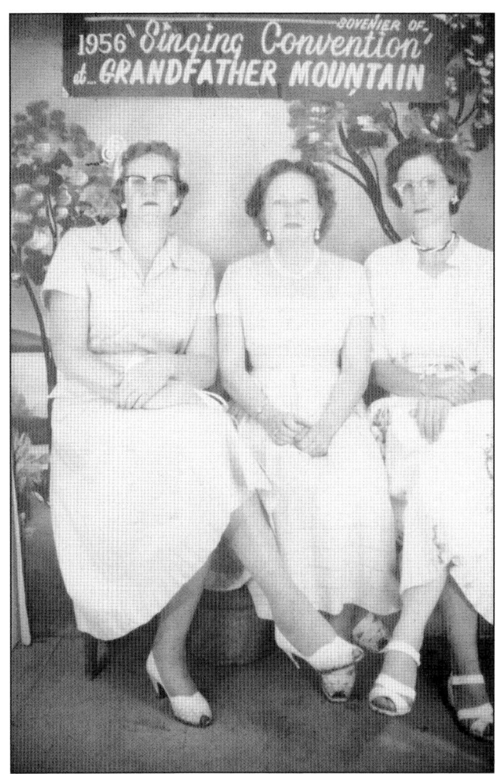

At many of the Singing on the Mountain events in the 1950s, Friday nights featured food vendors and even a photo booth. These three ladies are, from left to right, Willie Shell, Jean Hayes, and Mary Hayes, who visited that booth to have their image taken in 1956. (Courtesy of Floyd Hayes Photograph Collection.)

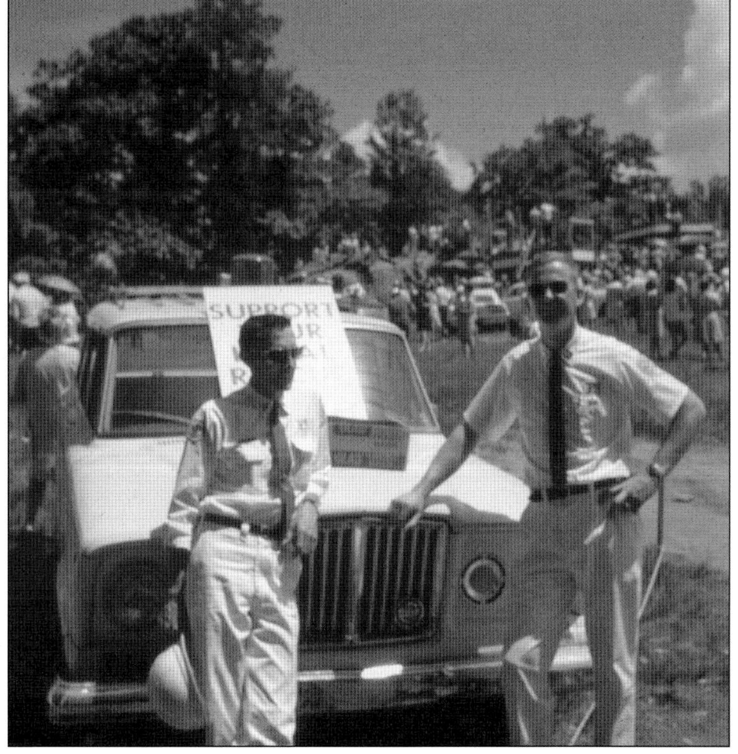

Harmon (left) and David Charles Vance of the Avery County Rescue Squad pose at the Singing on the Mountain. For decades, local volunteer fire departments have used the annual event for fundraising. (Courtesy of Floyd Hayes Photograph Collection.)

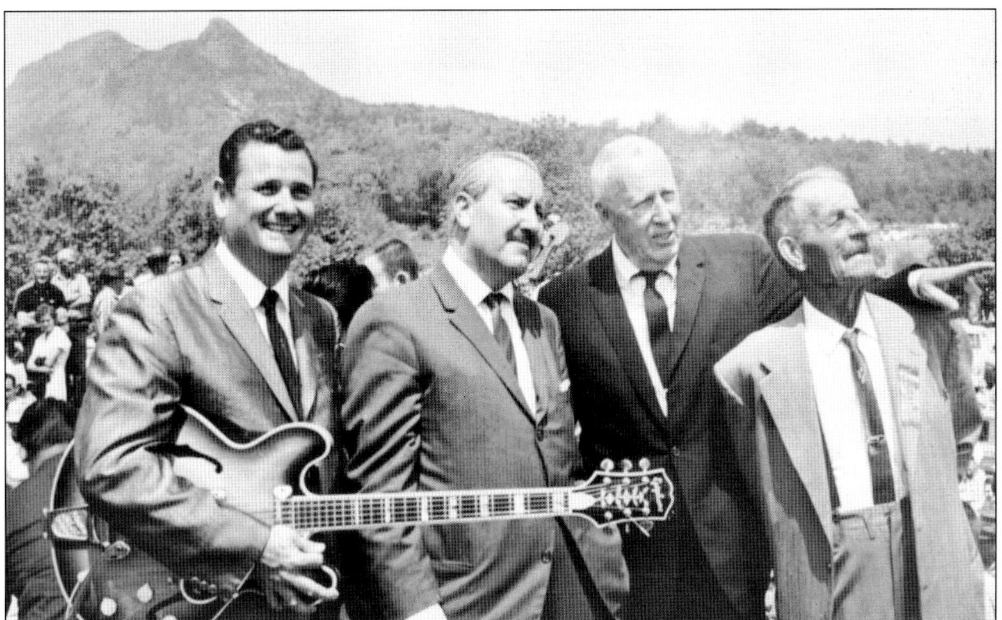

From left to right are legendary television performer and longtime music master of the Singing on the Mountain, Arthur Smith; John Parris, the noted Appalachian author; Joe Emerson, who led the Hymns of All Churches Choir; and Singing on the Mountain founder and chairman, Joe L. Hartley. (Courtesy of Lees-McRae College/Grandfather Mountain.)

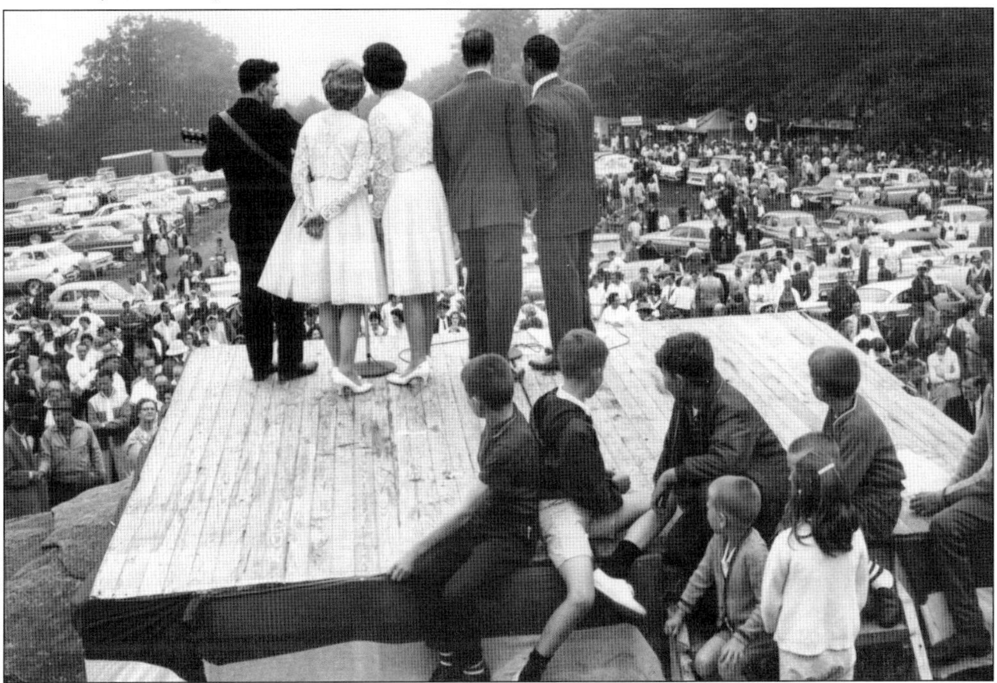

Not only has the musical lineup changed over the years at the annual Singing on the Mountain, but also the venue, at least slightly. In this photograph, a wooden platform covers the rock, and there are no chairs. Participants literally drove right up. The volunteer fire departments of Crossnore and Grassy Creek have booths in the background. (Courtesy of Avery County Historical Museum.)

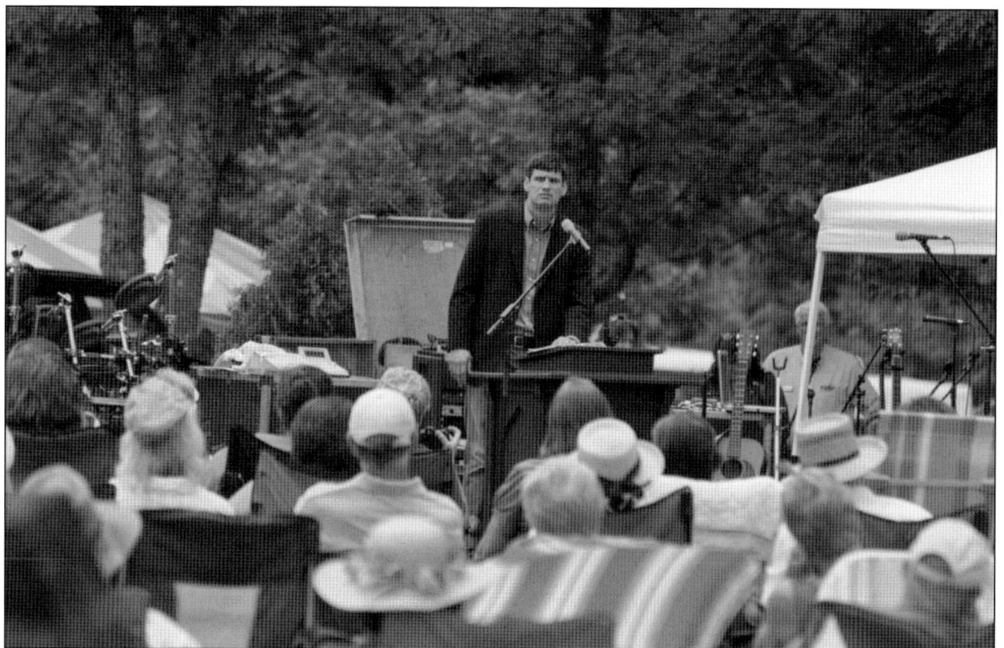

On June 23, 2013, at the 89th annual Singing on the Mountain, the Reverend Will Graham delivered the afternoon message. It was the first time a third-generation preacher had spoken at the event. The evangelist Rev. Billy Graham is Will Graham's grandfather, and noted philanthropist Franklin Graham is his father. (Courtesy of Michael Hardy.)

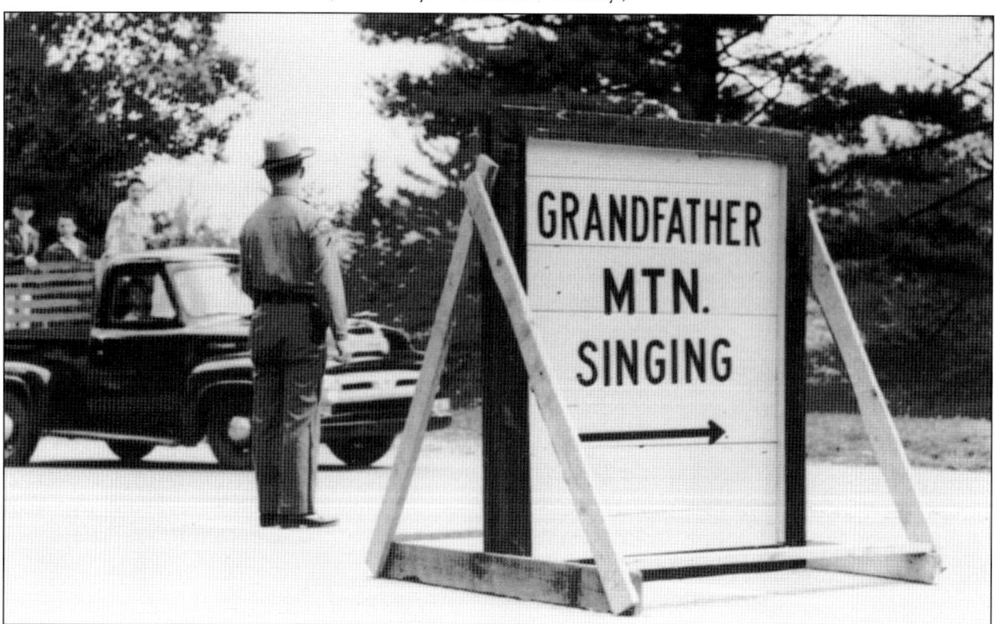

Getting to the annual Singing on the Mountain posed a problem some years. The years of 1962, 1968, and 1974 were especially bad, when Billy Graham, Oral Roberts, and Johnny Cash came to preach and sing. In those years, up to a five-hour wait, or closed roads altogether, greeted attendees. Local and state law enforcement are still on hand each year to help with any problems. (Courtesy of Grandfather Mountain.)

Six

Grandfather Mountain Highland Games

Although the roots of Scottish Highland Games come from the distant past, the modern games, as they are known today, date back about 200 years. The Grandfather Mountain Highland Games and Gathering of Scottish Games was founded by Donald MacDonald and Agnes MacRae Morton in 1956. There were 7,000 people at the first games, which were modeled on the Highland Games held in Braemar, Scotland, and included the shot put, caber toss, sprints, 440-yard dash, high jump, broad jump, pole vault, tug-of-war, and wrestling, along with Highland dancing. Over the decades, the games evolved from one Sunday afternoon to a Saturday and Sunday, and finally to a four-day event. They were also moved from August to July. The Grandfather Mountain Highland Games are the largest gathering of the clans in the United States. The events start on Thursday with a footrace up the mountain, a picnic, and a torchlight procession, with over 150 competitions in the heavy events on Friday, Saturday, and Sunday. There are also concerts, ceilidhs, and the *kirking* ("blessing") of the tartans on Sunday morning. Many people arrive in the area and camp for a week prior to the Grandfather Mountain Highland Games. Weddings have taken place, and in 1991, a baby was born there. Tens of thousands attend each year. Part of the lure of the Grandfather Mountain Highland Games is the setting, with its rhododendrons and laurel, trees, rocky terrain, and even thistles.

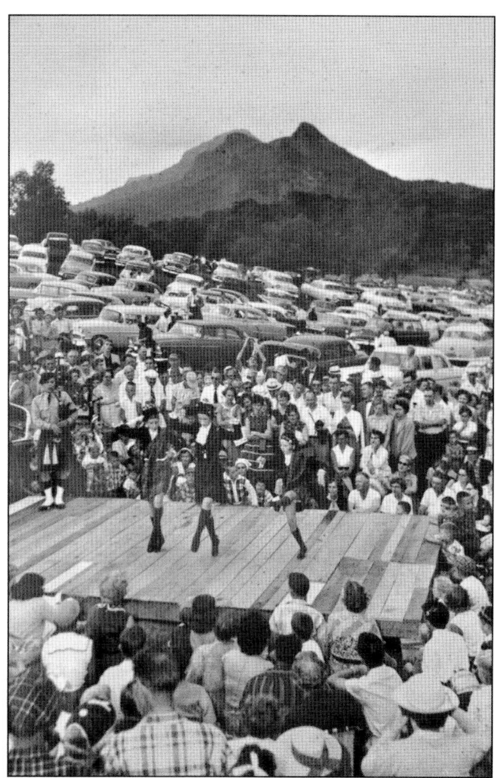

This early photograph, possibly of the first Grandfather Mountain Highland Games, shows young ladies competing in a dance contest. Over the years, the dance venues have evolved onto more elaborate, structured stages. (Courtesy of Grandfather Mountain Highland Games.)

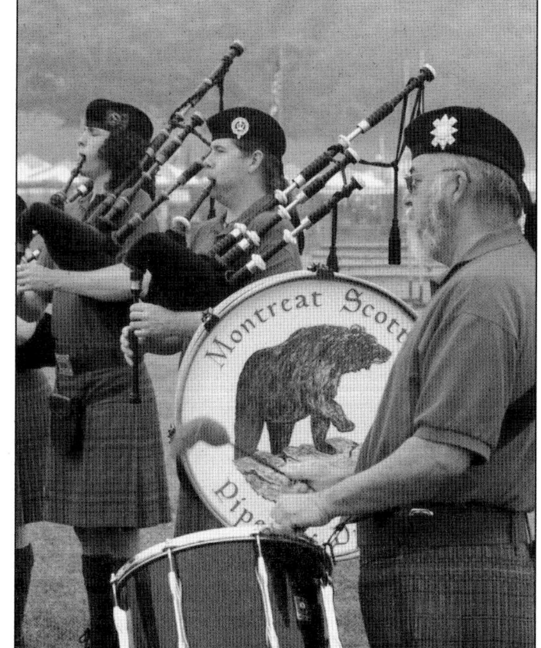

Piping bands are invited to come from all over the United States to perform each year at the Grandfather Mountain Highland Games. The Montreat Scottish Pipes and Drums come from the Asheville area. (Courtesy of *Avery Journal-Times*.)

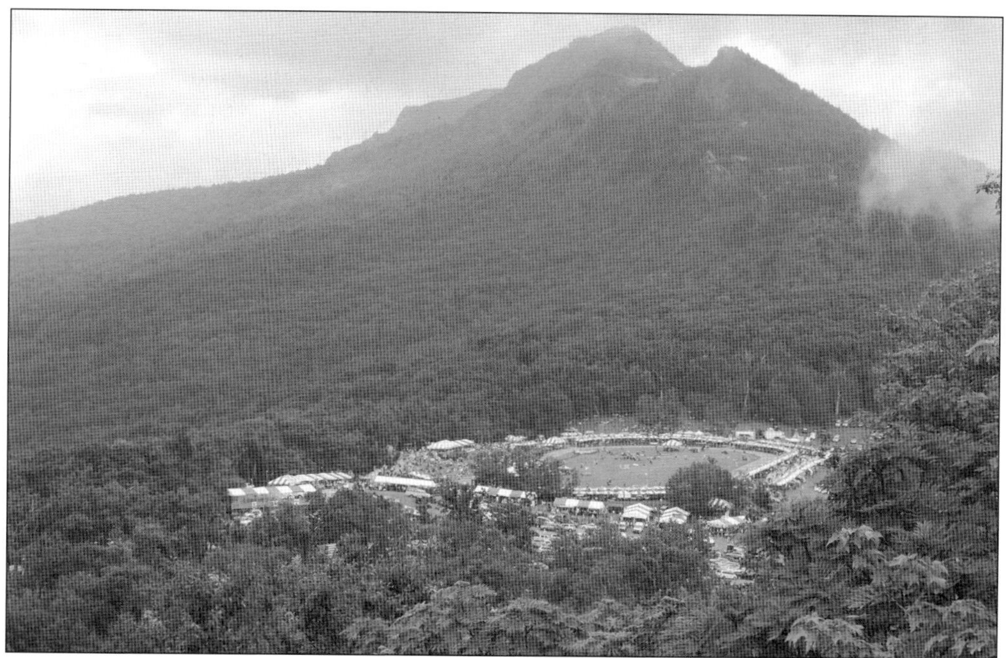

Here is an aerial view of the Grandfather Mountain Highland Games with Grandfather Mountain in the background overlooking the festivities. The many tents include displays on individual families, musicians, and vendors of a variety of food and other products. They also come in handy when the summer weather is foul rather than fair. (Courtesy of *Avery Journal-Times*/Helen Moss Davis.)

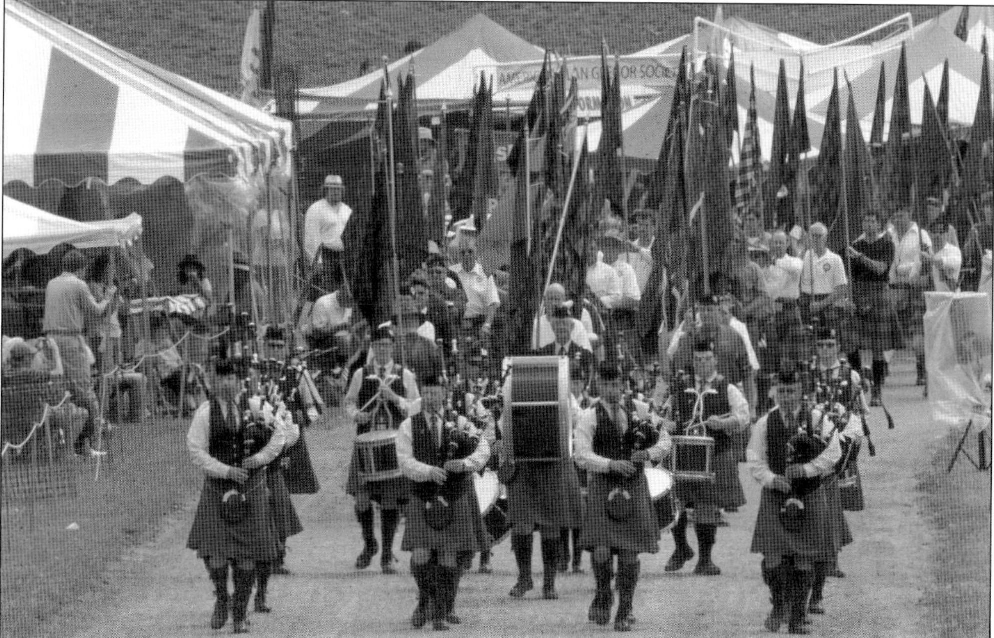

Pipers lead the parade of tartans at the July 2012 Grandfather Mountain Highland Games. Bagpipes are popular at many local gatherings, including the annual commencement for Mayland Community College. (Courtesy of *Avery Journal-Times*/Jeff Easton.)

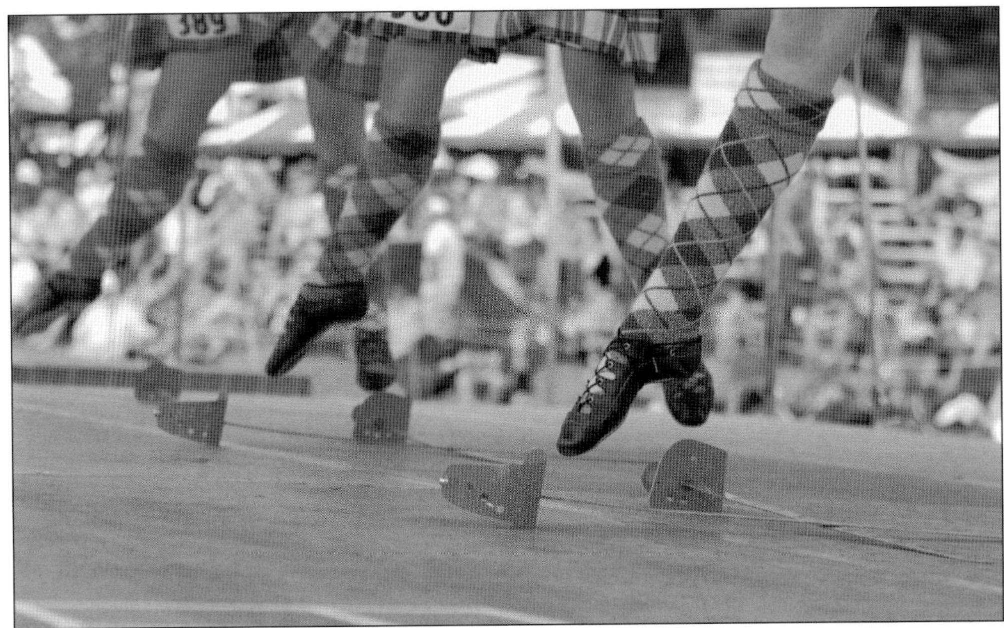

One of the most popular traditional dances at the Grandfather Mountain Highland Games is the Sword Dance, which, according to legend, is based on the victory celebration of Malcom, son of King Duncan, who defeated the treacherous Macbeth. Though William Shakespeare undoubtedly fictionalized a number of elements, Malcom and Macbeth were historic figures, and perhaps, Malcom did dance over his own and Macbeth's naked swords to commemorate his victory. (Courtesy of *Avery Journal-Times*/Helen Moss Davis.)

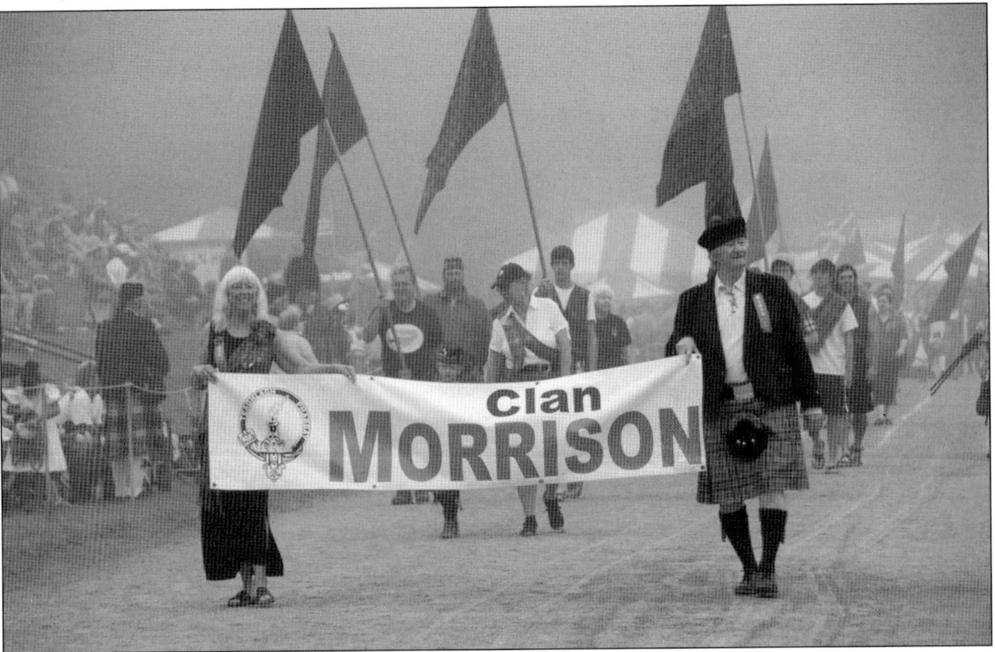

Local publisher Nancy Morrison and her husband, Bruce, lead the Morrison clan in the 2011 Grandfather Mountain Highland Games behind the massed pipe bands. (Courtesy of *Avery Journal-Times*/Helen Moss Davis.)

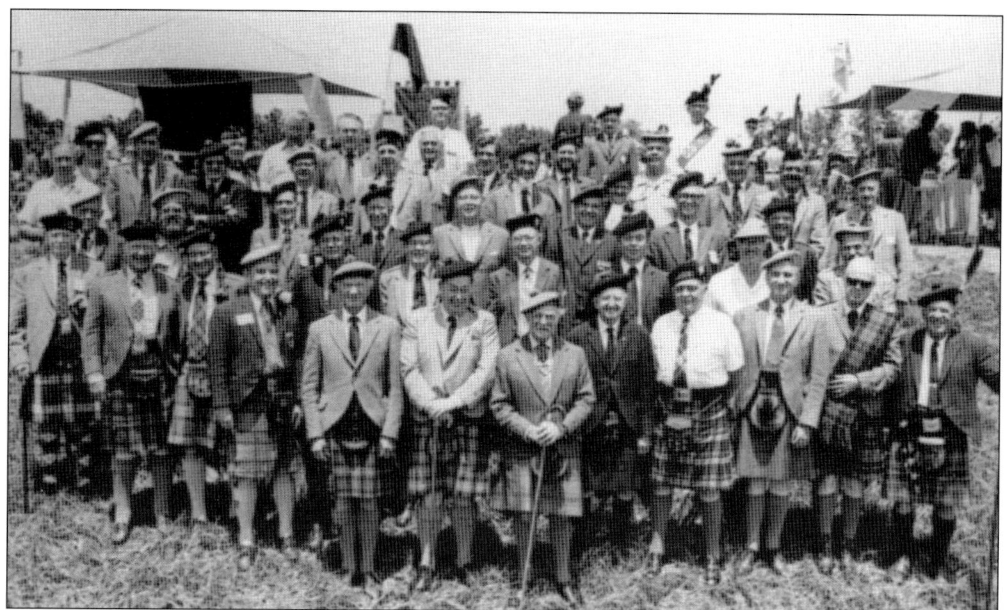

A group of kilted Highland chiefs poses for a photograph at one of the early Grandfather Mountain Highland Games. Such group photo opportunities are always a highlight of the games, as they bring together groups like these, family groups, or clan members who may only gather once a year. (Courtesy of Grandfather Mountain.)

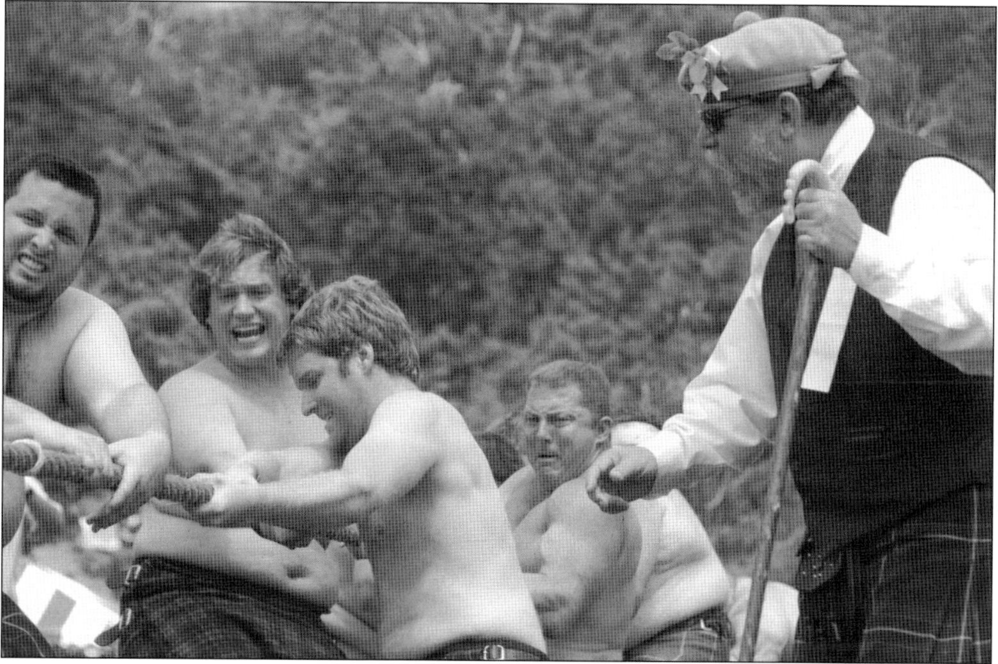

The tug-of-war has been a popular competition at the Grandfather Mountain Highland Games since the beginning. The contest pits clan, or allied clans, against another clan in this ancient competition. At the first Grandfather games, the crowd replaced spent participants, and the tug-of-war went on for some time. This image dates to the 2011 Grandfather Mountain Highland Games. (Courtesy of *Avery Journal-Times*/Helen Moss Davis.)

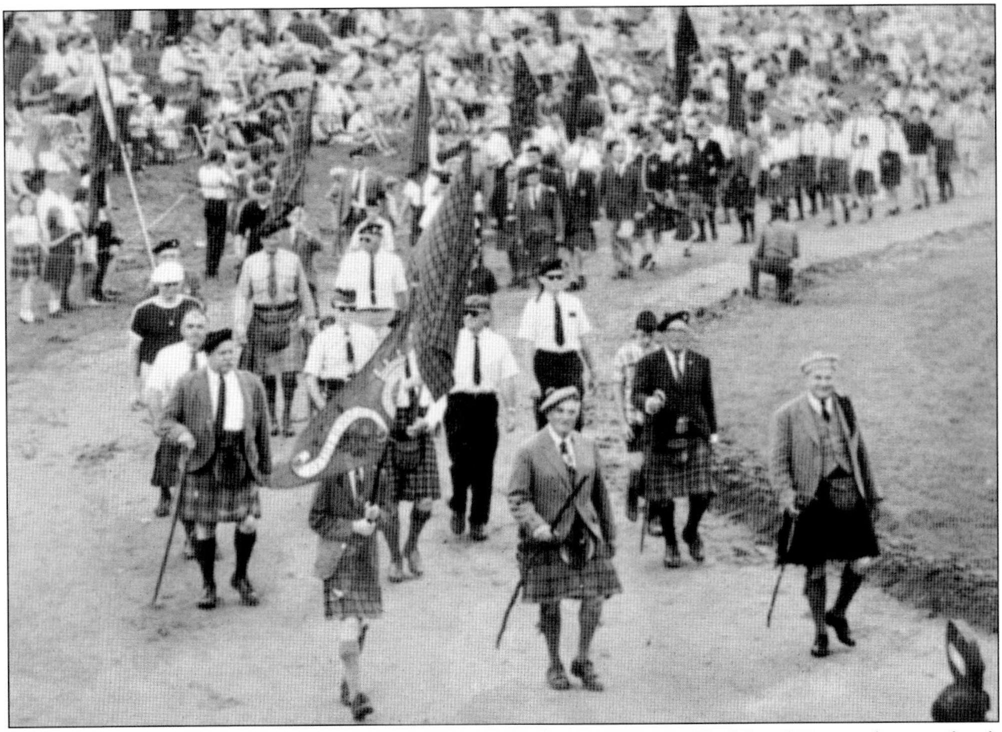

Over the years, the parade of tartans at the Grandfather Mountain Highland Games has evolved. Here, the marchers appear to be entirely male, while the crowd sits on the hillside. Toward the end of the 20th century, bleachers were used for the spectators, and the marchers began to include both male and female participants. (Courtesy of Grandfather Mountain Highland Games.)

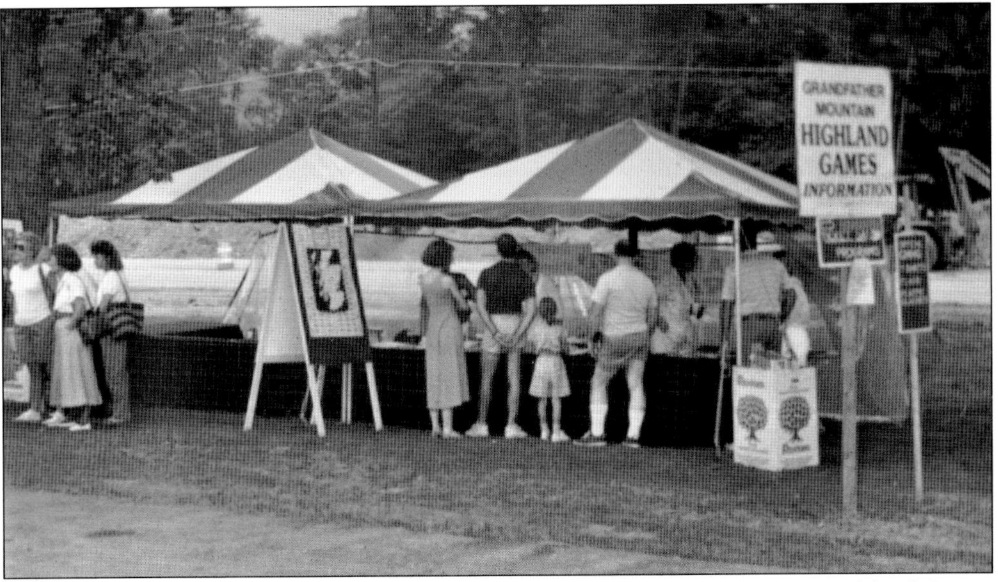

With tens of thousands of visitors coming to the annual Grandfather Mountain Highland Games every year, the information tent is vital. Local volunteers take on the duty of running the tent. In 2013, members of the *Avery Journal-Times* staffed the tent. (Courtesy of Grandfather Mountain Highland Games.)

A caber is a trimmed tree trunk, usually 16 to 20 feet long and weighing at least 90 pounds. Once upright, the caber rests on the shoulder of the athlete, who works his hands down toward the bottom. He then lifts and balances the caber, starts off on a run, and at the precise moment, as the caber starts to fall, gives it a heave. (Courtesy of Grandfather Mountain Highland Games.)

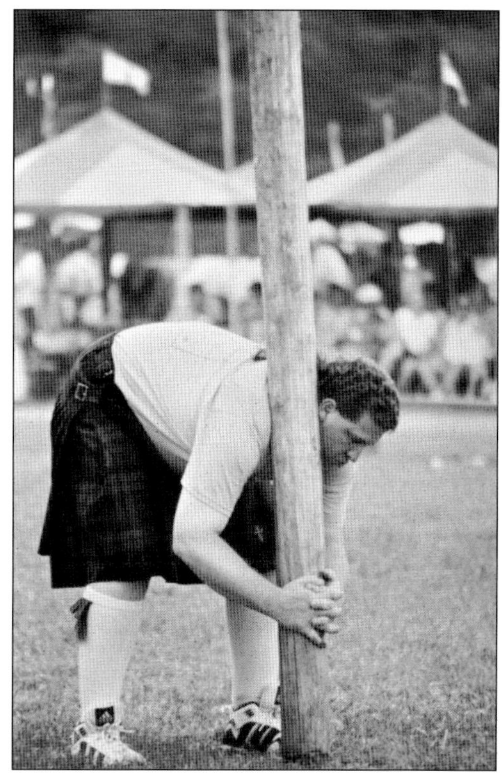

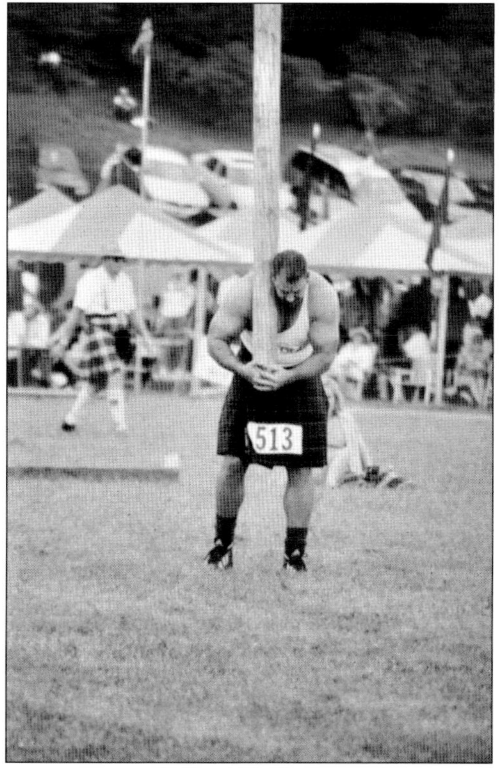

A judge follows the athlete and, once the caber is tossed, measures the spot from where the athlete stops and where the caber stops. Once the athlete tosses the caber, the caber is supposed to flip, pivoting on its heavy end. A toss that lands straight, in the 12 o'clock position, is scored as perfect. At times, championship cabers, weighing up to 160 pounds, are offered to challengers. (Courtesy of Grandfather Mountain Highland Games.)

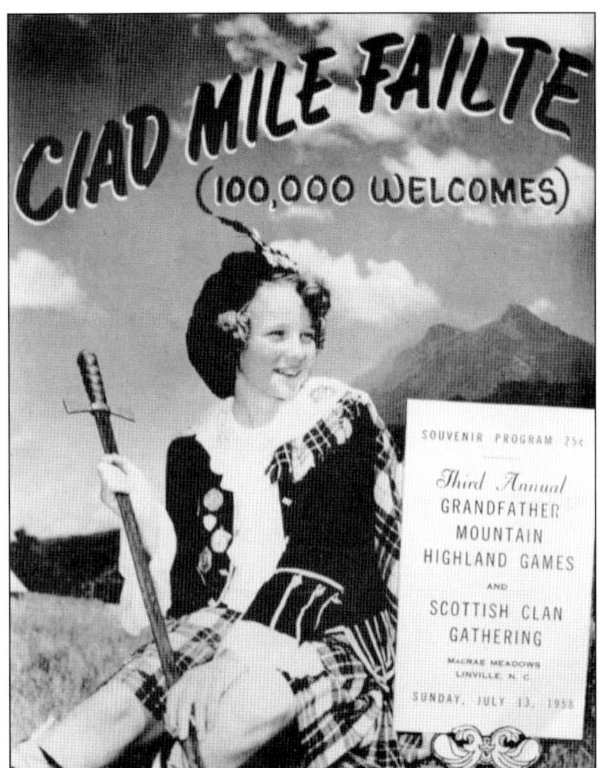

A souvenir program commemorates the third annual Grandfather Mountain Highland Games, held in 1958. The games were held on just one day until 1961, when two days were necessary for the competitions. In 1990, the games were held on three days, and beginning in 1995, at the 40th annual games, they went to four days. (Courtesy of Avery County Historical Museum.)

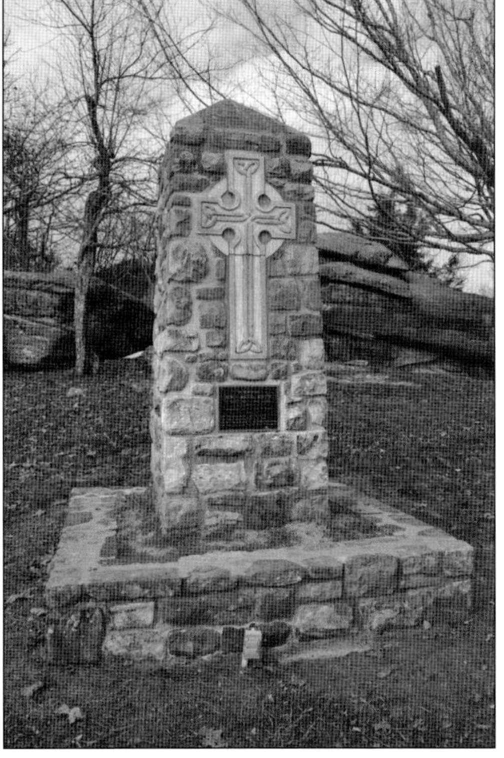

The Cofounders' Monument in the East Meadow is dedicated to Agnes MacRae Morton. The memorial was designed by Douglas Ferguson of Pigeon Forge, Tennessee, and constructed by Linville stonemason Clay Hartley. Morton, along with Donald MacDonald, cofounded the Grandfather Mountain Highland Games in 1956. The first games drew some 7,000 people. (Courtesy of Michael Hardy.)

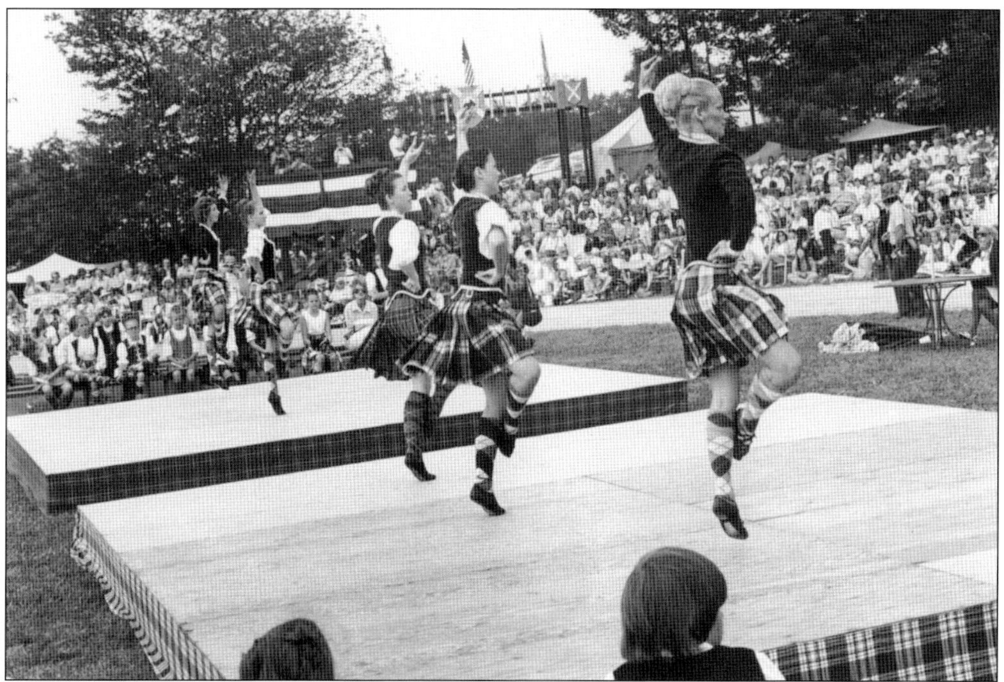

There are an estimated 15,000 different Scottish dances, including ceilidh dancing, country dancing, reeling dancing, Highland dancing, and step dancing. These competitors appear to be performing the Highland Fling, which was originally performed on a targe, a small round shield with a spike in the center. The spike taught the dancers to move with agility to avoid injury. (Courtesy of Grandfather Mountain Highland Games.)

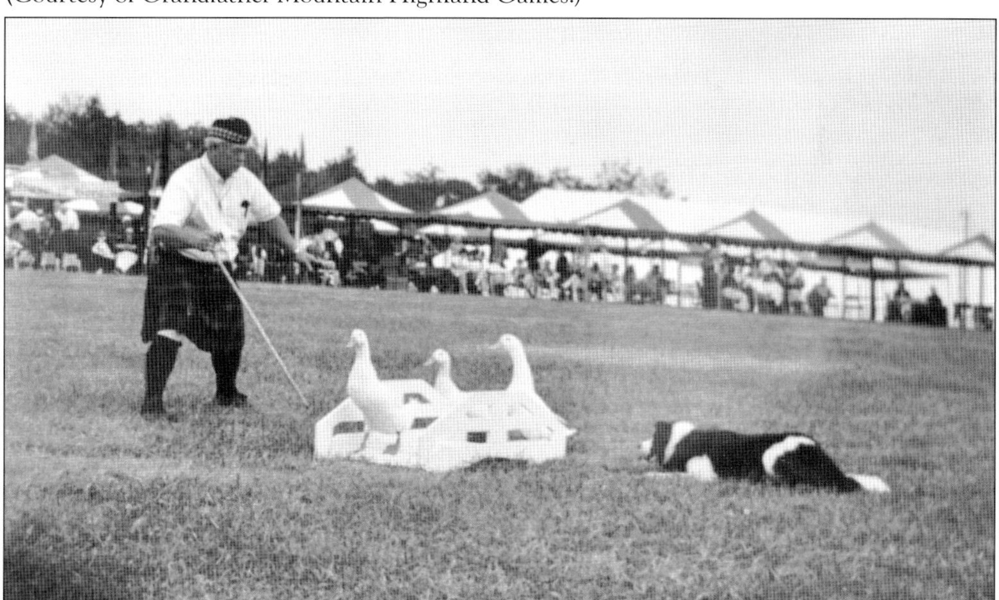

Not only does the Grandfather Mountain Highland Games feature demonstrations of sheep herding, but it also features demonstrations of herding ducks. Herder Stan Moore, from Philadelphia, Tennessee, shows off his national champion Border collie, Pete. (Courtesy of Grandfather Mountain Highland Games.)

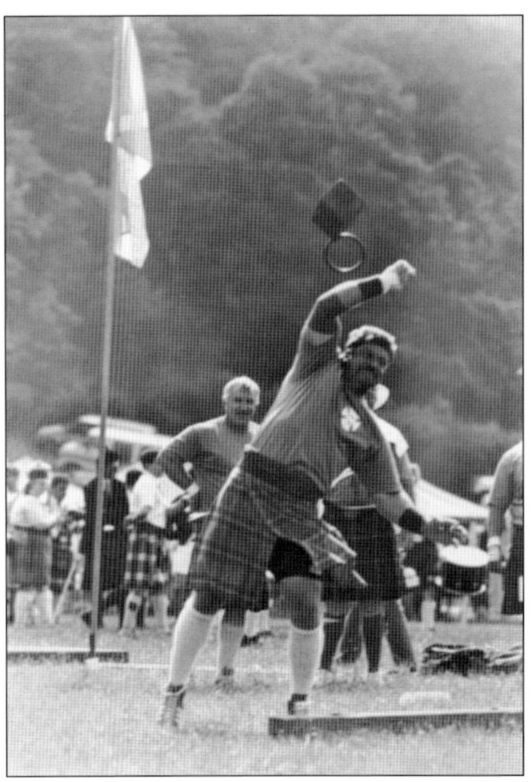

There are several different types of stone throws at the various Highland Games. These include the weight for height, weight for distance, and the stone throw, much like shot put. (Courtesy of Grandfather Mountain Highland Games.)

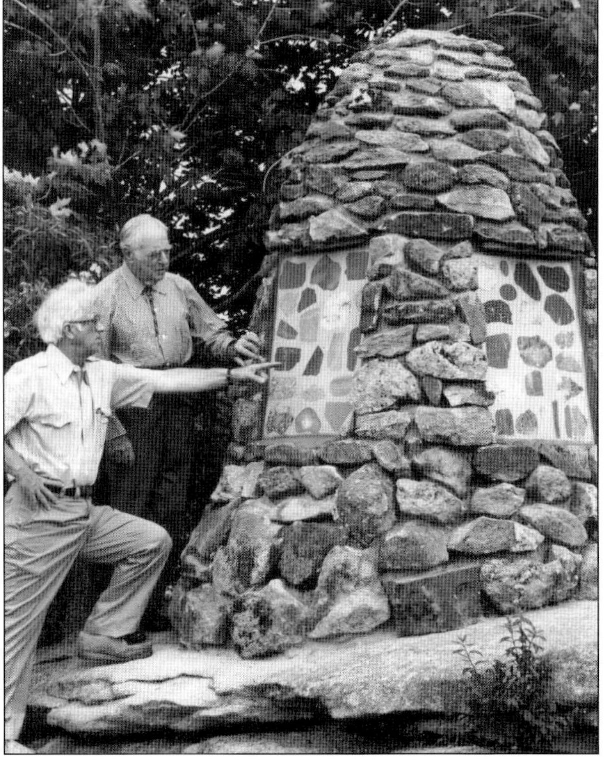

The memorial cairn at MacRae Meadows was dedicated in 1980. A series of panels features 74 polished stones contributed by different Scottish clans. The stones originally came from Scotland. At the dedication, Nestor McDonald read from Sir Walter Scott's "The Lay of the Last Minstrel." (Courtesy of *Mountain Times*/Grandfather Mountain.)

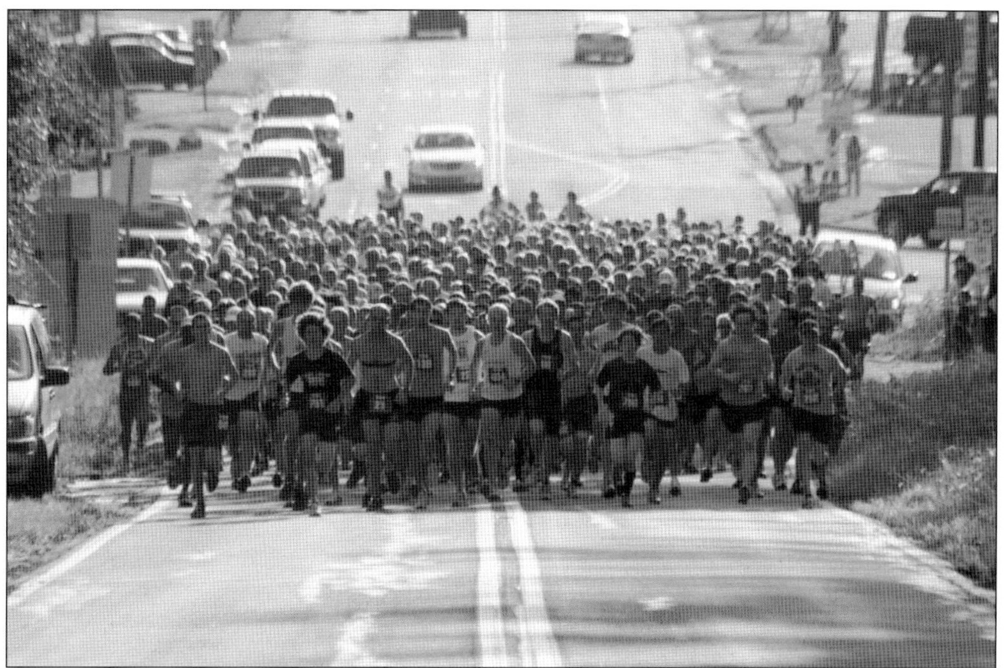

The Bear is a five-mile footrace that begins at the foot of Grandfather Mountain in Linville, works its way through the campground and MacRae Meadows, and ends at the Mile-High Swinging Bridge. In 2012, there were 700 runners registered. This image was captured just seconds after the start of the 2011 race. (Courtesy of *Avery Journal-Times*/James Shaffer.)

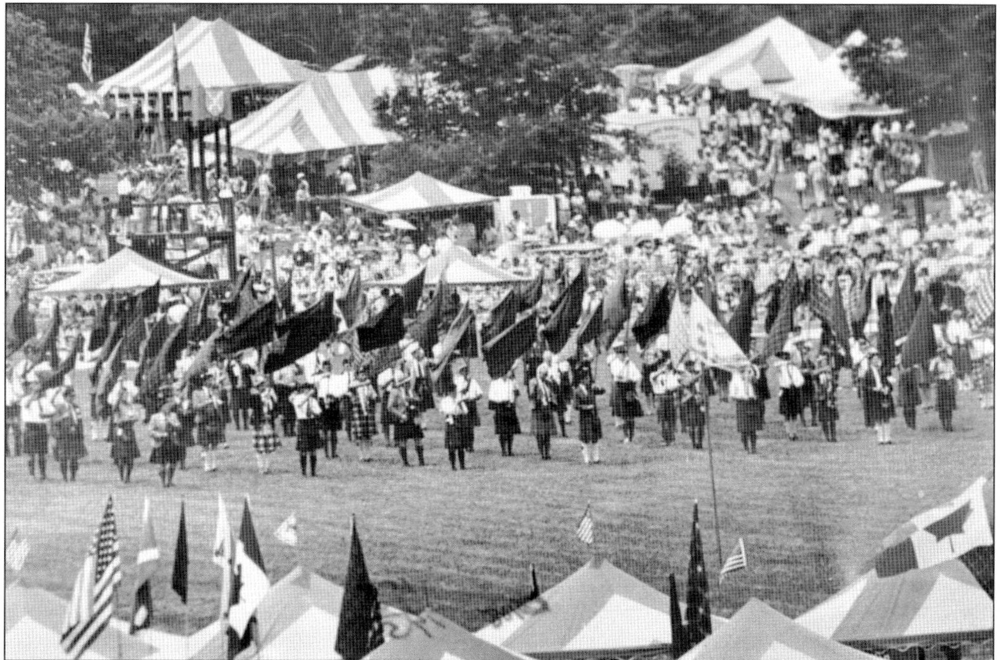

Members of each clan proudly display the tartans of their respective families. Those who wish to learn about their own families, or clans, can visit the clan tents to learn about family history, crests, and tartans. (Courtesy of Grandfather Mountain Highland Games.)

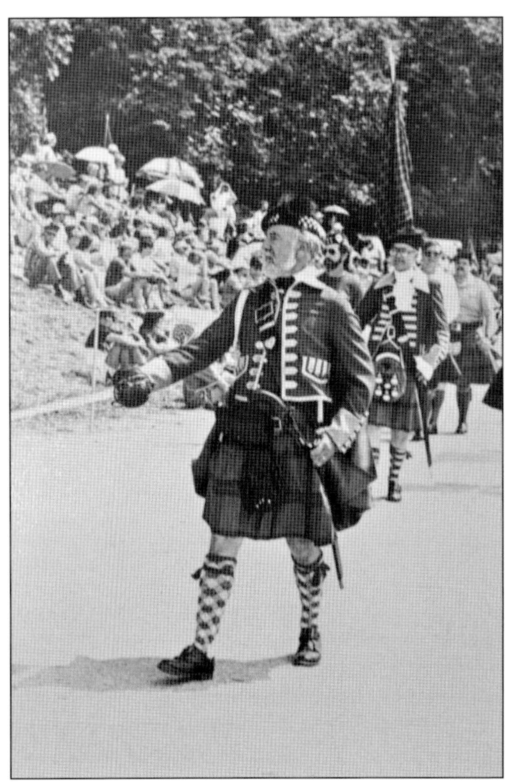

John Dall salutes the stand in the parade of tartans in 1987. Dall was a decorated British World War II veteran and, in 2010, received the Agnes MacRae Morton Award for service at the games. He served as director of the *kirking* and parade of tartans for a number of years. Dall, who passed in 2012, called Haywood County home. (Courtesy of Grandfather Mountain Highland Games.)

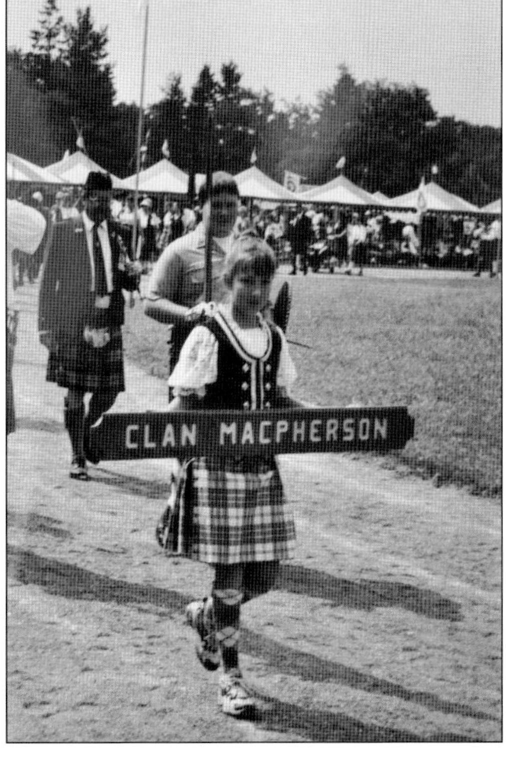

Every year, each of the clans can have representatives in the annual parade of tartans around the track at the Grandfather Mountain Highland Games. This photograph shows a young member of Clan MacPherson; she is watched over by arms-bearing clansmen. (Courtesy of Grandfather Mountain Highland Games.)

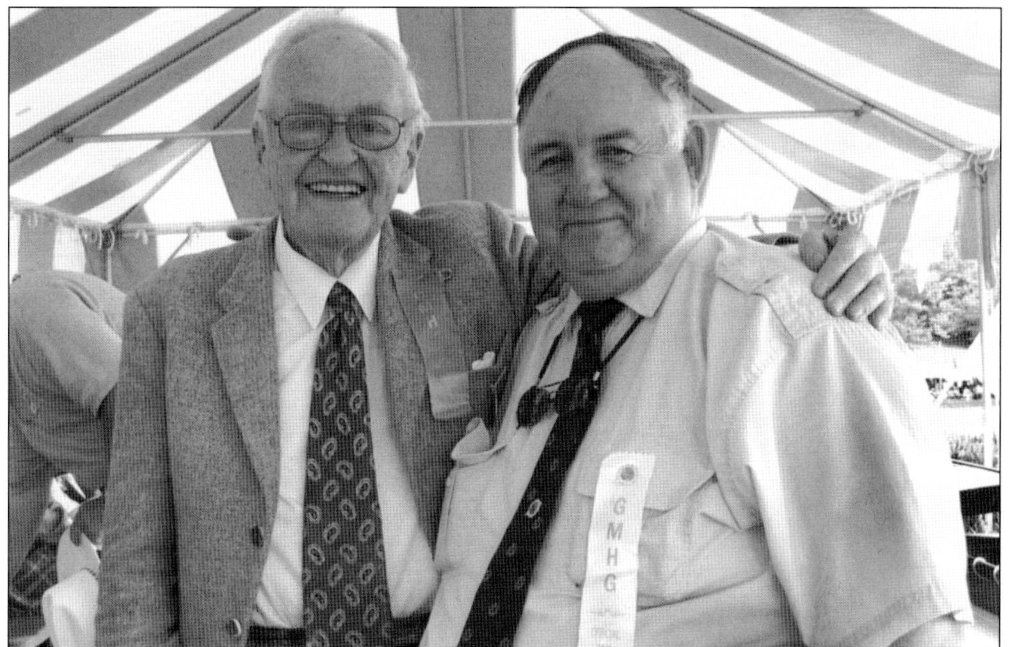

Former Charlotte journalist Donald McDonald, on the left, was a cofounder of the Grandfather Mountain Highland Games and served as the first president of the board, from 1956 until 1961. He is pictured with Frank Vance, general manager of the games for many years. (Courtesy of *Avery Journal-Times*.)

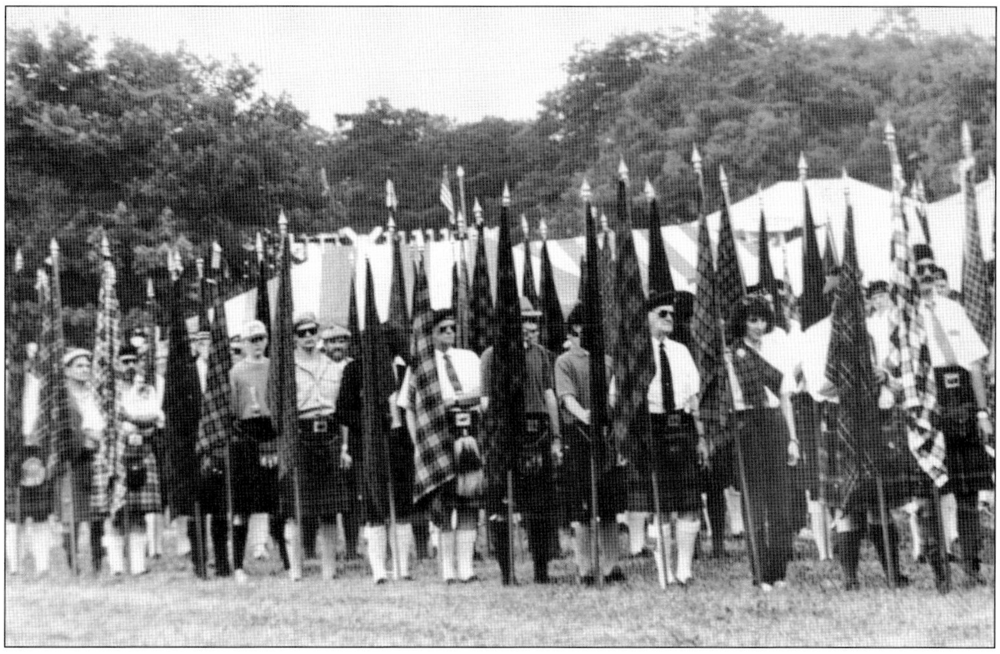

Tartan bearers line up for the parade of tartans, which immediately follows the *kirking* of the tartans on Sunday. Allowing families to display their iconic plaids, both events are highlights of the annual Grandfather Mountain Highland Games. (Courtesy of Grandfather Mountain Highland Games.)

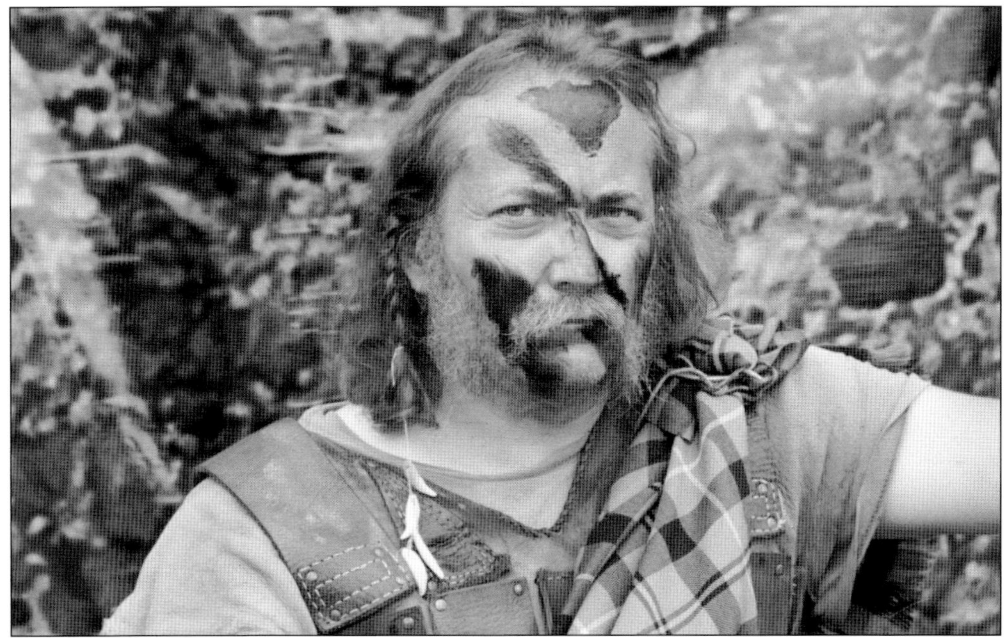

Tim Morris, the Clan Armorer for Clan MacNeil, goes beyond the normal attire for the Grandfather Mountain Highland Games. He dons clothing more in line for 12th-to-13th-century Scotland, around the time of famed William Wallace, one of the main leaders of the Wars of Scottish Independence. (Courtesy of *Avery Journal-Times*/James Shaffer.)

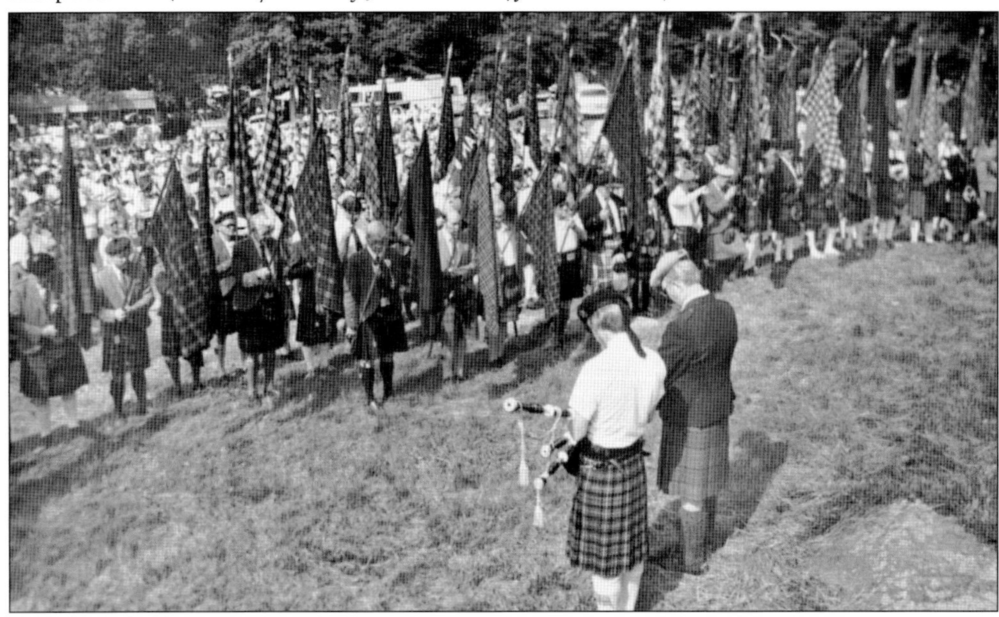

Traditionally, the *kirking* of the tartans takes place on Sunday morning at the Grandfather Mountain Highland Games. Some say that the *kirking*, a Gaelic word for blessing, dates to the mid-1700s, when Scots were forbidden to wear tartans. Scottish Highlanders hid pieces of tartan under their clothing and touched them when the minister offered a blessing. The ceremony, as it is known today, started in Washington, DC, in 1941. (Courtesy of Grandfather Mountain Highland Games.)

Seven

Grandfather Mountain State Park

For decades, everyone who saw the stately Grandfather Mountain wanted it turned into a park. Capt. Walter W. Lenoir proposed the idea in the 1870s and 1880s. In 1893, the press announced that there was legislation being introduced to acquire Grandfather Mountain as a national park. A newspaper article in July 1908 in the *Charlotte Observer* even referred to the entire 16,000-acre tract as "Linville Park." Later, that same newspaper reported that Hugh and Nelson MacRae had given the property to the state. That plan fell through, but almost a decade later, the press was reporting in 1917 that Hugh MacRae had given the property to the federal government. It appears that the federal government wanted to add the property to what is now known as the Pisgah National Forest. MacRae was opposed to the idea, and the plan never materialized. The North Carolina Board of Geology attempted to start a movement in 1922 to acquire the area for a state park. In fact, there were discussions every few years right up through World War II about Grandfather Mountain becoming a park. Even Hugh Morton, in an article in the *Greensboro Daily News* on January 31, 1943, wrote, "Obtaining Grandfather Mountain for a state park would be a wise utilization of the natural resources of North Carolina." However, once Morton became the sole owner of the mountain, the talk quickly subsided. Following the passing of Hugh Morton in 2006, his heirs chose to sell 2,456 acres to the state. This was finalized in 2009, and the Grandfather Mountain State Park was created, encompassing much of the backcountry. The attraction side of Grandfather Mountain came under the management of a new not-for-profit organization, the Grandfather Mountain Stewardship Foundation, and the state park's office opened in nearby Foscoe.

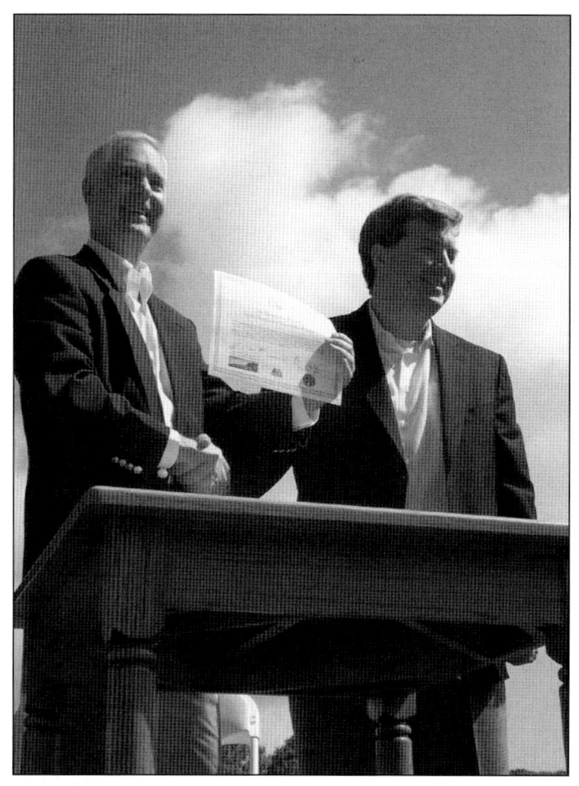

In September 2009, North Carolina governor Mike Easley, on the left, signed an agreement to purchase a large portion of Grandfather Mountain from the Morton family. Grandfather Mountain president Hugh MacRae "Crae" Morton III, on the right, signed the document on behalf of the family. The state acquired over 2,000 acres that would become the Grandfather Mountain State Park. (Courtesy of *Avery Journal-Times*.)

Grandfather Mountain president Crae Morton, with the mountain in the background, spoke at length at the official ceremony in September 2009. Morton recalled that his grandfather, Hugh Morton, once asked, "Who can really own a mountain?" Morton felt that he was just a "steward and caretaker, but the mountain belonged to God and citizens." (Courtesy of Marilyn Ball.)

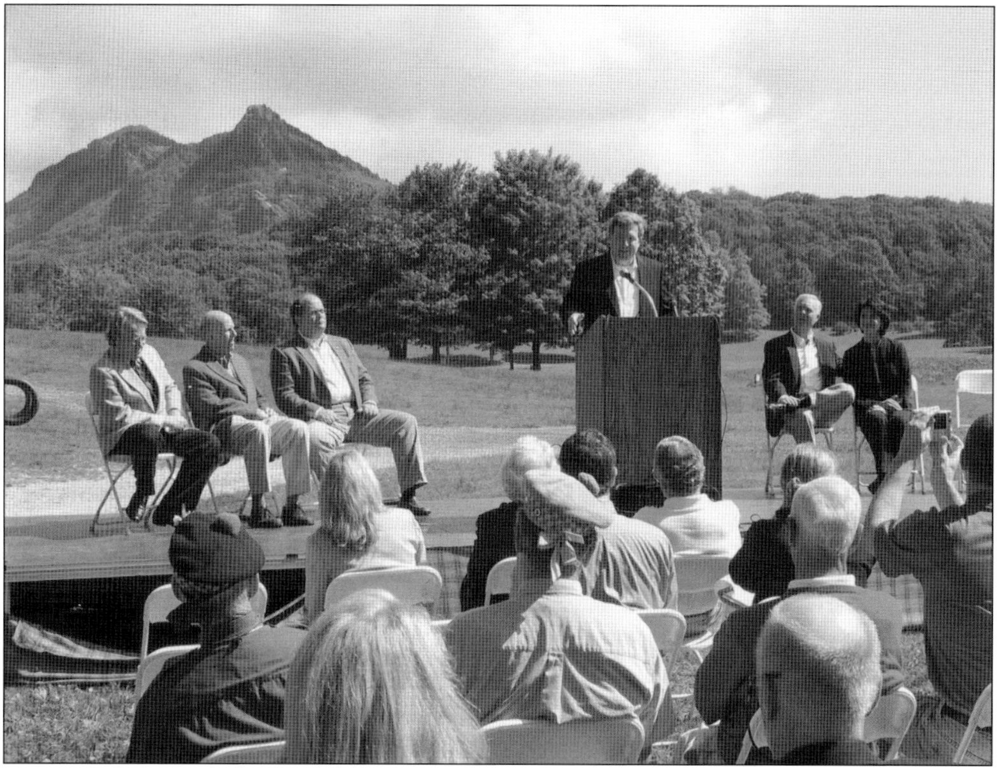

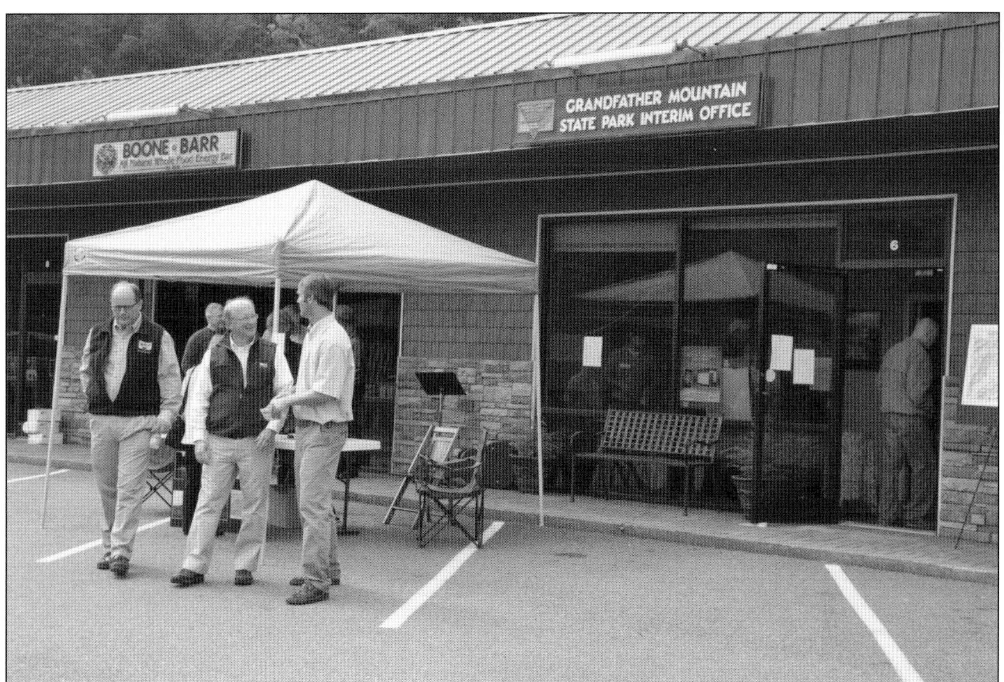

The official opening of the Grandfather Mountain State Park brought dignitaries such as Rep. Mitch Gillespie and Lewis Ledford, director of the North Carolina State Park Service. Grandfather Mountain State Park became the 34th state park in the North Carolina State Park system. (Courtesy of Michael Hardy.)

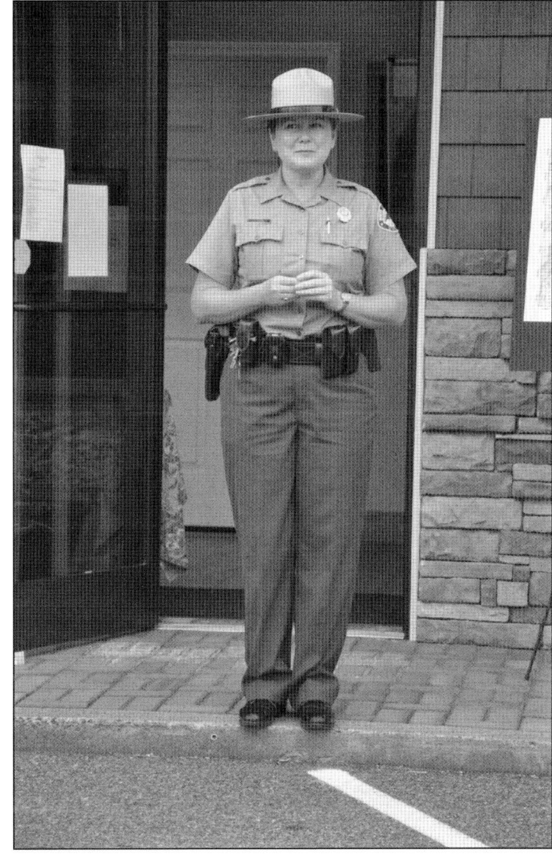

Susan McBean, superintendent of the Grandfather Mountain State Park, welcomes visitors on September 18, 2011, to the official opening of the Grandfather Mountain State Park. The offices of the park are located on Highway 105 in the Foscoe community. Visitors were invited to tour the offices, and the rangers provided several different games for children. (Courtesy of Michael C. Hardy.)

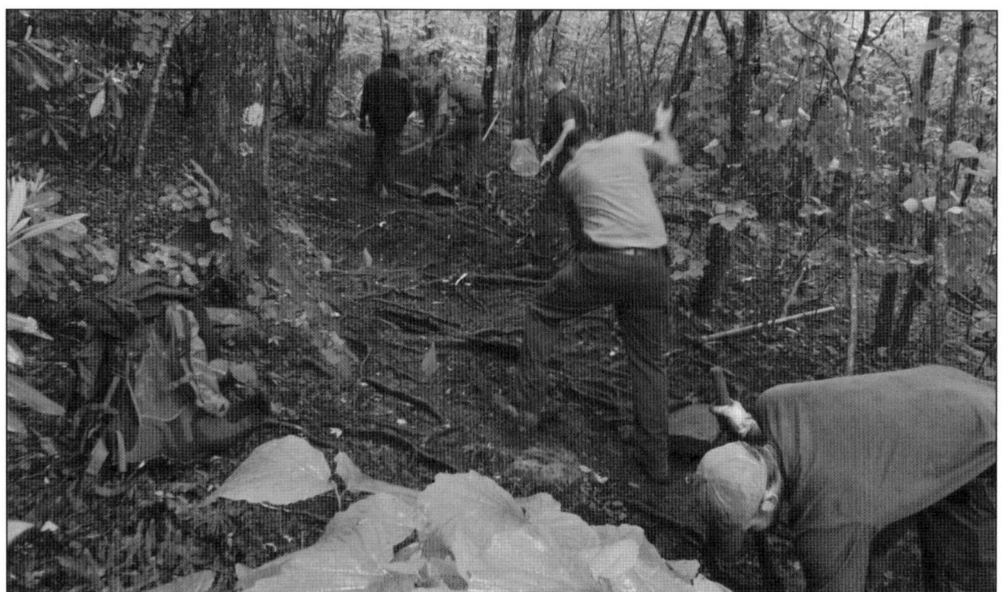

There are many trails within the confines of the Grandfather Mountain State Park. The rains in the spring and summer and the winter snows often play havoc on these trails. Here, members of the Grandfather Mountain Stewardship Foundation join the Grandfather Mountain State Park staff for a workday on the Daniel Boone Scout Trail in June 2013. (Courtesy of Grandfather Mountain State Park.)

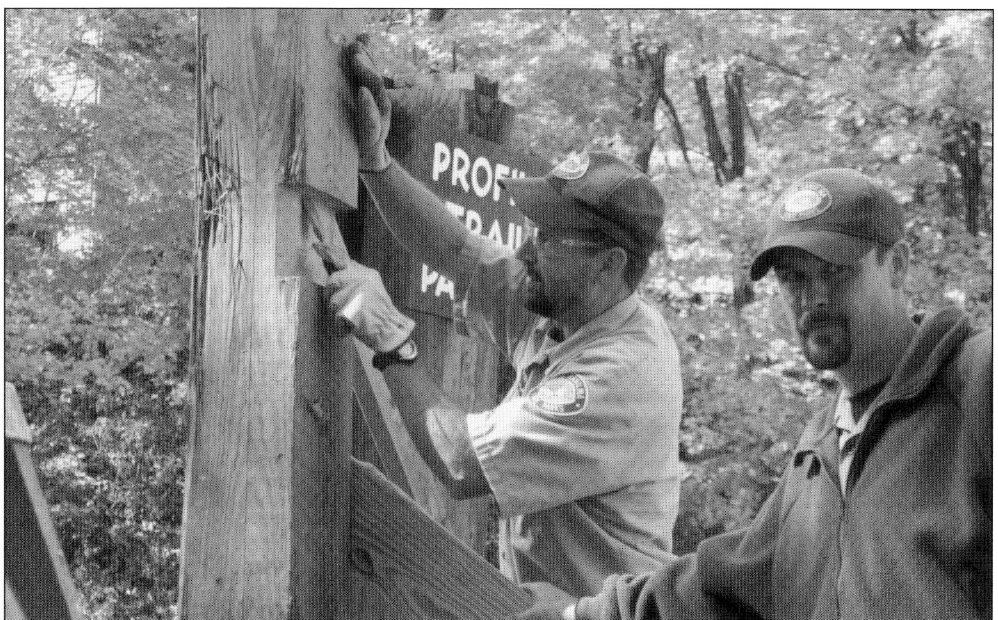

In the 1980s, the Profile Trail replaced the older Shanty Spring Trail. Winding from a US 221 parking area, along the headwaters of the Watauga River and Shanty Spring, the trail ends at Calloway Gap, 2.8 miles later. At several different points are breathtaking views of the profile of Grandfather Mountain. Here, state park maintenance mechanics Daniel Baumgarner and Jason Jerrell install new signage at the Profile Trailhead. (Courtesy of Grandfather Mountain State Park.)

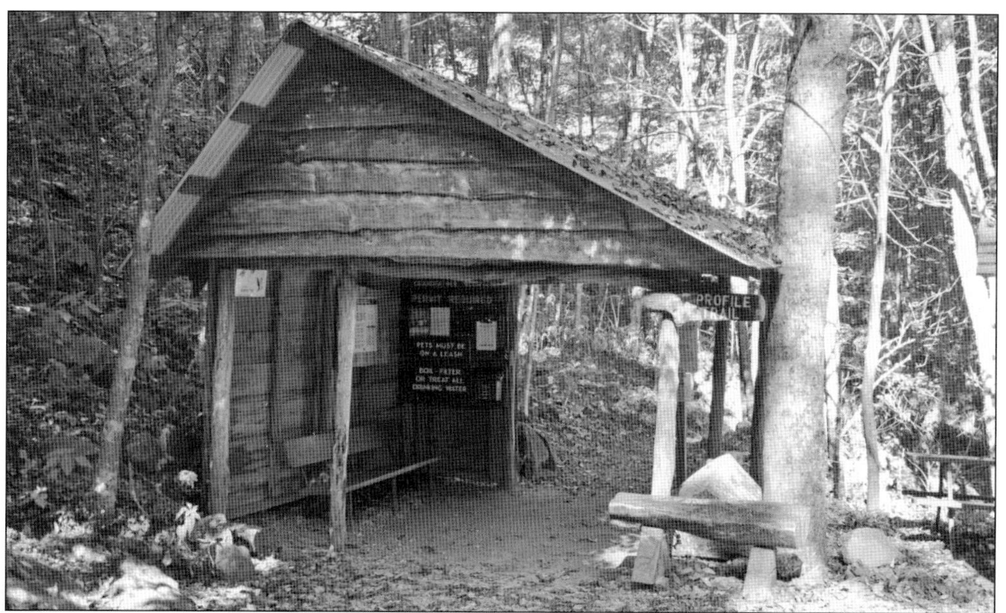

The Profile Trail, located off Highway 105, is a popular destination for hikers from the surrounding area. This trail was built in the latter half of the 1980s to replace the badly worn Shanty Springs Trail. Hikers start by passing over the Watauga River and slowly working their way up Grandfather Mountain. There are several places to get a glimpse of the profile of Grandfather Mountain before arriving at the top of the mountain. (Courtesy of Michael Hardy.)

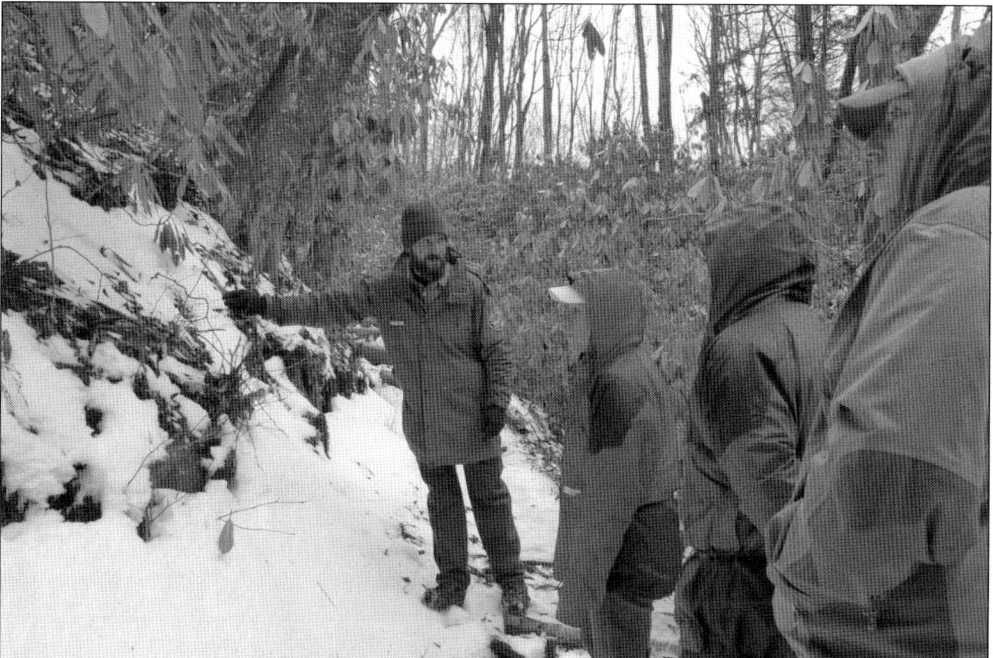

Grandfather Mountain State Park head ranger Luke Appling leads a "First Day Hike" on January 1, 2013, along the Profile Trail on Grandfather Mountain. The Profile Trail is just one of several trails within the state park that combine to make 12 miles of challenging, rocky hiking trails along the mountain. (Courtesy of Grandfather Mountain State Park.)

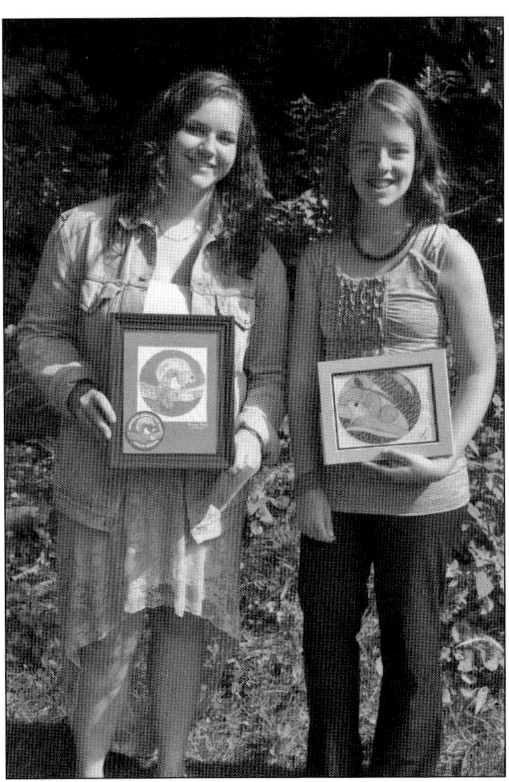

In 2013, Grandfather Mountain State Park announced a contest for the best design for a new junior ranger patch. Brandi Haney, a student at Avery County High School, submitted an image of the endangered Carolina Northern flying squirrel, which was selected and incorporated into the new design. She is pictured here, on the left, with contest runner-up Katherine Tufts. (Courtesy of Michael Hardy.)

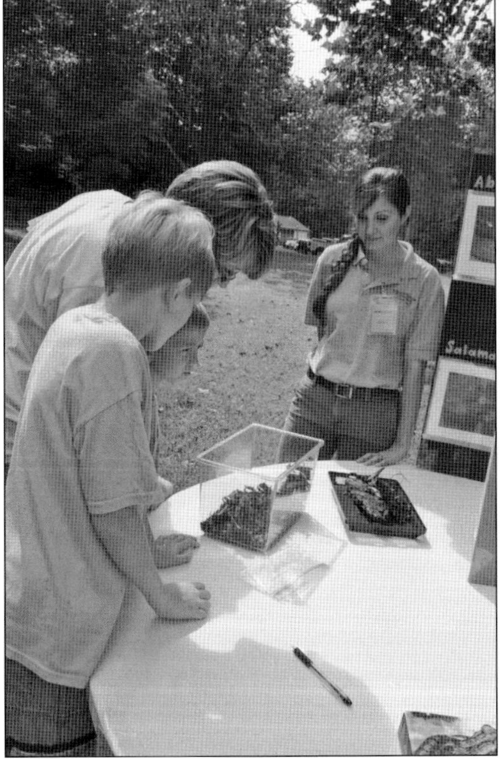

Each fall, the Grandfather Mountain State Park hosts a family fun day. The rangers and park volunteers set up booths on wildlife and other activities in the park. As an added bonus, groups, including the Gardens of the Blue Ridge and NASA, present displays. Here, visitors learn about salamanders. (Courtesy of Michael Hardy.)

Eight

Flora and Fauna

Grandfather Mountain and the surrounding region host a very diverse collection of life forms. There are 16 distinct habitats on Grandfather Mountain, supporting one of the most diverse groups of flora and fauna in the South. Not only are there fir, spruce, and oak forests, but also rich cove forests, acidic cove forests, and Canada hemlock forests. Driving up the mountain is often compared to driving from North Carolina to Newfoundland. Temperatures are frequently 5 to 10 degrees different between the top and the bottom. Grandfather Mountain has numerous rare and endangered plant, insect, and animal species. Extremely rare globally are the spruce fir moss spider, Blue Ridge goldenrod, and *Frullania appalachiana* (liverwort) species, and considered imperiled globally due to rarity are Heller's blazing star, Roan Mountain bluet, and spreading avens, all plants; the Grandfather Mountain lepodontium, a moss; velvet vovert and high mountain supercoil, both mollusks; the rock gnome lichen; and *Bazzania nudicaulis*, *Plagiochila sullivantii*, and *Sphenolobopsis*, all liverworts. Rare globally are the bog turtle, Eastern small-footed bat, Appalachian woodrat, Weller's salamander, and the pigmy salamander along with numerous plants, including trailing wolfsbane, wretched sedge, tall larkspur, Gray's lily, and roan rattlesnake root. Animals considered imperiled or critically imperiled in North Carolina include the Virginia big-eared bat, magnolia warbler, Peregrine falcon, the Carolina Northern flying squirrel, Southern water shrew, sharp-shinned hawk, Northern saw-whet owl, and black-billed cuckoo. Throughout the years, Grandfather Mountain has worked to help protect the fragile ecosystem. Two bears were brought in 1968 to be released into the wild. The male bear disappeared into the woods, while the female bear hung around in the area. Learning that the female bear was hand-raised by humans at the Atlanta Zoo, Hugh Morton adopted her, naming her Mildred. Eventually, an animal habitat was built, providing homes for bears, eagles, otters, cougars, and deer.

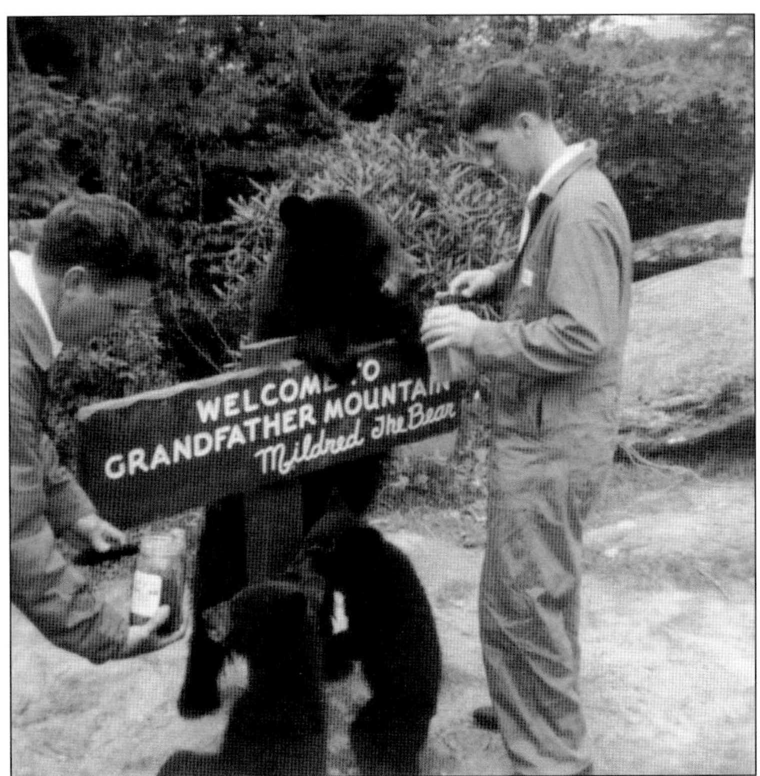

Born in 1966 at the Atlanta Zoo, Mildred the Bear came to Grandfather Mountain two years later in order to be released into the wild. She quickly demonstrated that she was better suited to live with people than fend for herself in the great outdoors. Over the years, Mildred gave birth to a number of her own cubs and fostered others. (Courtesy of Lori Benfield.)

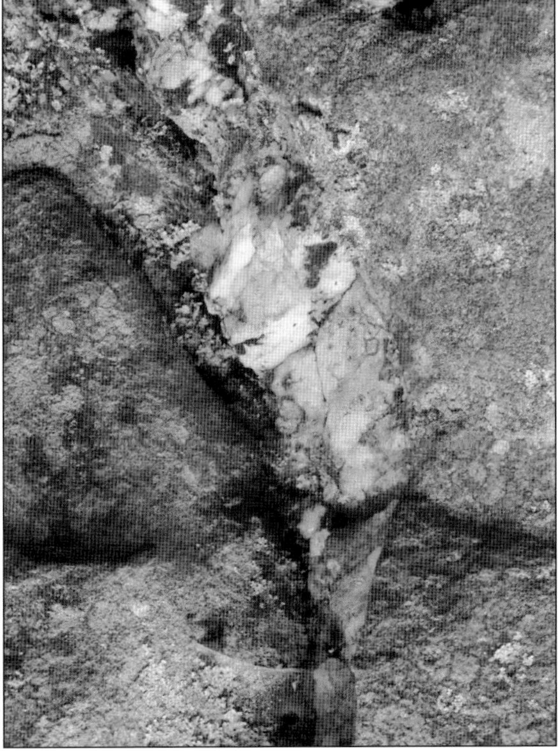

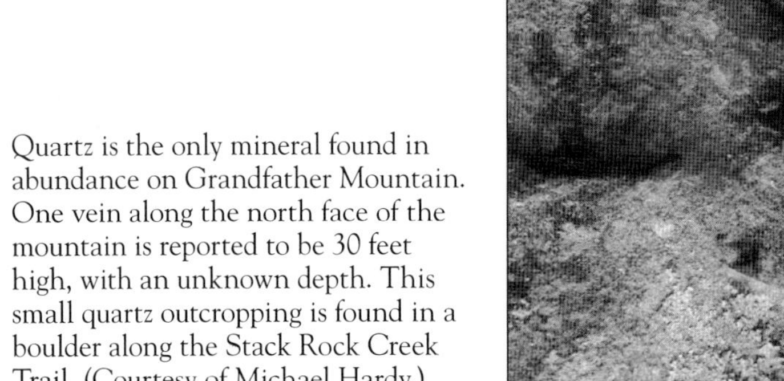

Quartz is the only mineral found in abundance on Grandfather Mountain. One vein along the north face of the mountain is reported to be 30 feet high, with an unknown depth. This small quartz outcropping is found in a boulder along the Stack Rock Creek Trail. (Courtesy of Michael Hardy.)

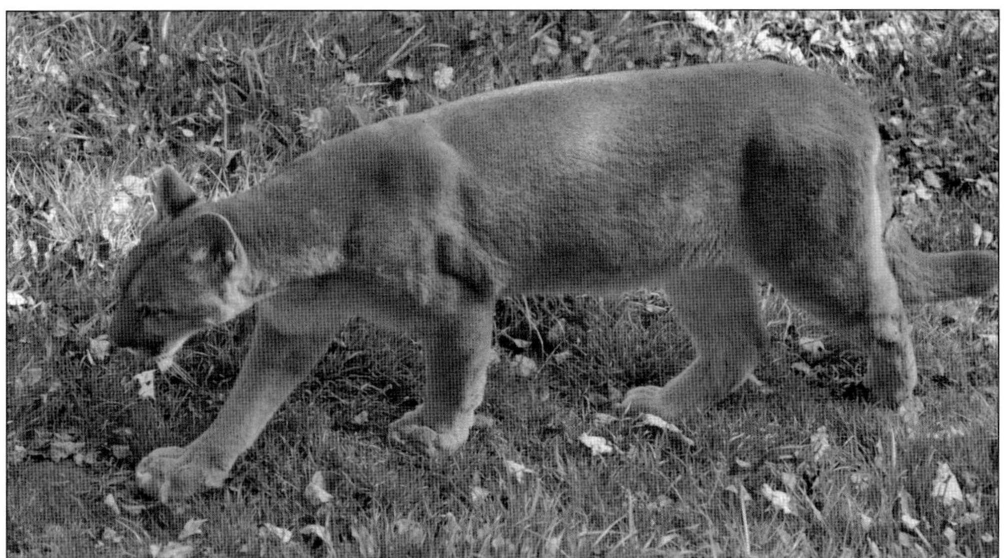

For centuries, panthers roamed the Southern Appalachian Mountains. The scream of these big cats often evoked terror. However, hunting and loss of habitat made them virtually extinct. In 1980, the animal habitat at Grandfather Mountain introduced a pair of western cougars, representing the large felines that once inhabited the area. The last possible wild "painter" sighting on Grandfather Mountain may have come in 1922. (Courtesy of Michael Hardy.)

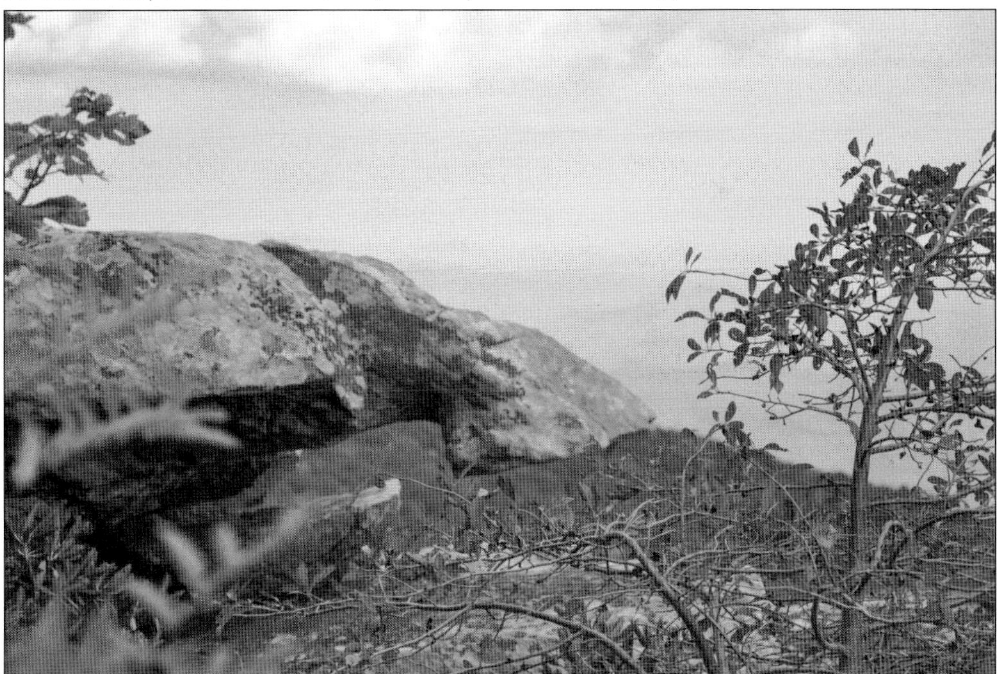

Over the eons, erosion has taken its toll on Grandfather Mountain. Some estimate that the mountain was once 10 miles tall, instead of the 5,945 feet that it is today. Examples of this erosion can be found at various places within the attraction, the state park, and the national park. This wind-worn rock is on the Tanawha Trail, on the way to Rough Ridge. (Courtesy of Michael Hardy.)

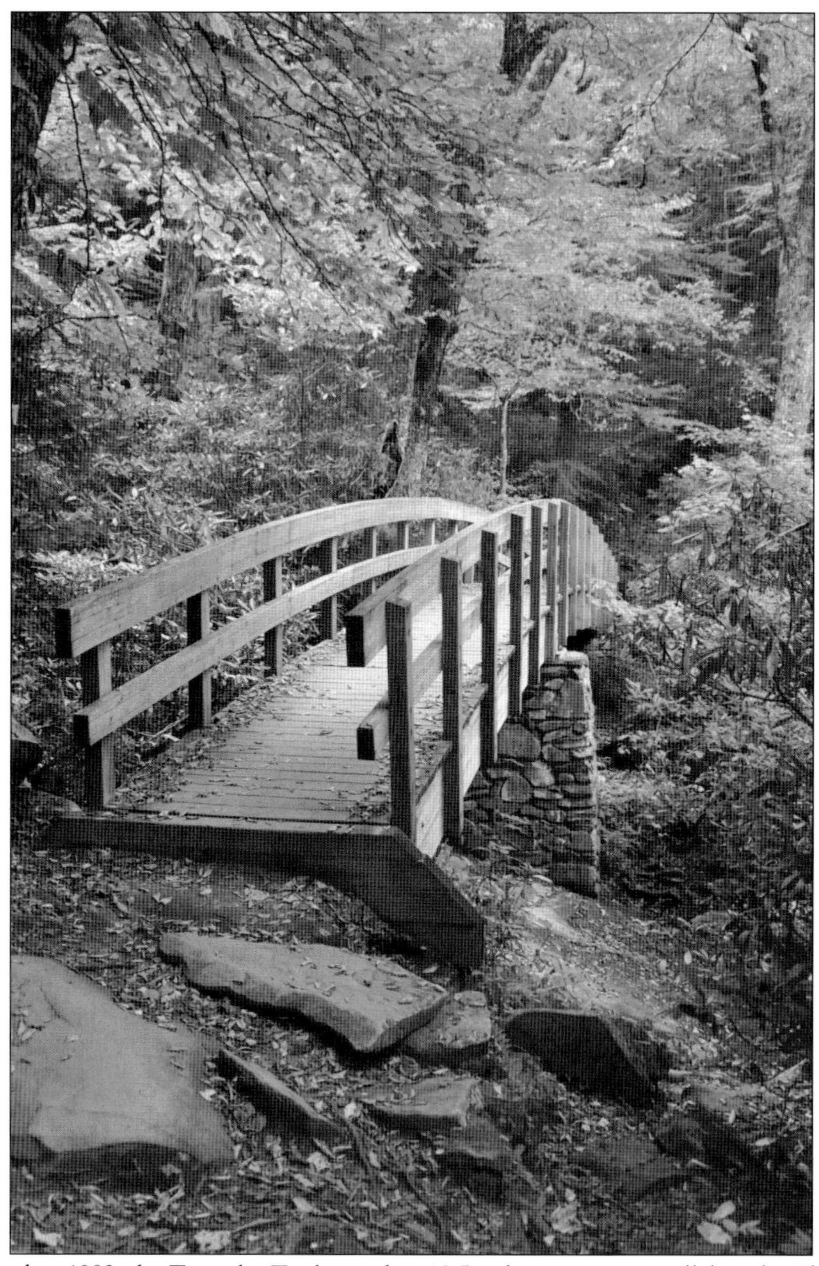

Completed in 1993, the Tanawha Trail stretches 13.5 miles, running parallel to the Blue Ridge Parkway. The trail starts at Julian Price Park, ends at Beacon Heights, and cost $750,000 to complete. *Tanawha* is a Cherokee word for fabulous hawk or eagle, the same name that the tribe supposedly called Grandfather Mountain. The Tanawha Trail crosses a fragile and ancient ecosystem, passing through a diverse range of biological and geological terrains, including thickets of rhododendron and laurels, hardwood covers, evergreen glens, and boulder fields. Several creeks, like the Boone Fork and Wilson Creek, are also passed. The Tanawha Trail provides access to several of the Grandfather Mountain State Park trails, including the Daniel Boone Scout Trail and the Nuwati Trail. Several bridges, some of which were built intact and lowered into place by a helicopter, help protect the delicate ecosystem. (Courtesy of Michael Hardy.)

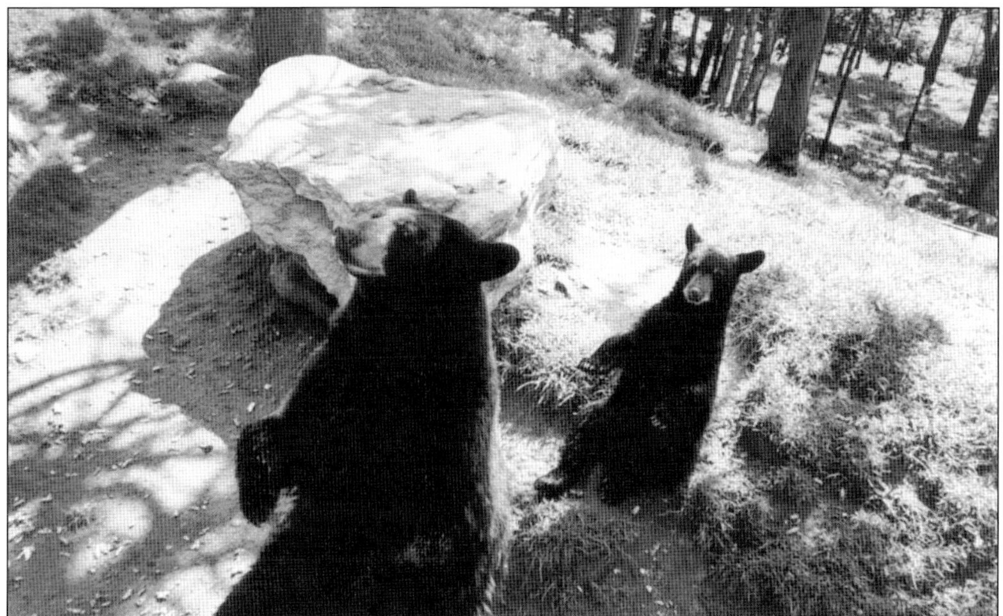

A newspaper in St. Louis printed in 1894 a story of a lost fisherman who spent the night in a cave on Grandfather Mountain. The next morning, something pulling at his coat woke him. It was a bear cub, with momma and another cub watching. The fisherman lay still for about three hours before the bears lost interest and ambled off. The fisherman then "beat a hasty retreat." (Courtesy of Martha Hicks.)

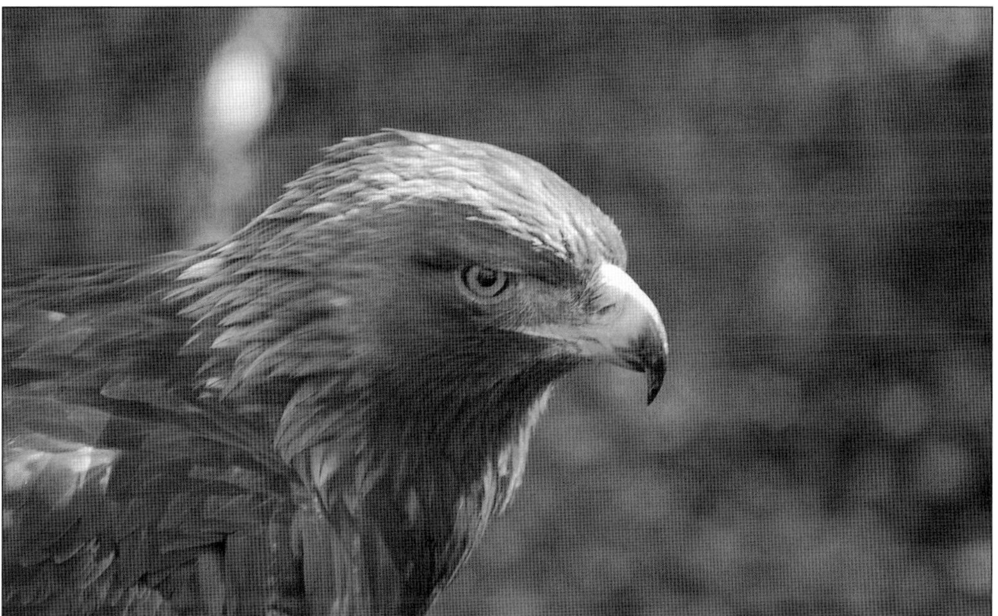

The golden eagle is North America's largest bird of prey. Like bald eagles, they might have once been spotted in the Grandfather Mountain area. Loss of habitat has greatly reduced their numbers in the Eastern portions of the United States. The golden eagles that have been at Grandfather Mountain were often birds that were damaged in accidents, left unable to fly or to return to the wild. (Courtesy of Michael Hardy.)

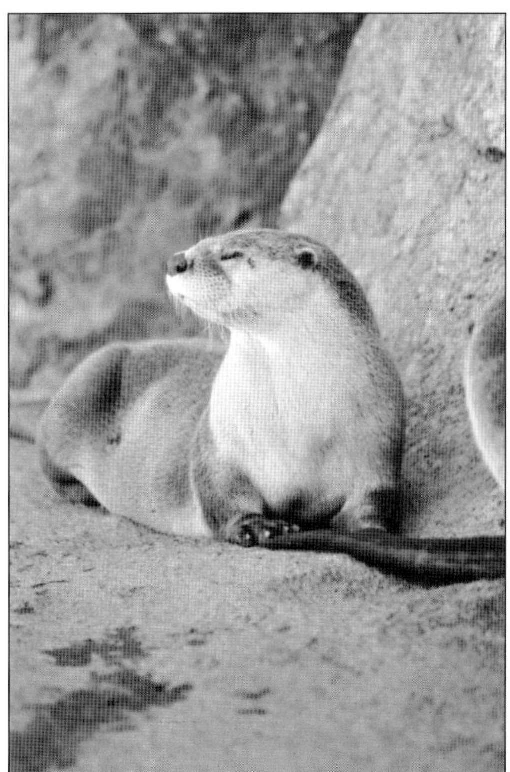

Beside bears, the river otters in the habitat at Grandfather Mountain are some of the most entertaining animals to watch. In the Southeastern United States, otters are rarely seen, having lost most of their original habitats. These winsome animals, related to weasels and minks, mate for life and can live for 10 to 15 years. (Courtesy of Michael Hardy.)

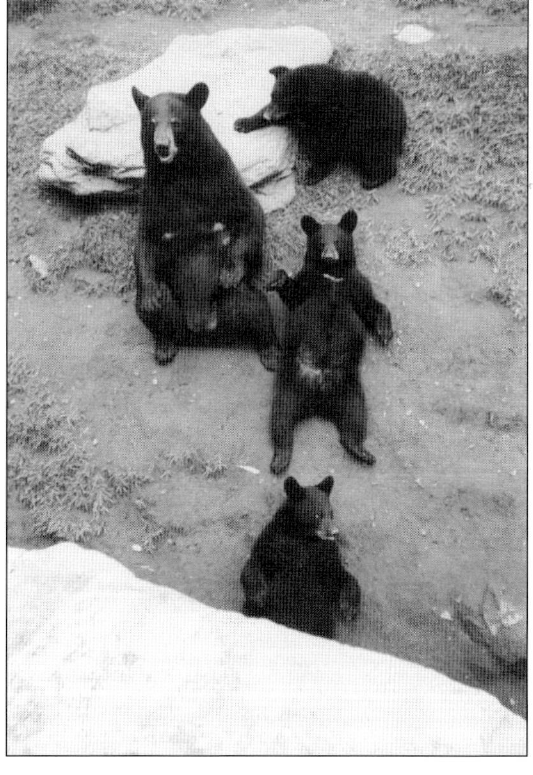

For years, visitors could purchase snacks, like peanuts, for Mildred and her offspring and friends to eat. Many visitors saw this sight, the bears waiting for the treats. Eventually, it was determined that the irregular feeding schedule was bad for the bears, and the practice stopped. (Courtesy of Martha Hicks.)

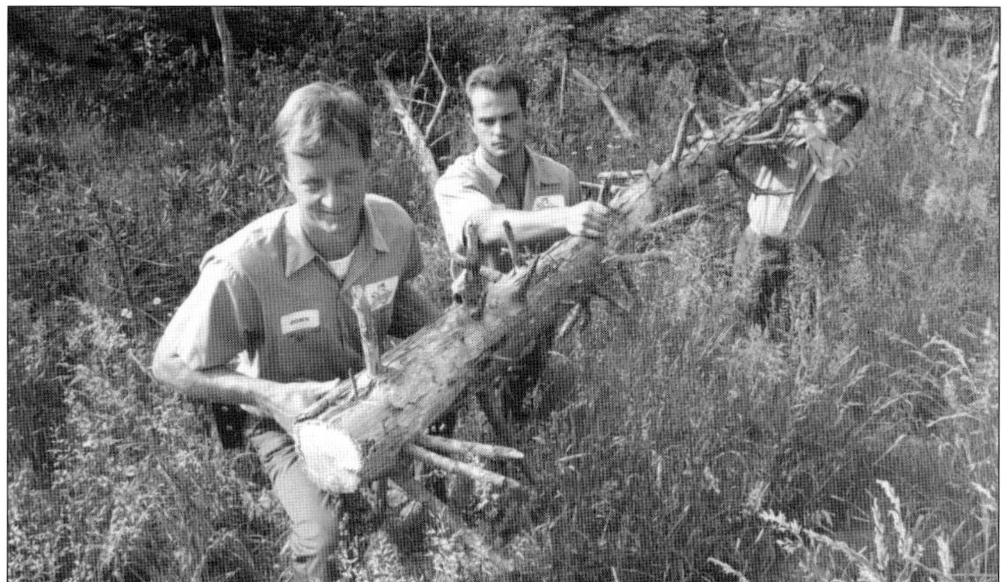

Acid rain has posed a problem to the to the spruce-fir trees on Grandfather and surrounding mountains for several decades. Here, Grandfather Mountain employees remove two dead spruce trees to be used as centerpieces in an exhibit that toured different Eastern European countries. (Courtesy of *Mountain Times*.)

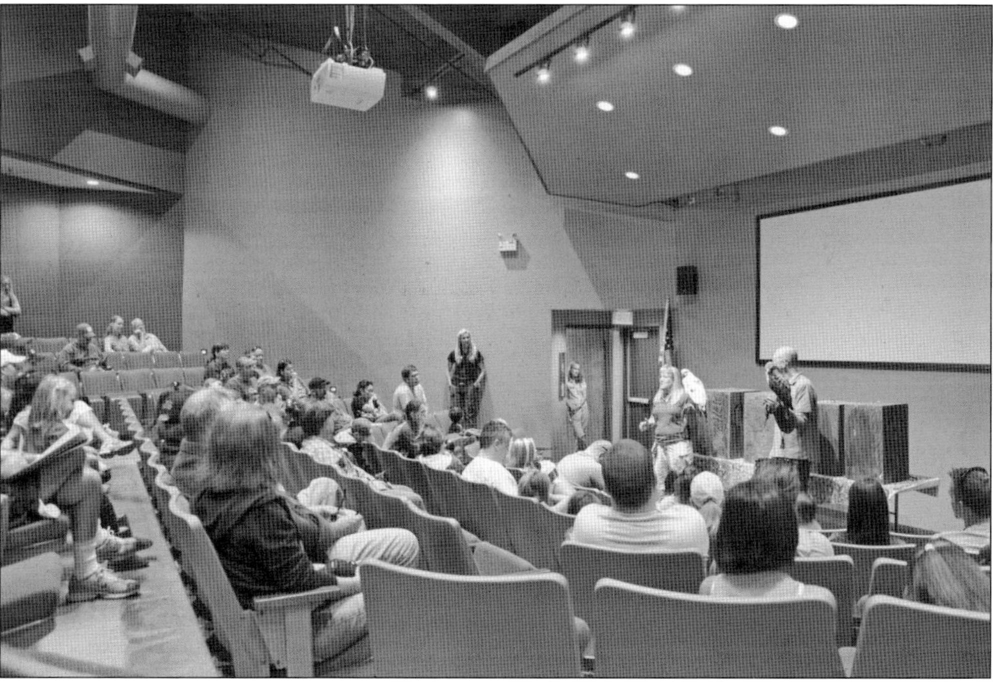

The auditorium within the Nature Museum at Grandfather Mountain holds numerous special events every year. These include annual events, like the Naturalist Weekends, Kids' Day activities, and even musical concerts. Plus, award-winning films are shown through the day during normal park hours. Here, members of the Blue Ridge Wildlife Institute from Banner Elk present an educational program with two of their animal ambassadors. (Courtesy of Michael Hardy.)

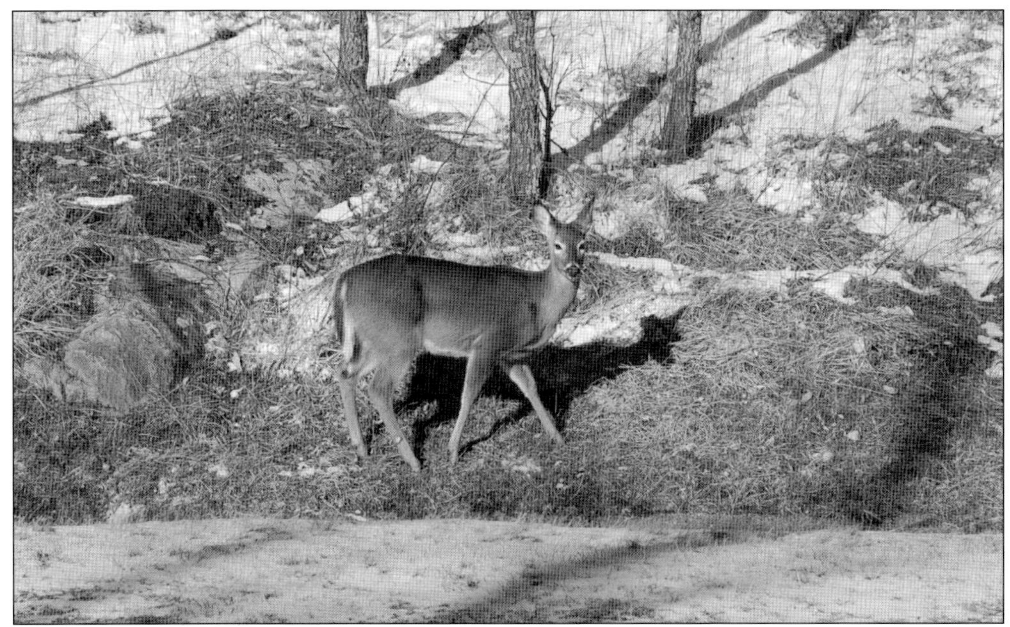

A deer this like, photographed in 2008 at the intersection of US 221 and the Blue Ridge Parkway, used to be a rare sight in the Blue Ridge Mountains. Deer populations thrived during first contact with European settlers but quickly declined due to hunting. Proper management brought the herd back up to 1.25 million animals by 2012. (Courtesy of Michael Hardy.)

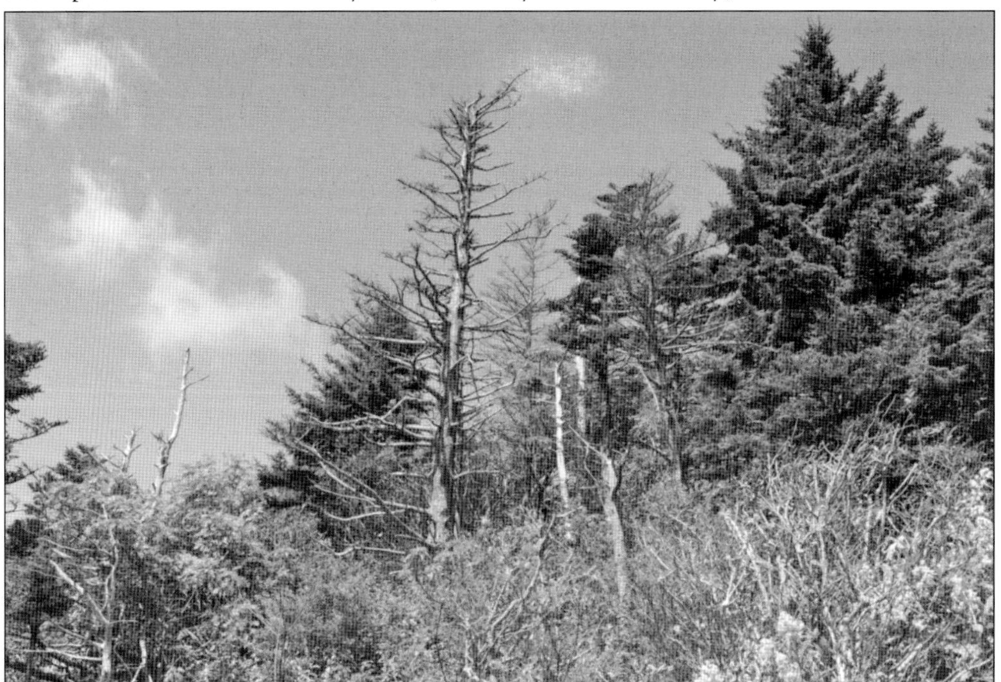

In the first few decades of the 20th century, blight struck the chestnut trees found so commonly in the southern Appalachian Mountains. Likewise, in the first few years of the 21st century, the hemlock trees, like the ones pictured here near the Mile-High Swinging Bridge, were decimated, falling victim to a pest called the woolly adelgid. (Courtesy of Michael Hardy.)

Smokey Bear was a well-known mascot for the National Forest Service. Smokey was hurt in a fire in New Mexico in 1950. Later, the bear went to live at the National Zoo in Washington, DC. Always looking for publicity opportunities, Hugh Morton posed Mildred with a forestry service hat and a sign. (Courtesy of *Mountain Times*.)

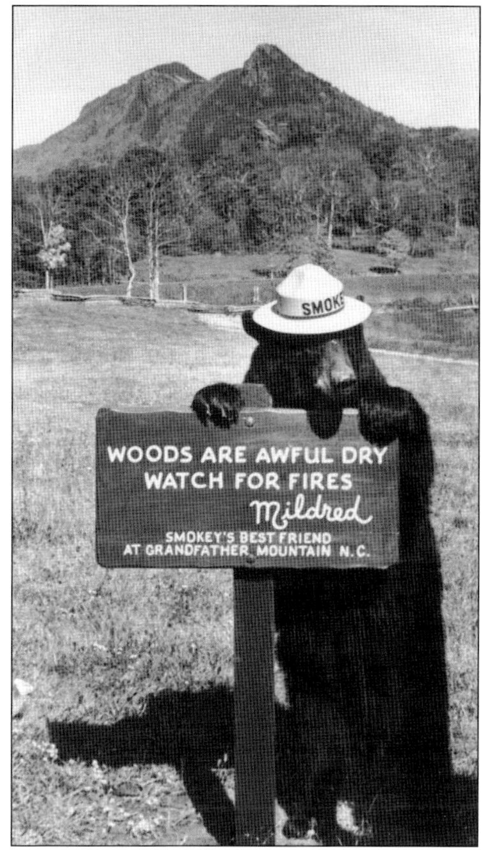

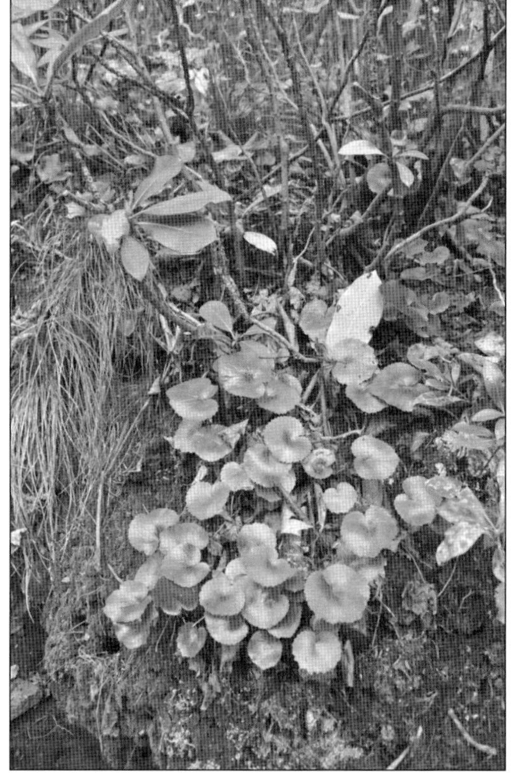

A writer for the *Greensboro Record* recorded in October 1927 that "under the trees along the roadsides the earth is covered with a carpet of large galax leaves, for Grandfather Mountain is distinguished by the great beauty and abundance of its galax." Galax is used both in the floral industry and by herbalists to treat cuts and kidney ailments. (Courtesy of Michael Hardy.)

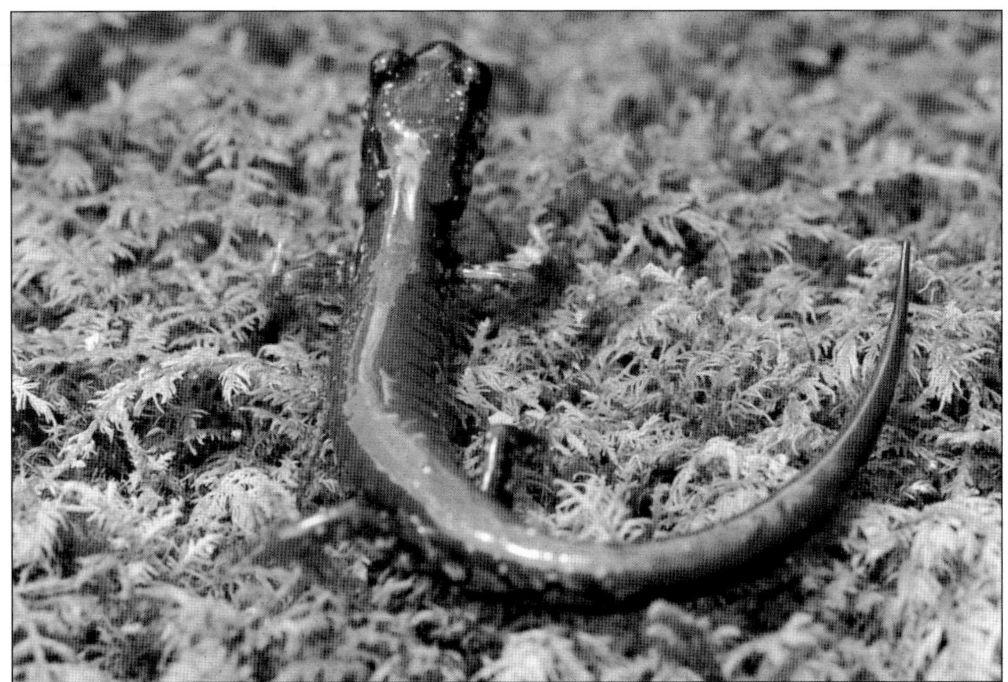

Grandfather Mountain has numerous native salamander species, including the Yonahlossee salamander, which serves as the mascot for the attraction's programs for children. (Courtesy of Grandfather Mountain.)

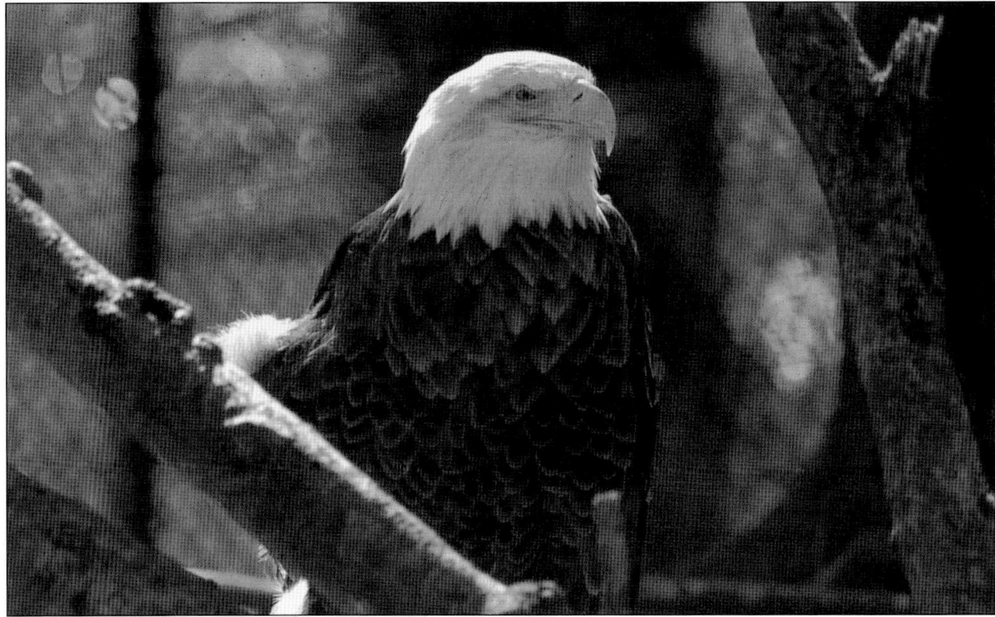

According to an article in the *Greensboro Daily* News (October 8, 1981), it took Hugh Morton more than a year to gain permission to keep bald eagles in the animal habitat at Grandfather Mountain. The original pair, a male and female, had been damaged, having lost wings, but were rescued by the Audubon Society's Eagle Protection Program and came from St. Louis. (Courtesy of Michael Hardy.)

Nine

Visitors from Near and Far

Grandfather Mountain was being billed as "Carolina's Top Scenic Attraction" as early as 1947. Visitors could pay a small fee to drive up the mountain and park at an observation deck. Numerous trails could also be utilized to explore more of the mountain. A decade later, the Grandfather Mountain attraction had changed drastically. While the observation platform was still available, the road had been widened and extended all the way to the top. Visitors could now stroll across the Mile-High Swinging Bridge. Other changes continued to keep bringing new and returning visitors back year after year. Mildred the Bear performed three times a day. In 1973, the first two acres of an animal enclosure were opened to the public, and Mildred and other bears had their own homes. Later, the area was expanded to include animal habitats for eagles, cougars, deer, and otters. Soon thereafter, the Nature Museum opened to the public. This facility has numerous displays on the natural history of the area surrounding Grandfather Mountain. Dr. Rolland Hower, of the Smithsonian Institution, designed exhibits. Visitors can learn about North Carolina gems and minerals, early explorers like Daniel Boone and André Michaux, and the many different types of plants and animals that call Grandfather Mountain home. The facility also has an auditorium, along with a snack bar. The Grandfather Mountain attraction continues to expand. There are now several picnic areas, a woodworking shop, hiking trails of different skill levels, a butterfly garden, and a fudge shop. In 2010, a new Top Shop opened next to the Mile-High Swinging Bridge. The new shop has an elevator, providing access to the bridge area for those not able to manage the stairs. There are also plans for a historical display to document the Grandfather Mountain area. Visitors come for many reasons: to see the animals, to brave the Mile-High Swinging Bridge, and to hike many of the trails, both at the Grandfather Mountain attraction and in the adjacent Grandfather Mountain State Park. In addition, special events, such as Scout Days, sporting events, and family gatherings, draw guests to the mountain.

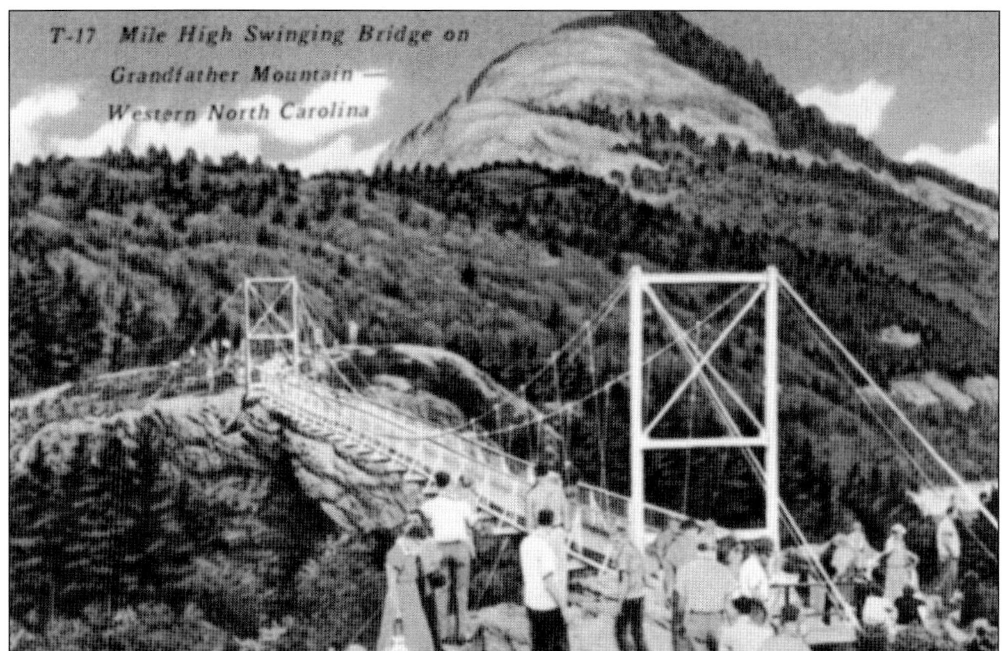

The mountain's main attraction, advertised far and wide, is the Mile-High Swinging Bridge. At an elevation of 5,280 feet above sea level, it truly is a mile high, yet it only stands 80 feet above the chasm below. This view is from an early linen postcard. (Courtesy of Sandra Blankenship.)

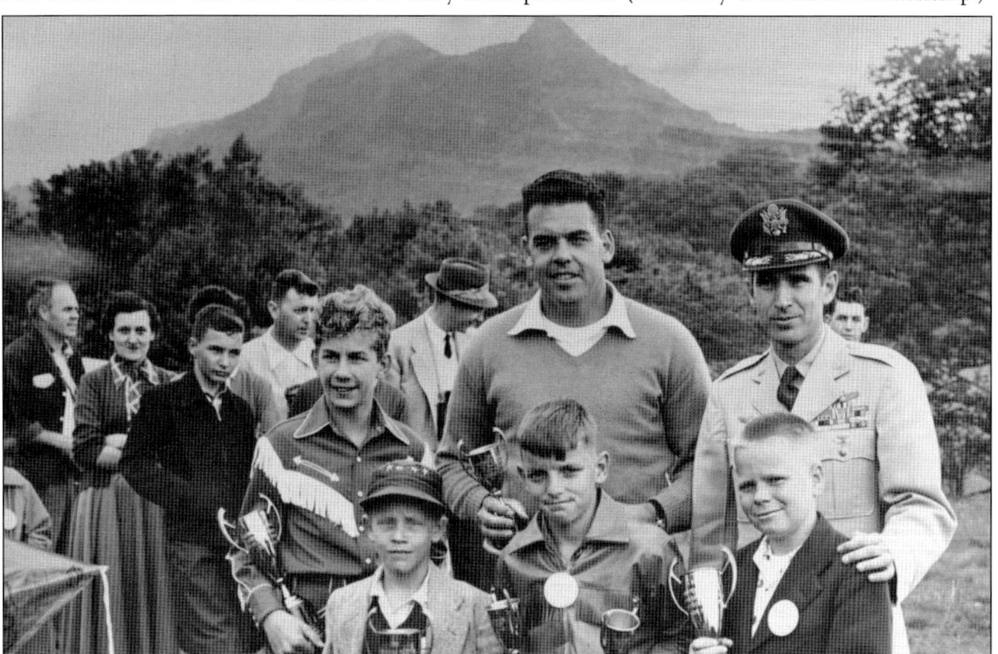

For three years in the 1950s, Grandfather Mountain held a kite-flying contest. The contest was originally scheduled to be held at the top of the mountain, but strong winds forced the contestants down to MacRae Meadows. This photograph dates from 1955. On the left in the cowboy shirt is Clive Rice. The man in the sweater is Otto Graham, and the man in uniform is Col. Dean Hess. (Courtesy of Patricia Combs.)

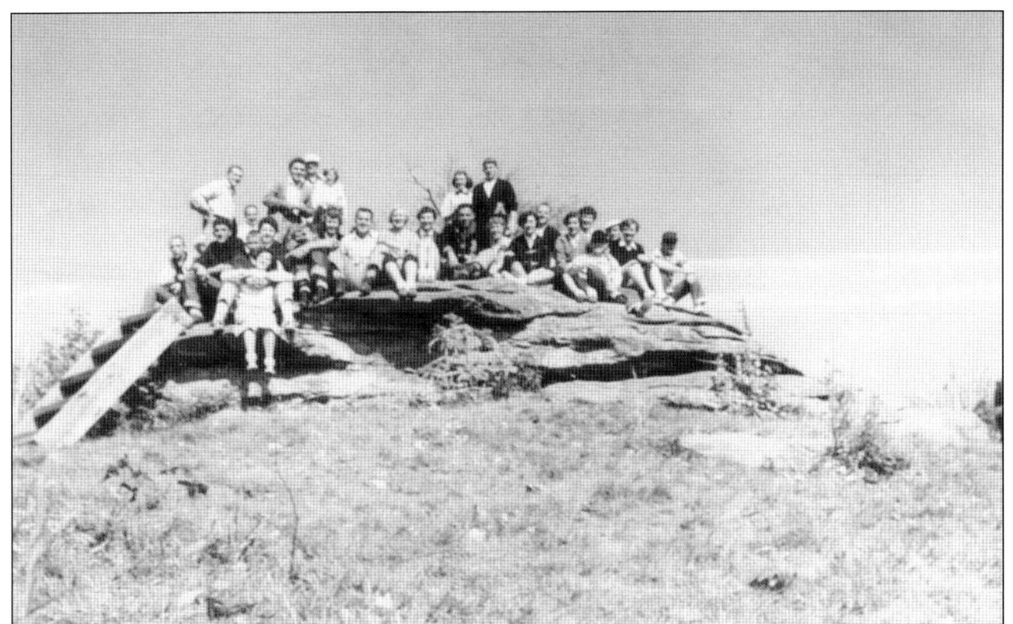

Many groups visit Grandfather Mountain every year, both to enjoy the natural vistas and to learn about conservation efforts. Members of what was then Appalachian State Teachers College's (now Appalachian State University's) football program visited the area in 1951. (Courtesy of Grandfather Mountain Highland Games.)

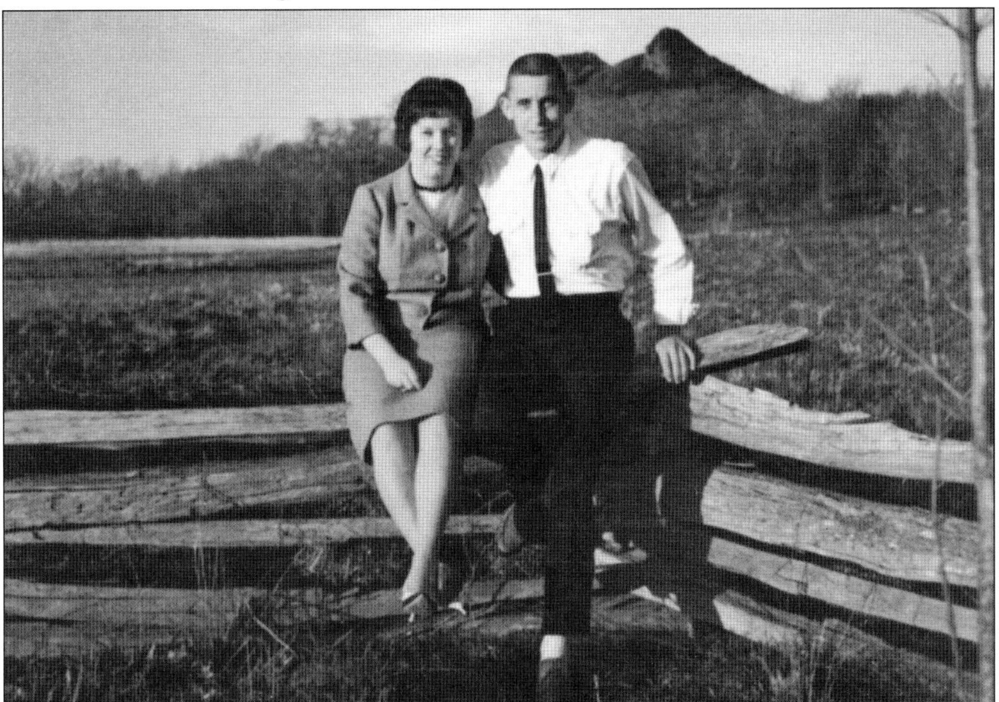

Ken Waycaster and his wife, Sandra White Waycaster, pose at MacRae Meadows around 1965. The split rail fence on which they were perched was typical of those used all along the Blue Ridge Parkway. (Courtesy of Marilyn Ball.)

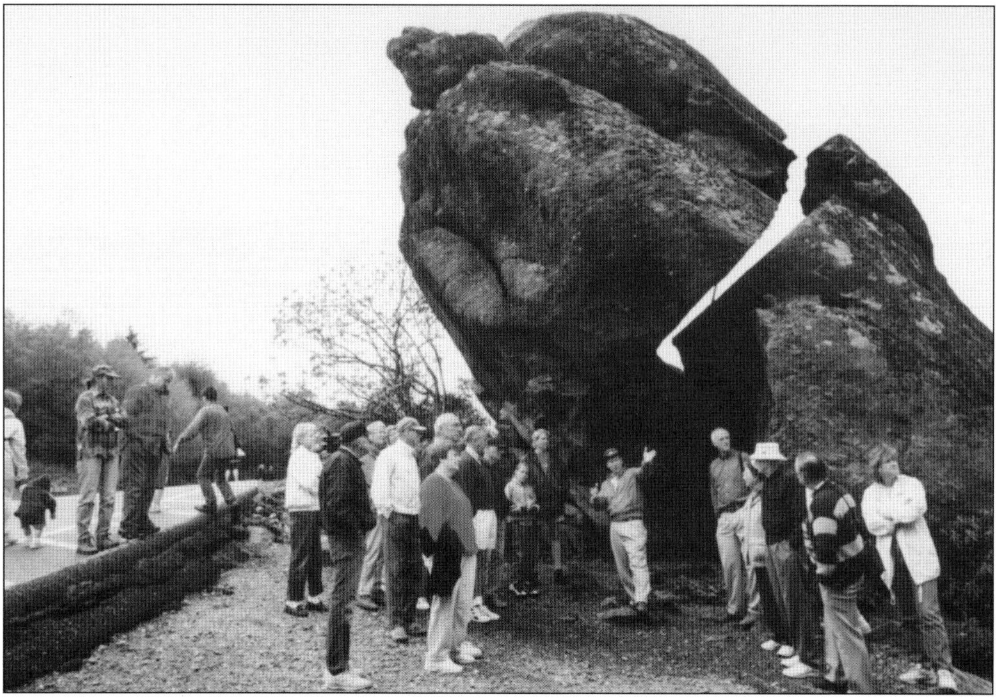

One of the Grandfather Mountain park rangers gives a lecture with the famous split rock as a backdrop. Split Rock is made of metamorphosed conglomerate. If a visitor looks closely at the rock, he or she can see pebbles embedded in it. The split occurred over time as water and erosion made the crack larger. (Courtesy of *Mountain Times.*)

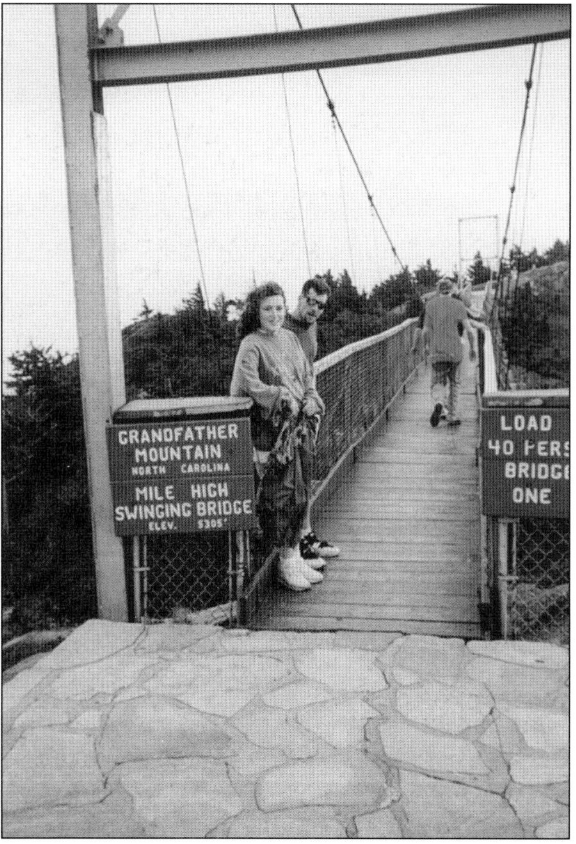

The sign denoting the altitude of the Mile-High Swinging Bridge at Grandfather Mountain is a popular spot to stop and have a photograph taken. Michelle and Michael Diciuccio from Maiden, North Carolina, have posed to show their accomplishment. (Courtesy of Martha Hicks.)

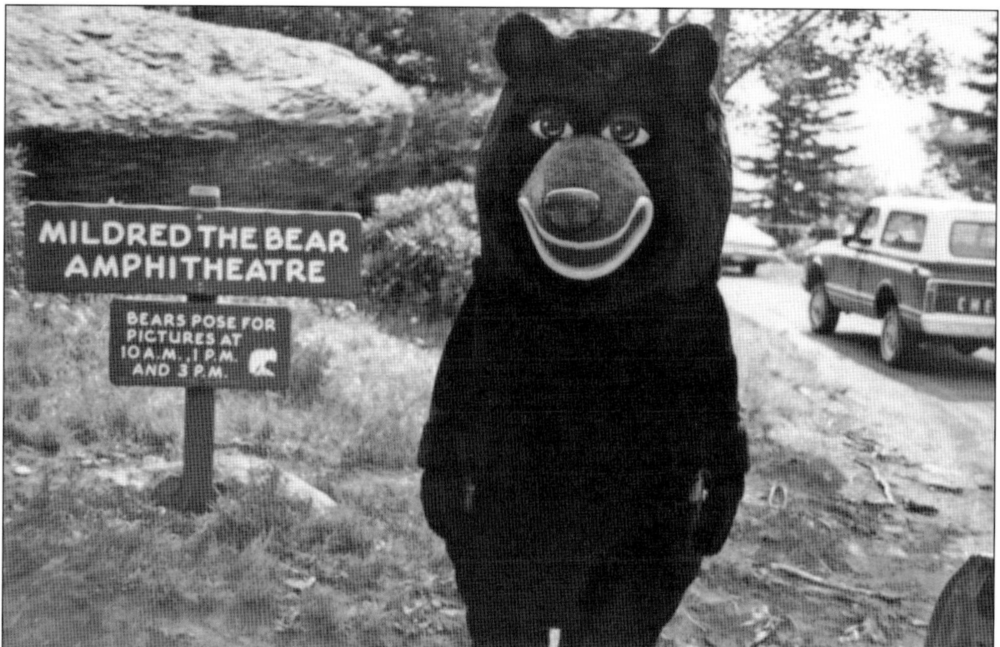

Holmes Harding wore this bear suit in the summer of 1972. It was the job of the mascot to wave to visitors as they traveled up and down the mountain, in an effort to get them to stop at the animal habitat. As the sign attests, guests could take photographs of the bear three times a day. (Courtesy of Suzanne Tucker.)

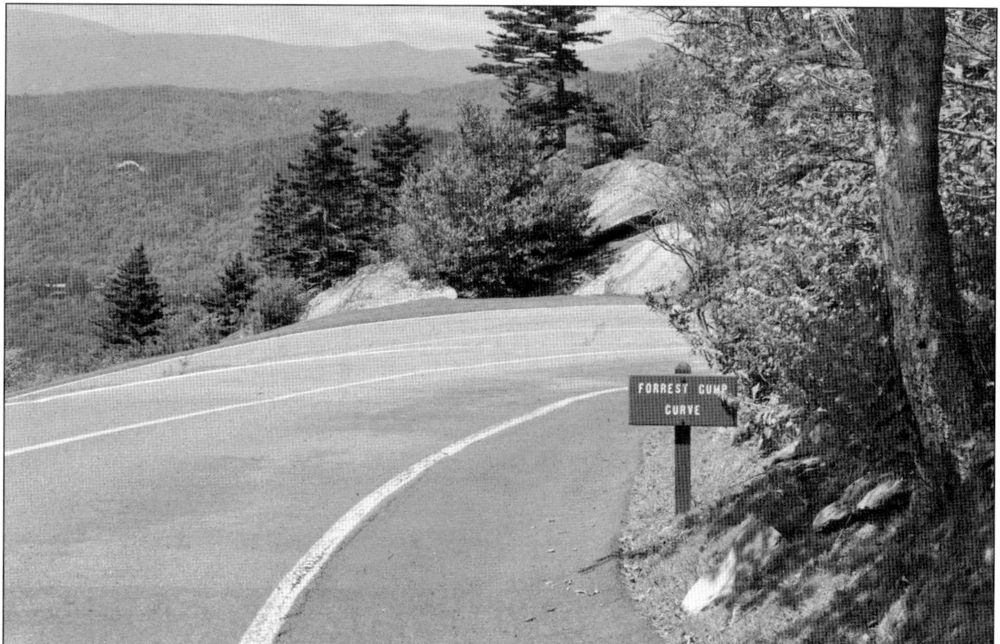

Released in 1994, *Forrest Gump*, starring Tom Hanks, was filmed in a variety of locations, including Grandfather Mountain. The movie later won six Academy Awards. During his climatic run across America, the ubiquitous Gump (played by Hanks's brother, his stunt double) was seen running on a curve that now bears his name. (Courtesy of Michael Hardy.)

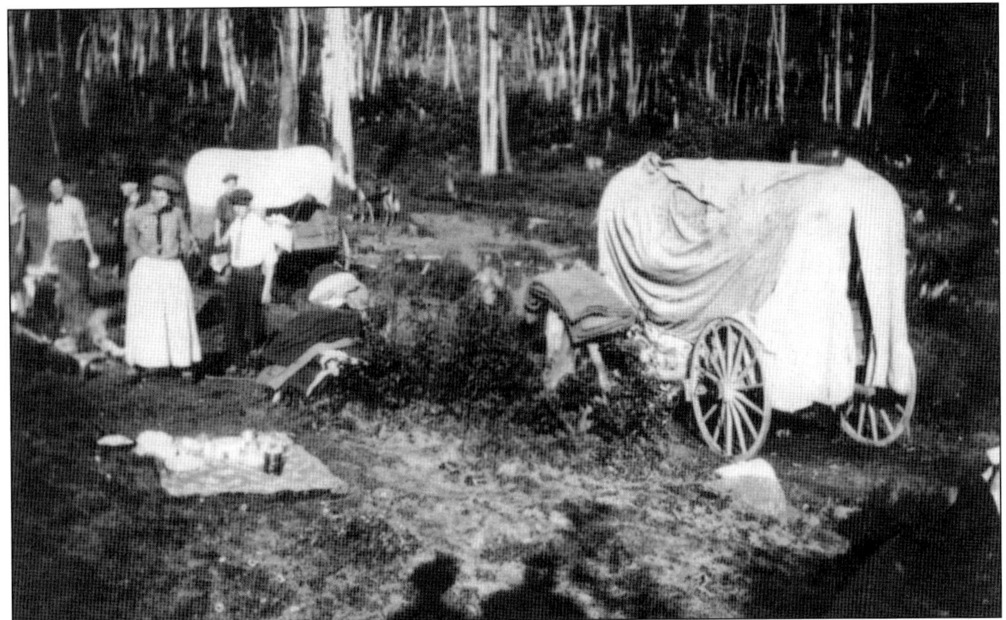

In the late 19th century, Grandfather Mountain was a popular camping destination. People, like this family from Burke County, would load their wagons and journey up the mountain. These visits could last for days or even weeks. (Courtesy of Nancy McMurray.)

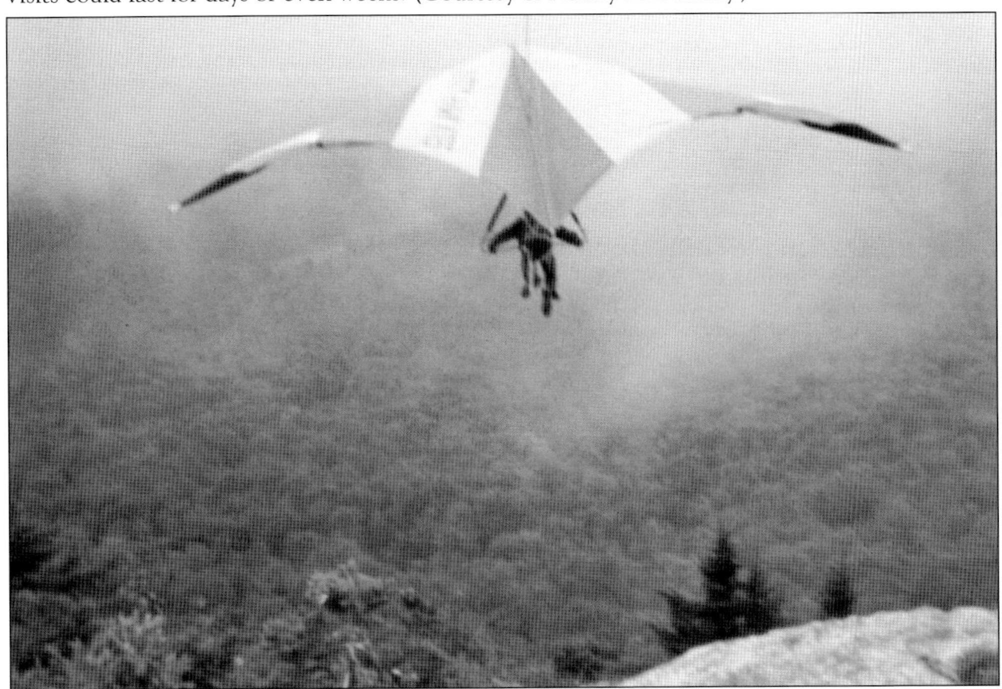

Hugh Morton brought the first Masters of Hang Gliding Championship to Grandfather Mountain in 1976. It was an invitation-only event, drawing the best hang glider pilots in the world. In 1986, hang gliding legend Stu Smith was killed during the Masters of Hang Gliding event at Grandfather Mountain. In 1984, Smith had made the longest flight ever in the Appalachian Mountains, some 112 miles. (Courtesy of Jonathan Lindsey.)

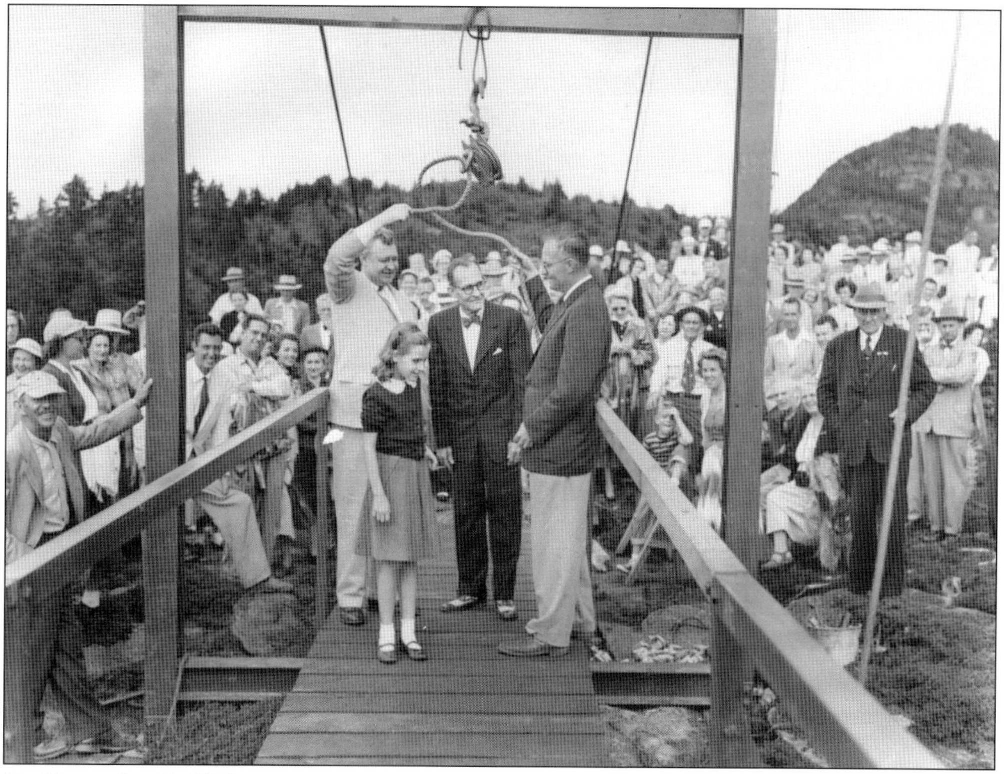

On September 2, 1952, gubernatorial candidate William B. Umstead and his nine-year-old daughter Merle became the first tourists to cross the Mile-High Swinging Bridge. Grady Cole of WBT in Charlotte (left) and Hugh Morton removed the rope so the Umsteads could pass. Countless other visitors followed in their footsteps in the ensuing decades. (Courtesy of *Mountain Times*/June Glenn Jr.)

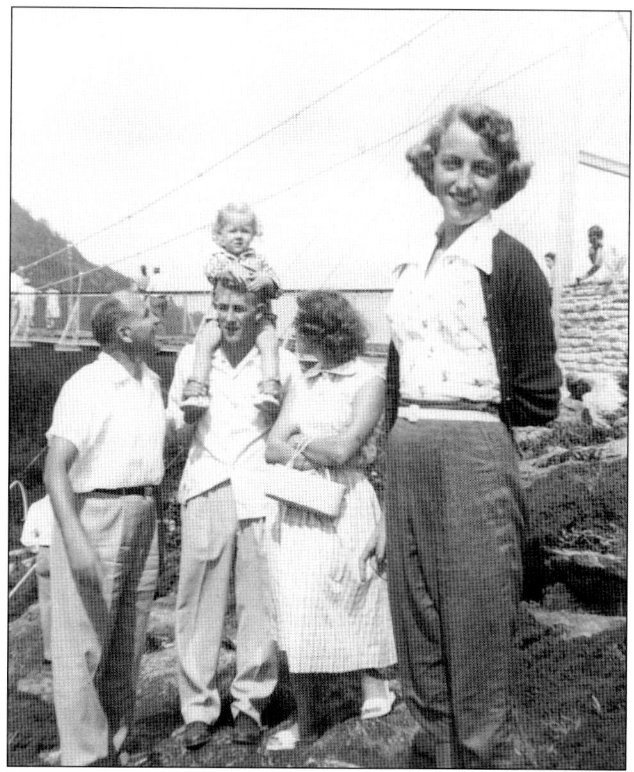

Lolita Buchanan and her family visited the Mile-High Swinging Bridge on Grandfather Mountain in 1955. The family included, from left to right, Tyson Buchanan, Herschel Buckner, Teresa Buckner (on shoulders), Amy King Buckner, and Lolita. Behind them is the less-often-used backdrop of the left side of the bridge. (Courtesy of Beth Davis.)

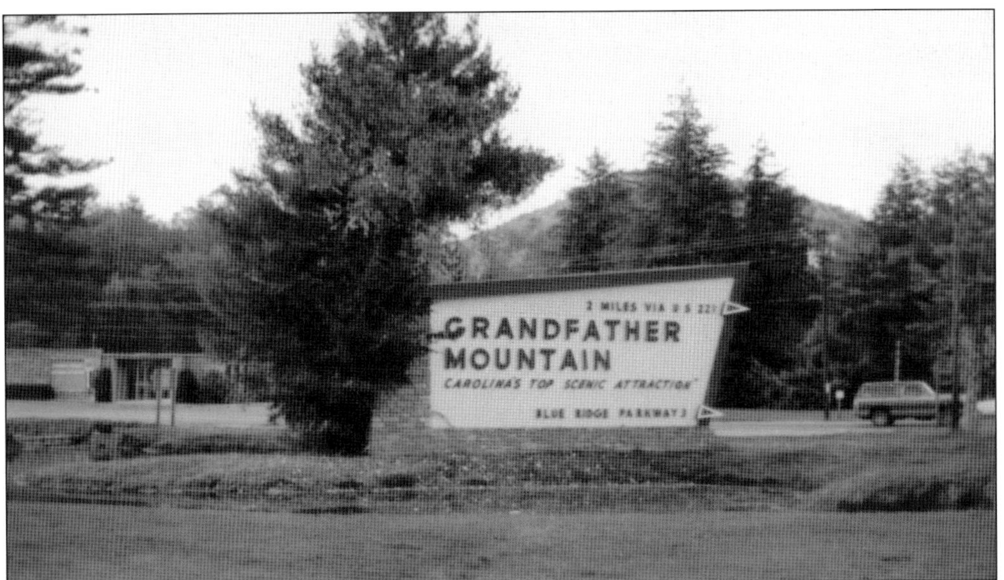

There are two large signs directing visitors to Grandfather Mountain. One is at the intersection of Highway 105 and Highway 184. The other sign, pictured here, sits at the intersection of US 221 and Highway 105. For decades, the signs have proclaimed Grandfather Mountain "Carolina's Top Scenic Attraction." This sign was constructed in 1959. (Courtesy of Patricia Townsend Brookbank.)

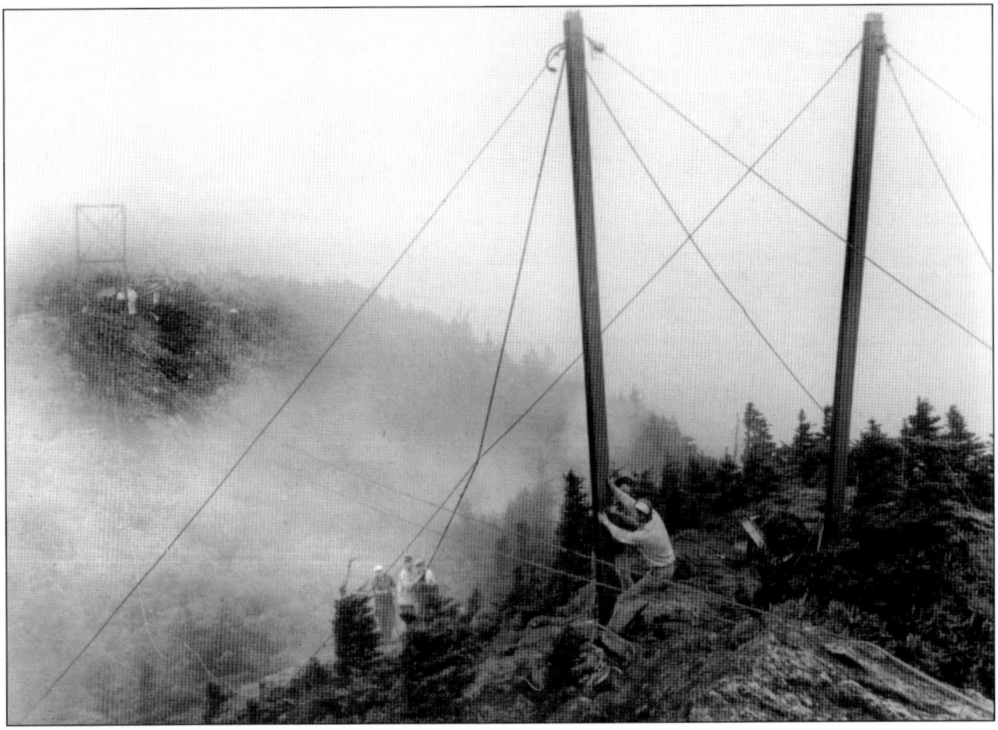

The original Mile-High Swinging Bridge was designed by Charles Hartman Jr. and constructed in Greensboro. It was then disassembled and brought to Grandfather Mountain where, due to the inclement weather, it took three weeks to put together. The bridge cost $15,000 to build originally and was rebuilt in 1999. (Courtesy of Appalachian Collection.)

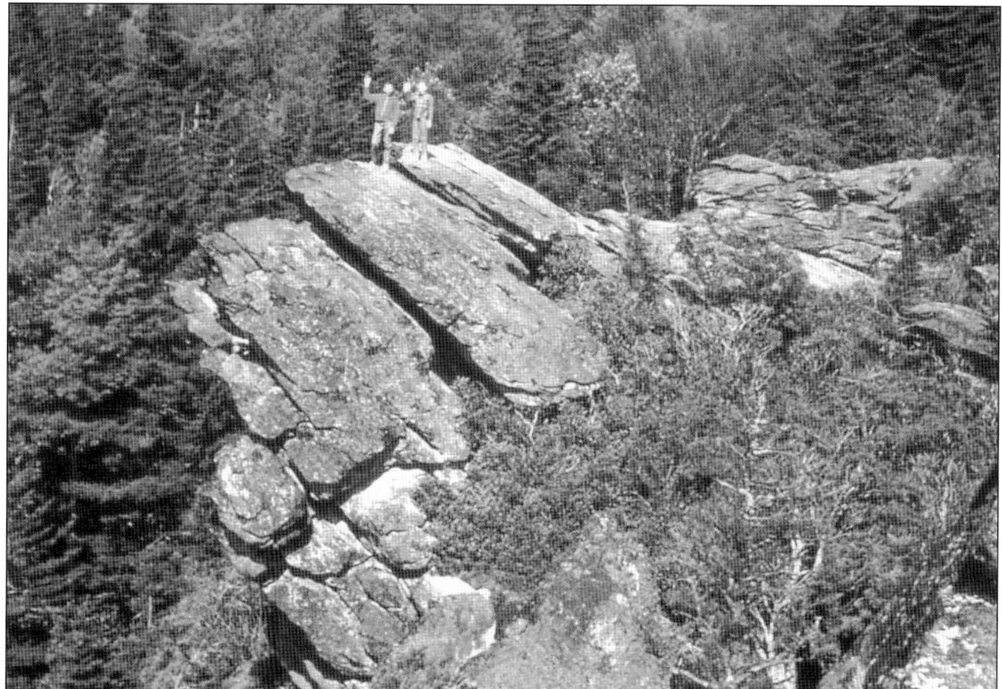

It would be difficult to find any spot in or around Grandfather Mountain that has not felt the tramp of at least one human's boot. Like these adventuresome individuals, some visitors relish the thrill of reaching one of the highest outcroppings. (Courtesy of Floyd Hayes Photograph Collection.)

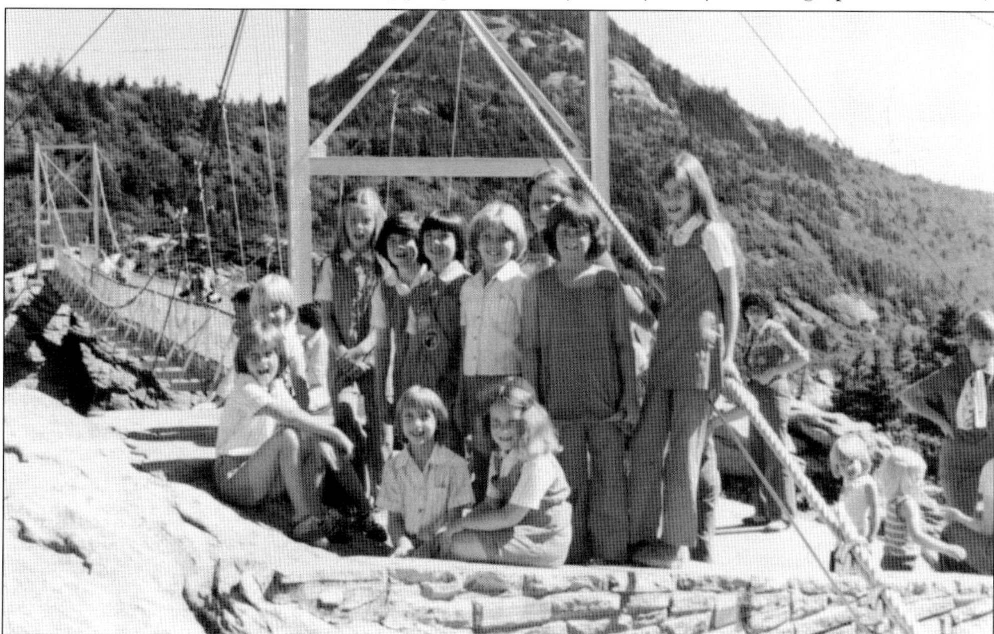

In September 1971, Grandfather Mountain began holding an annual Girl Scouts of America day. The girls were invited to the mountain to learn about Grandfather Mountain and the Blue Ridge. Members of the Newland Brownie Troop visited the Mile-High Swinging Bridge in 1978. (Courtesy of Marilyn Ball.)

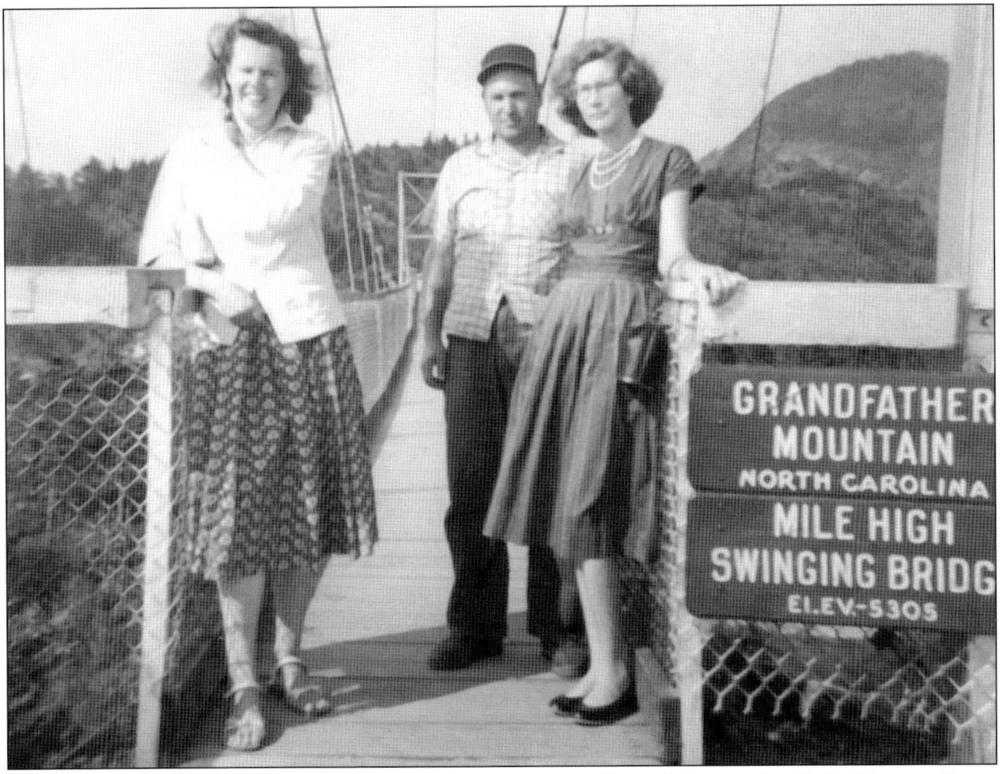

From left to right, Sally Hagan, Guy Ollis, and Beverly Ollis selected the popular elevation sign for this 1955 photograph, taken by Sally's husband, Russell Hagan. Russell and Guy had served together in the Merchant Marines during the turbulent years of the World War II. (Courtesy of Doyle Ollis.)

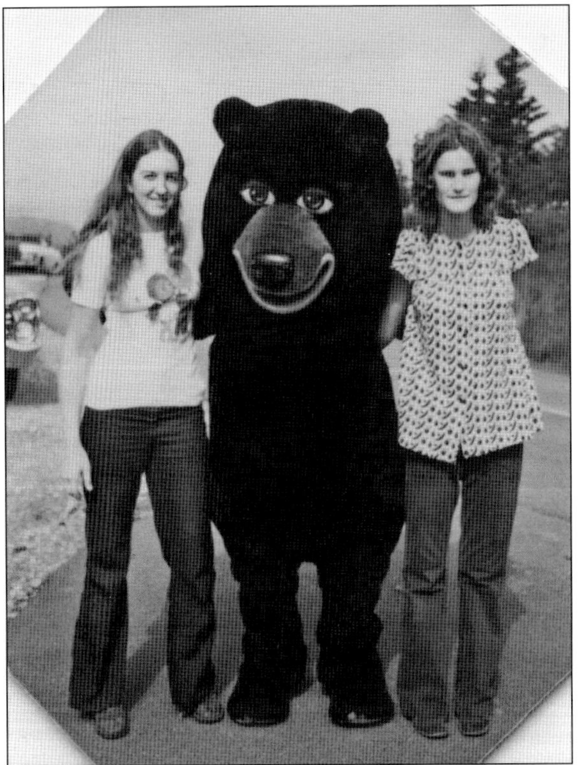

For more than a couple of generations, local residents have found seasonal employment working at the Grandfather Mountain attraction. Pictured in this 1972 photograph are, from left to right, Suzanne Hayes Tucker, Randy Edwards (in bear suit), and Jane Franklin Calloway. Wearing the bear suit could be miserable on warmer days. (Courtesy of Suzanne Tucker.)

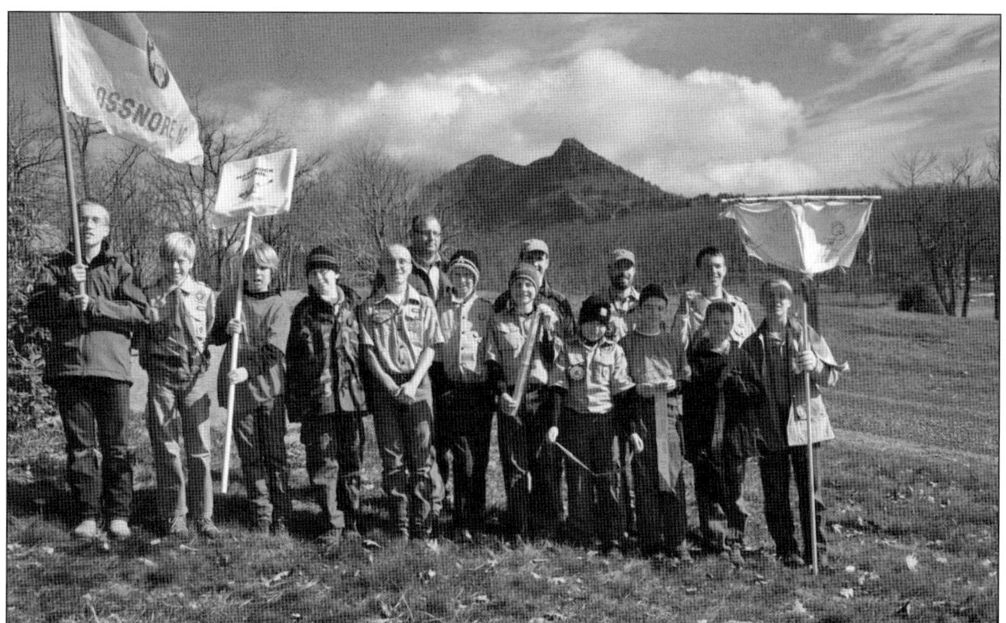

For many years, MacRae Meadows has played host to the annual Boy Scout Klondike Derby. Scout troops from across the Southeast build "sleds" to hold their supplies while completing a course around the meadow. Different stations challenge the Scouts' knowledge of building temporary shelters, orienteering, fire building, and more. Pictured here is Troop No. 814 of Crossnore, North Carolina, in 2012. (Courtesy of Michael Hardy.)

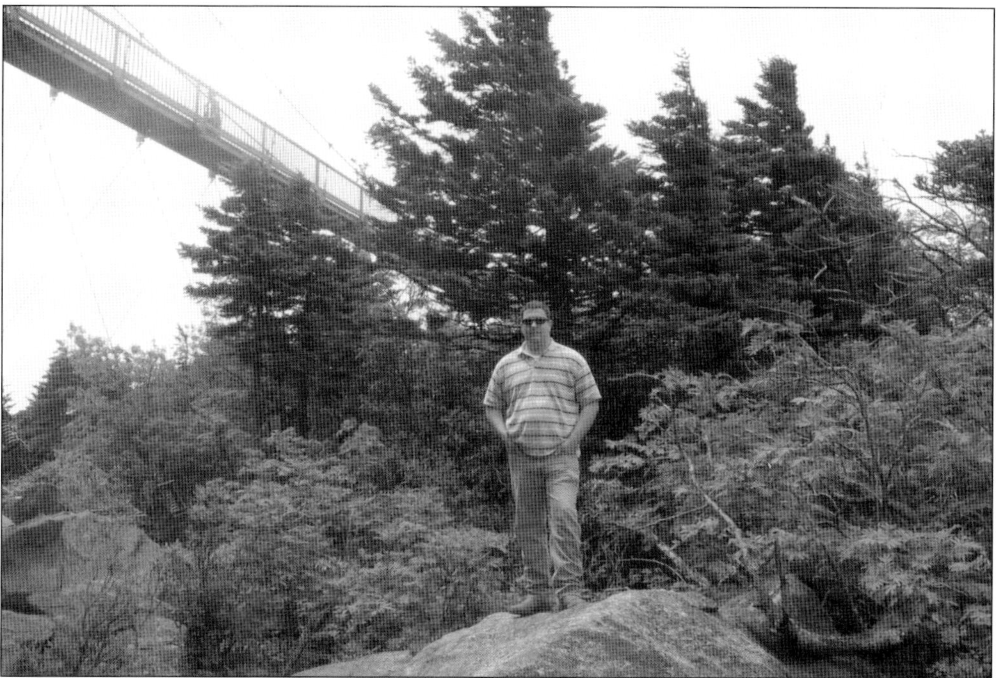

There are many different ways to view the Mile-High Swinging Bridge, like from Highway 105 or from other areas within the Grandfather Mountain attraction. Here, Craig Pippen is checking out the famous bridge from underneath. (Courtesy of Craig Pippen.)

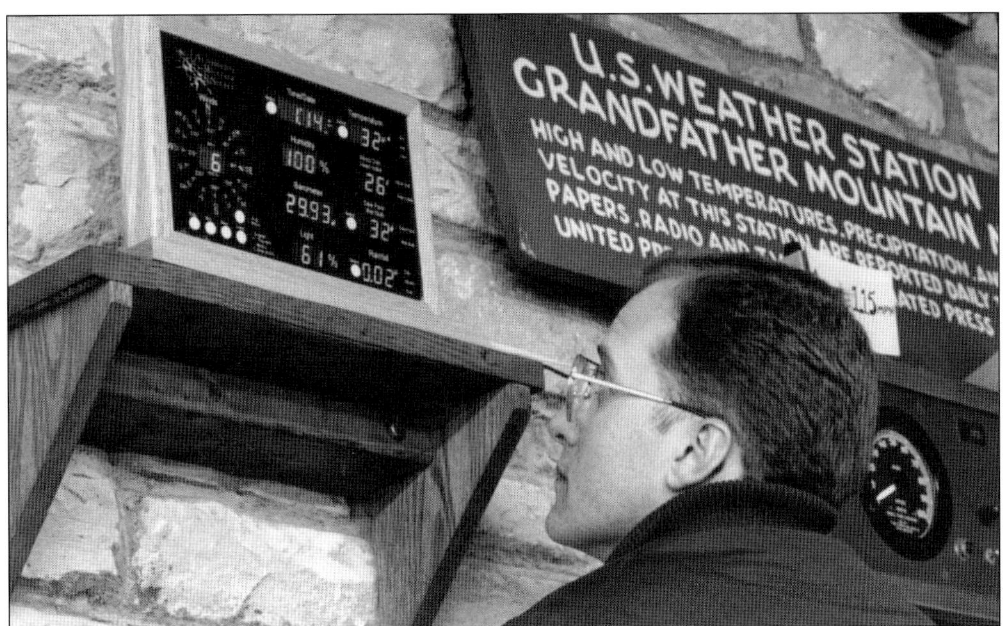

A National Weather Service reporting station at Grandfather Mountain was established in 1956. Information gathered at the station is sent once a month to the US Department of Commerce. In 2008, a second weather collection system was installed. This system is supported by Grandfather Mountain and Appalachian State University. Here, Billy Story examines information from the station at the Mile-High Swinging Bridge gift shop. (Courtesy of *Mountain Times*.)

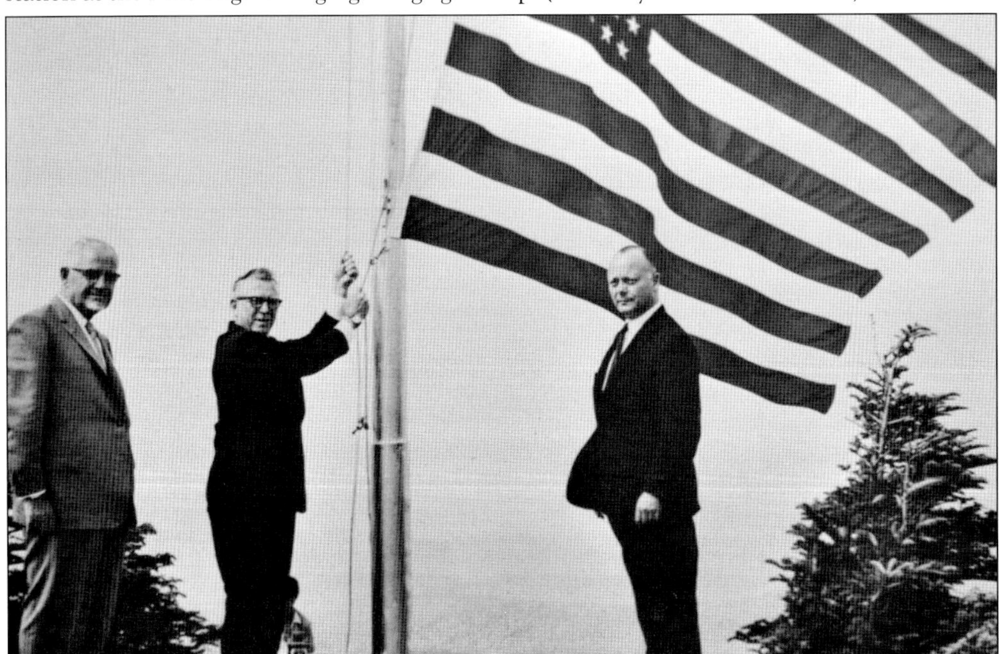

On January 3, 1959, Alaska officially became the 49th state to join the Union. J.E. Broyhill (right), leader of the North Carolina Republican Party, brought Secretary of Interior Fred Seaton (left) and Congressman Charles R. Jonas (center) to Grandfather Mountain to raise a new 49-star flag. (Courtesy Avery County Historical Museum.)

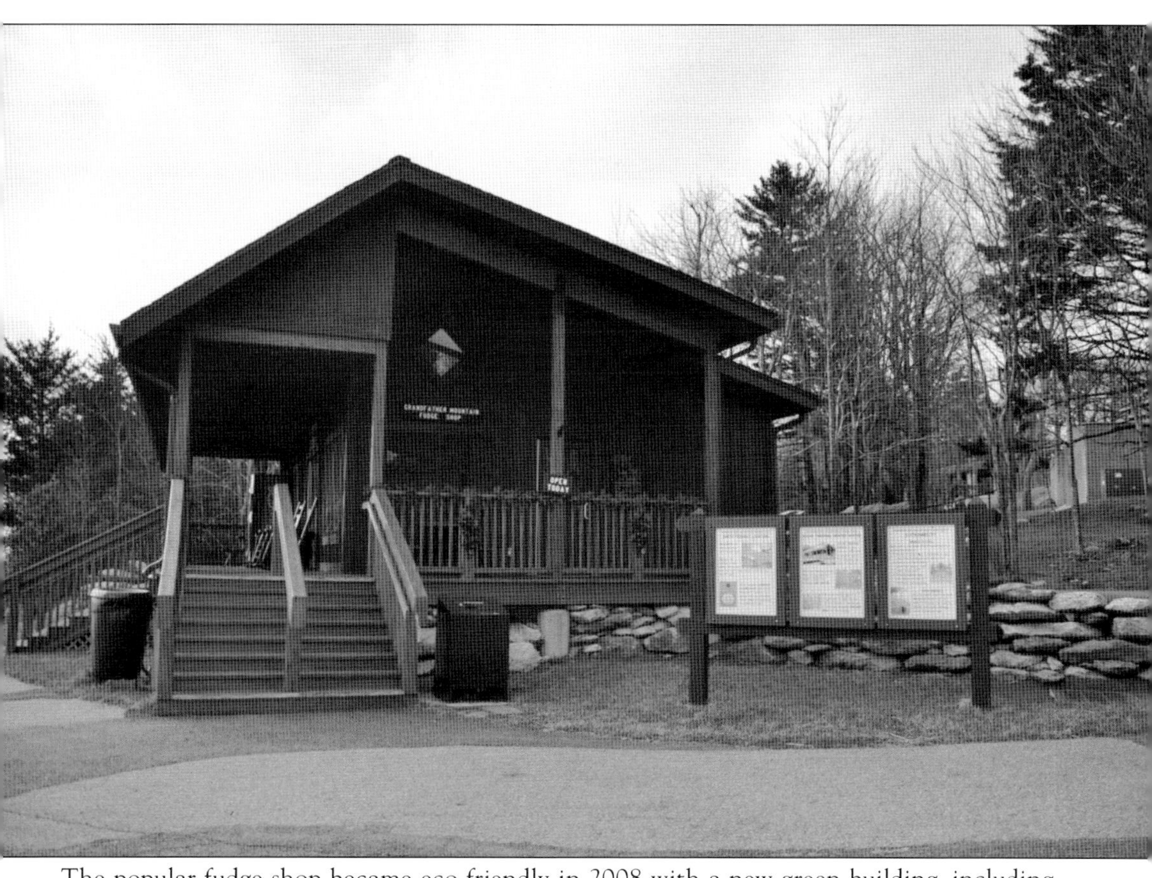

The popular fudge shop became eco-friendly in 2008 with a new green building, including renewable materials like bamboo, solar heating, rainwater collection, and skylights supplemented by efficient compact florescent lightbulbs. Now, visitors can feel guilty about the fudge they eat but not about their carbon footprints. (Courtesy of Michael Hardy.)

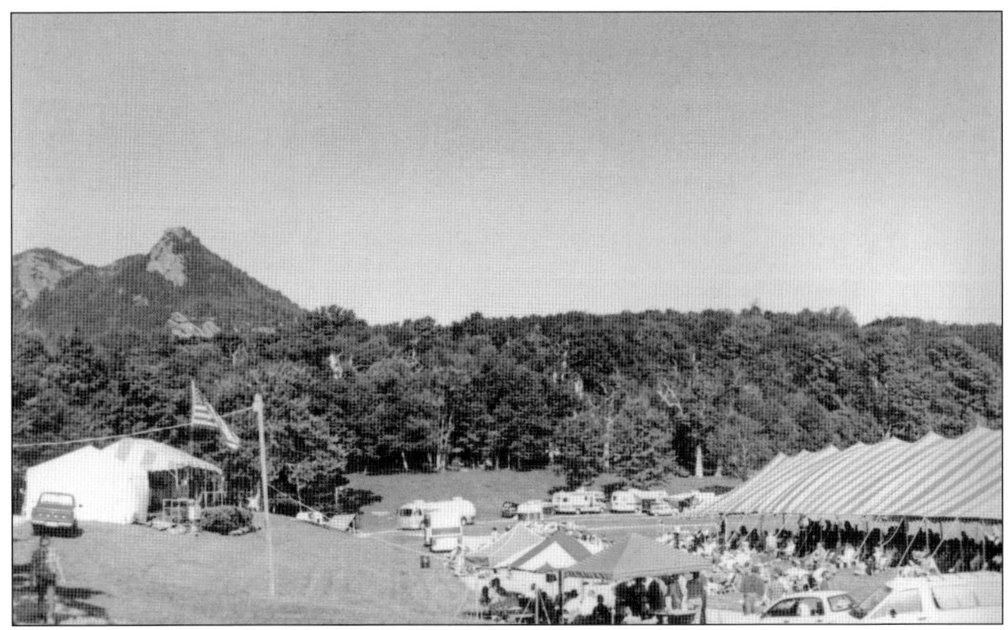

Among the participants at the 1993 Bluegrass Festival at MacRae Meadows were Generation Gap, the Nashville Bluegrass Band, Tim O'Brien and the O'Boys, Tony Rice, and the Del McCoury Band. (Courtesy of Patricia Townsend Brookband.)

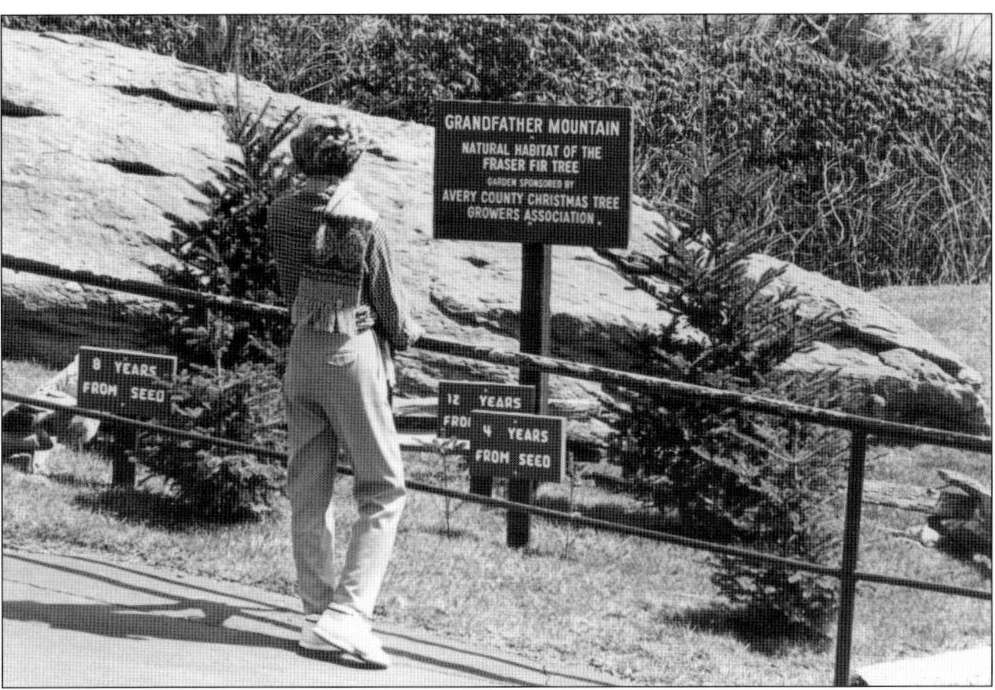

Growing Christmas trees in Western North Carolina has been an important business for half a century. At Grandfather Mountain, this display shows Fraser fir trees in their "natural habitat." About 95 percent of the Christmas trees grown in North Carolina are Fraser firs. (Courtesy of *Mountain Times*.)

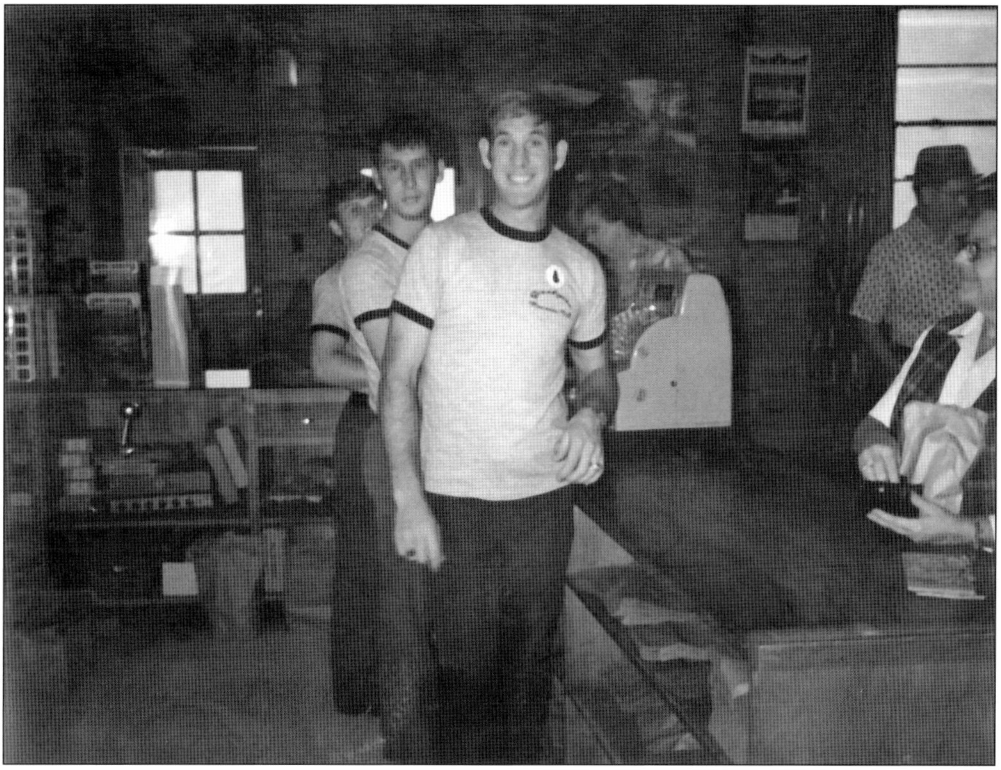

Though the products sold have changed over time, the gift shop has been a mainstay at Grandfather Mountain for decades. Here, some of the seasonal employees assist customers in 1972. (Courtesy of Suzanne Tucker.)

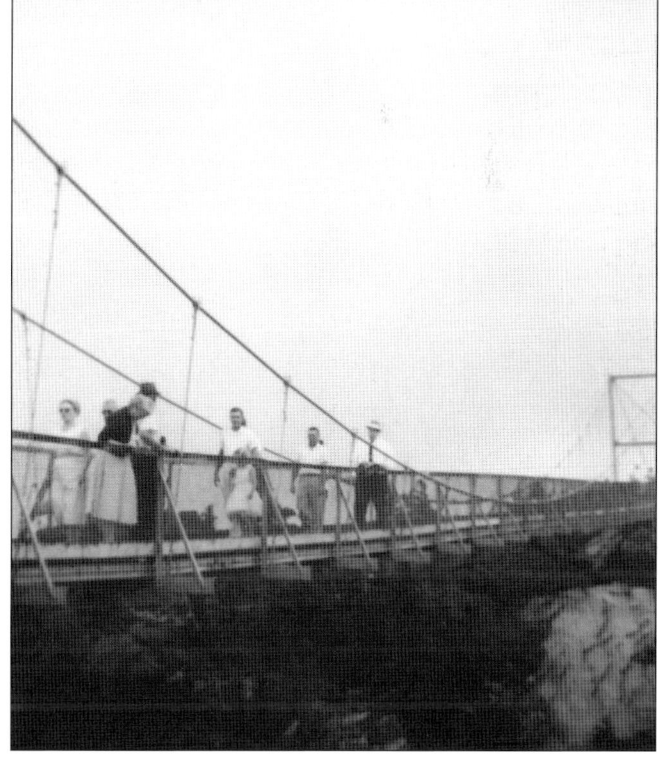

In this 1958 photograph, a few people stop long enough to peer over the edge of the Mile-High Swinging Bridge. Others walk swiftly, trying to not look down into the chasm below. These two different approaches can be seen every day on the bridge. (Courtesy of Wanda Rabb.)

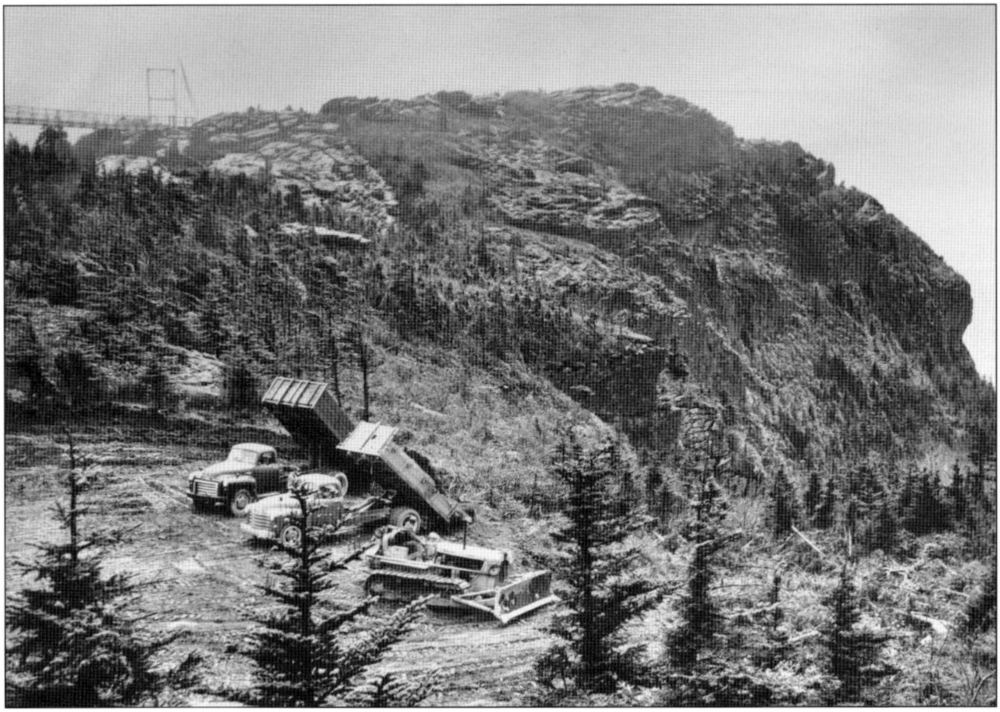

Upon taking ownership of Grandfather Mountain, Hugh Morton widened the road and extended that road to the top. He then carved out a parking lot and constructed the Mile-High Swinging Bridge between two peaks. (Courtesy of Patricia Combs.)

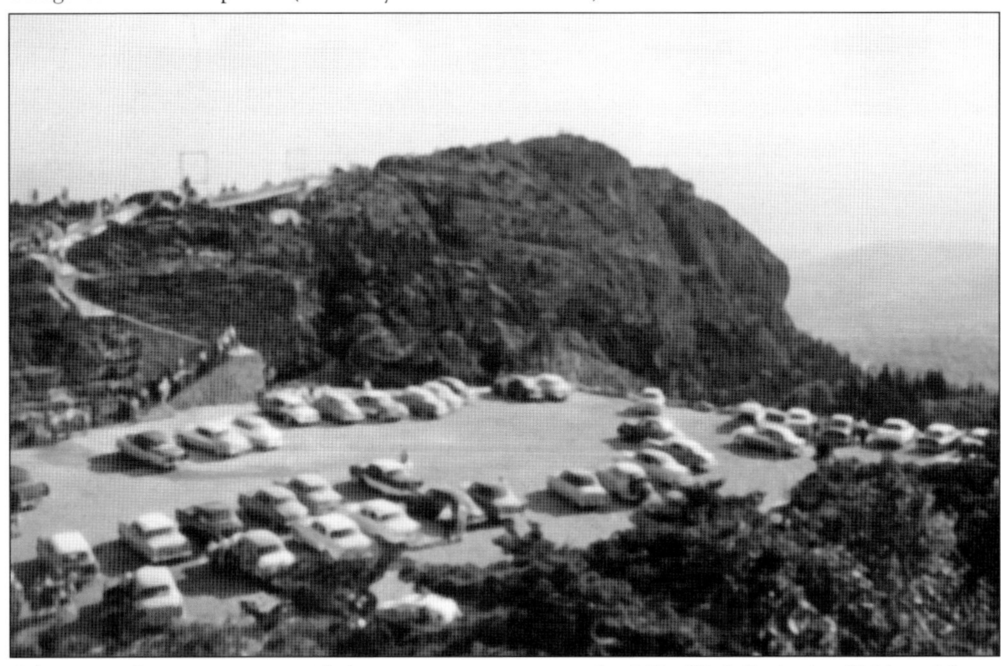

A long set of stone stairs provided guests a way to access the Mile-High Swinging Bridge. Also, a wooden structure was built, serving as a shop, with a set of restrooms located nearby. (Courtesy of Appalachian Collection.)

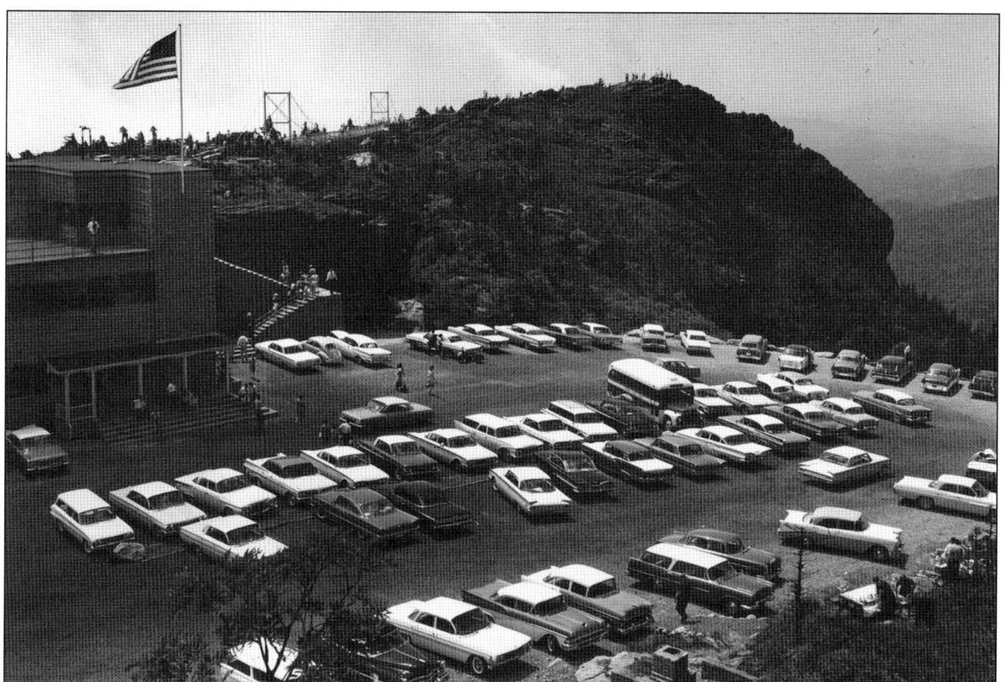

Over time, a visitor center was constructed on the site, near the Mile-High Swinging Bridge. There, visitors can buy a souvenir or hide out while their family and friends cross the bridge. (Courtesy of Michael Hardy.)

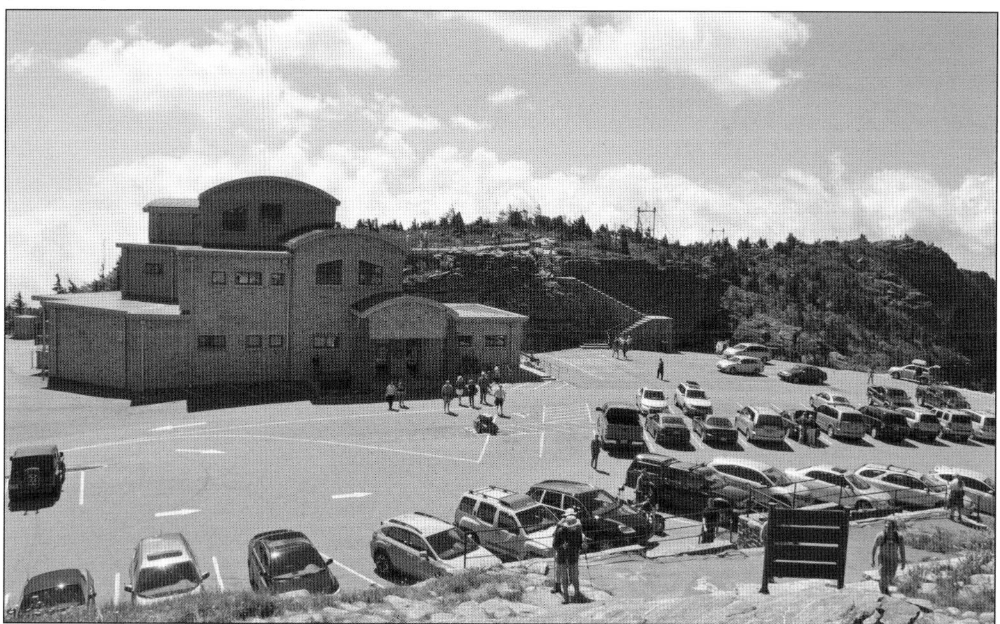

The new Top Shop was completed in 2010. The three-story, 6,000-square-foot building was constructed partially of salvaged materials from the old Top Shop, constructed in 1961. The building, designed by Bill Dixon of Appalachian Architecture and built by Greene Construction of Boone, was designed to blend more into the natural surroundings. The building provides wheelchair access to the Mile-High Swinging Bridge. (Courtesy of Michael Hardy.)

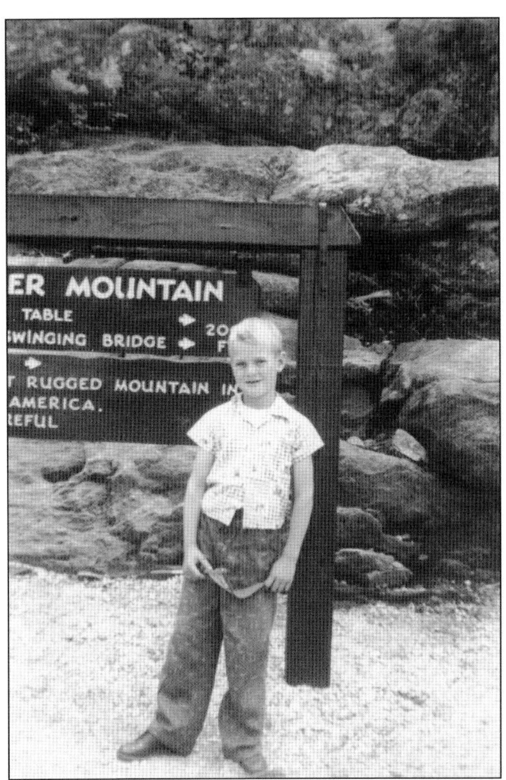

Rodger Richardson poses in the early 1950s at a sign near the Mile-High Swinging Bridge. The sign exhorted visitors, like young Roger, to be careful on the most rugged mountain in the eastern United States. (Courtesy of Johnny Graybeal.)

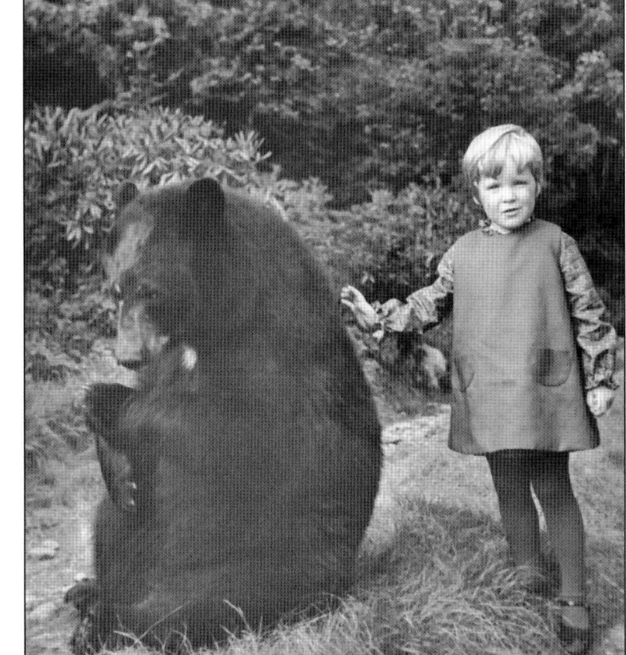

On many occasions, Hugh Morton brought Mildred the Bear out to pose with special guests. Here, she poses with Linda Wiseman, daughter of legendary musicians Lulu Belle and Scotty. She seems a little hesitant as she reaches out with her hand. (Courtesy of Avery County Historical Museum.)

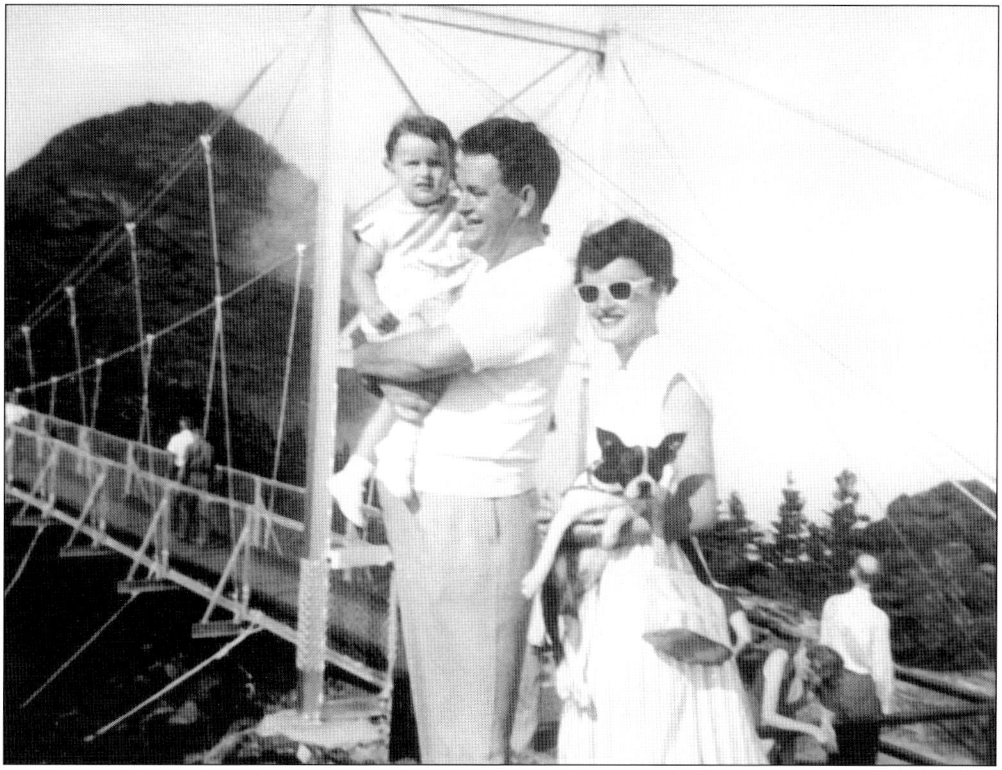

Members of the Buchanan family visited the Mile-High Swinging Bridge in 1953. They are, from left to right, Myria Buchanan, Ted Buchanan, and Ted's sister Tess Buchanan. (Courtesy of Terry Buchanan.)

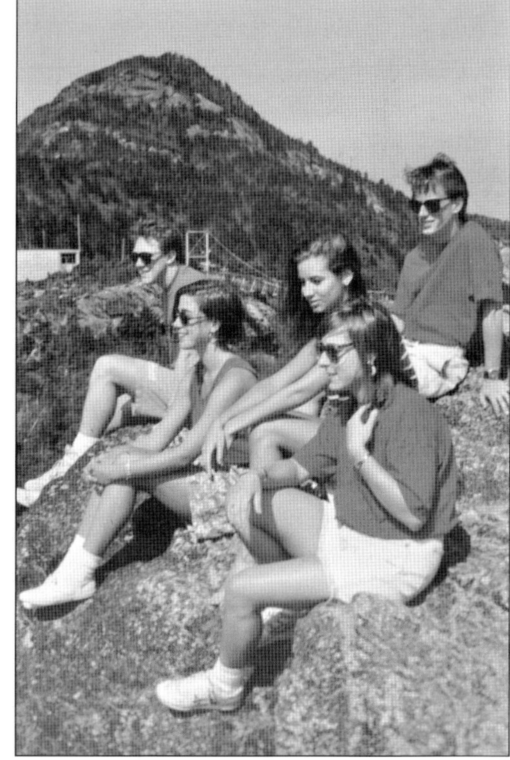

For decades, Lees-McRae College students, from nearby Banner Elk, have enjoyed individual and group visits to Grandfather Mountain. Here, a group of students poses for a shot in the 1990s. (Courtesy of Lees-McRae College.)

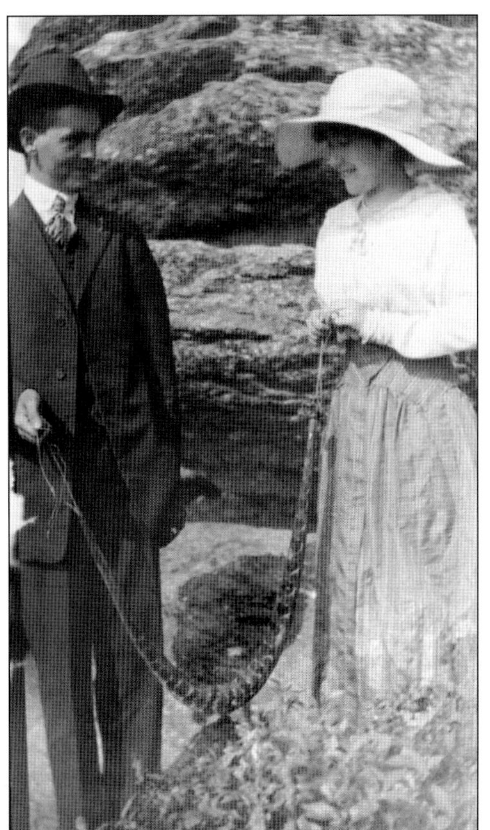

Jete W. and Louise (Hughes) Johnson, at View Rock on the Yonahlossee Road, hold a dead rattlesnake. The photograph was taken shortly after their April 3, 1920, wedding. The Johnsons lived in the Hughes community of Avery County, and Jete was known for his skill and accuracy with small rocks, probably bringing about the death of the snake. (Courtesy of Denise Baird Schwartz.)

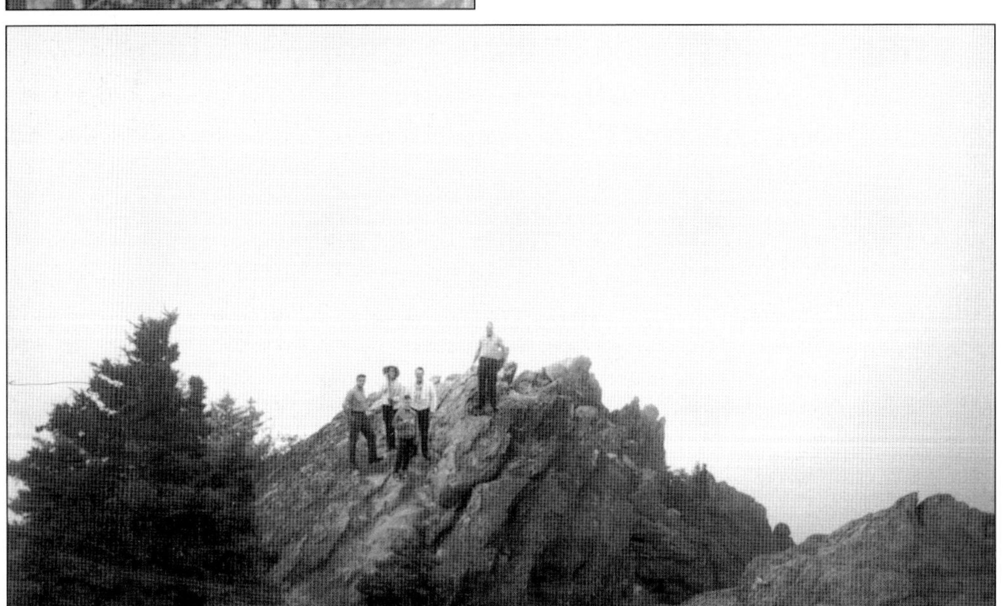

This photograph, snapped in August 1969, shows a group of visitors exploring some of the rock formations at Grandfather Mountain. Though they seem to be enjoying themselves, such climbs do pose real risks, and visitors are urged to wear proper shoes and stay on safe locations. (Courtesy of Historic Boone Collection.)

Ruth Richardson, with her daughter Betty Lou Richardson, looks a little windblown at the Mile-High Swinging Bridge at Grandfather Mountain in June 1955 or 1956. (Courtesy of Erma Dean Graybeal.)

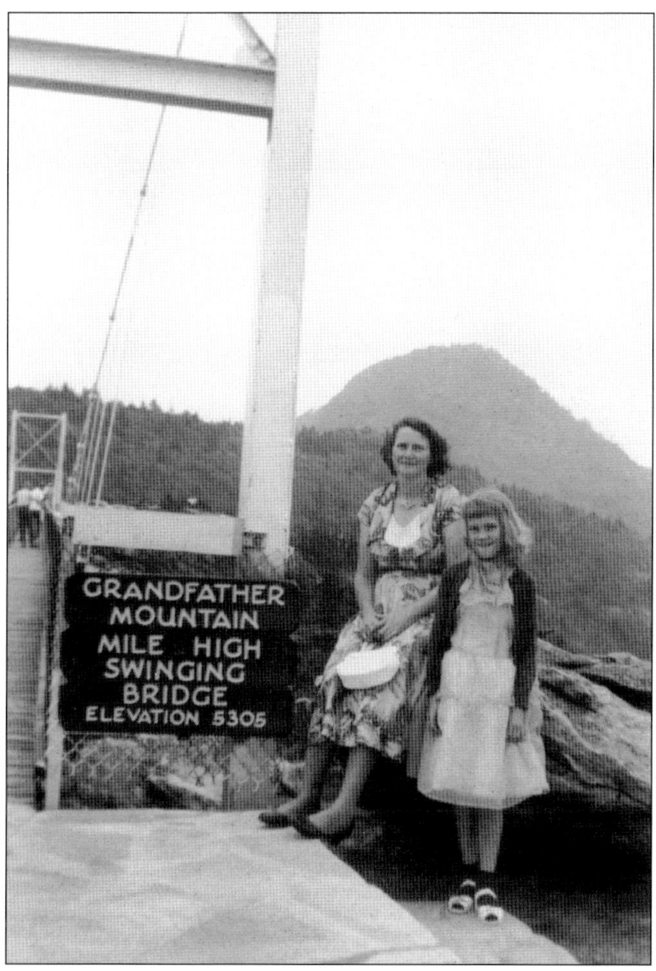

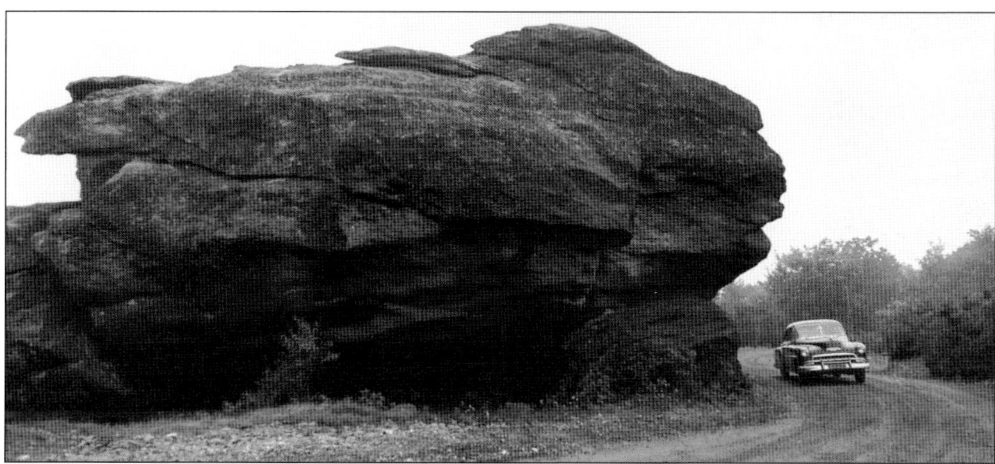

Prior to the widening of the road to the top of Grandfather Mountain, visitors had to navigate a one-lane gravel road to the Cliffside observation deck. That in itself was an adventure. Cars passed not only the Split Rock, but the Sphinx Rock as well, as illustrated in this early photograph. (Courtesy of Appalachian Collection.)

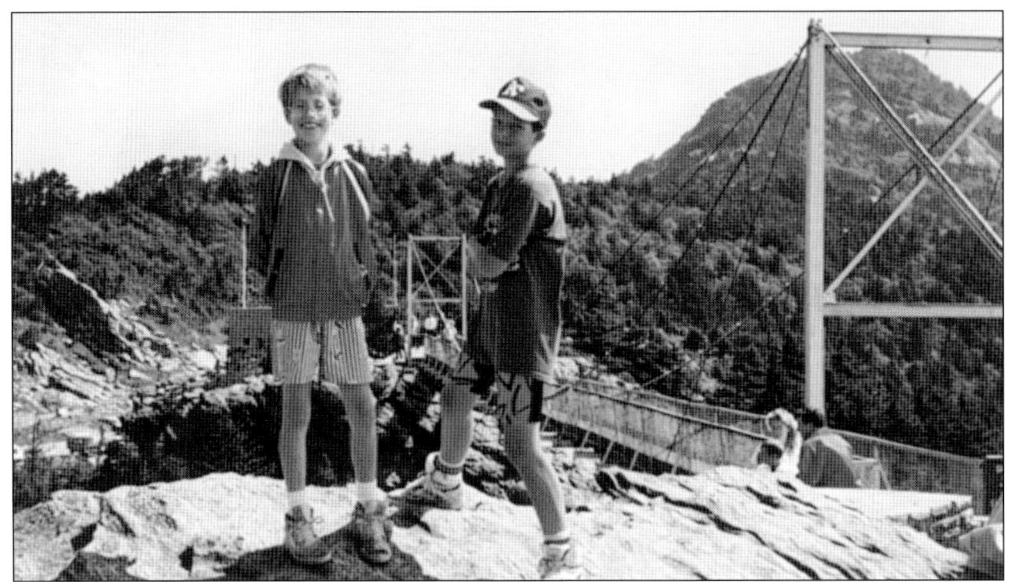

These two young men appear to be enjoying themselves and the view at the entrance to the Mile-High Swinging Bridge. Many people take one look at the bridge, especially on a windy day, and choose not to cross. (Courtesy of Martha Hicks.)

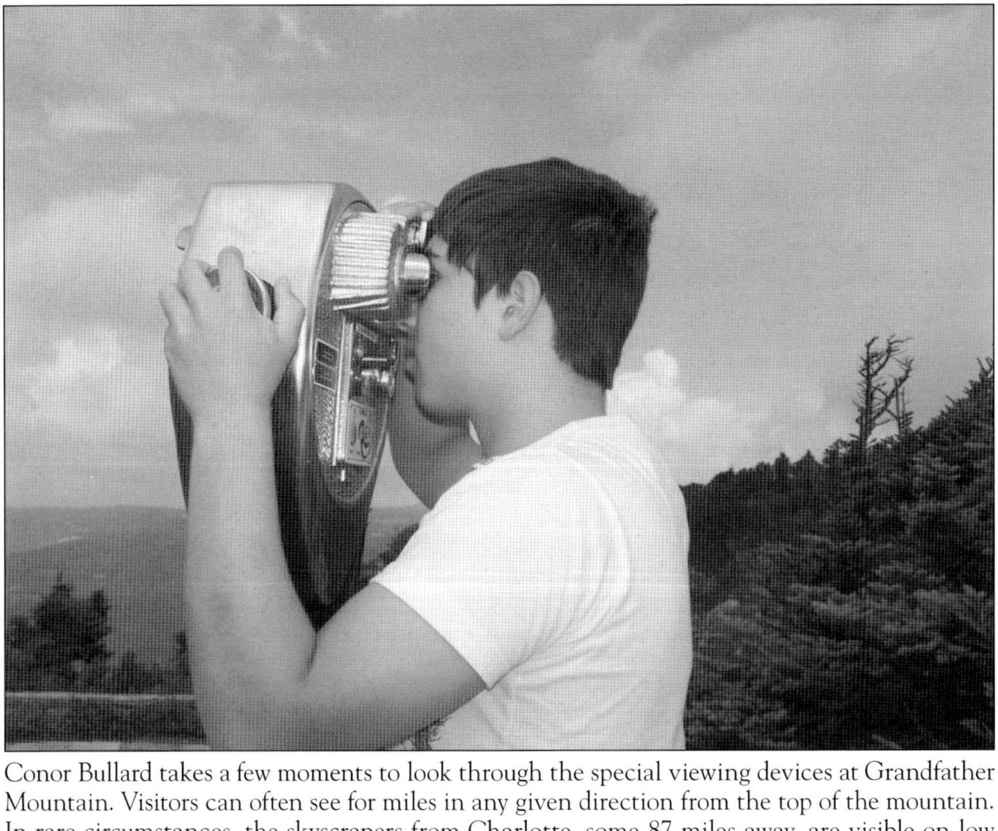

Conor Bullard takes a few moments to look through the special viewing devices at Grandfather Mountain. Visitors can often see for miles in any given direction from the top of the mountain. In rare circumstances, the skyscrapers from Charlotte, some 87 miles away, are visible on low humidity mornings. (Courtesy of Tim Bullard.)

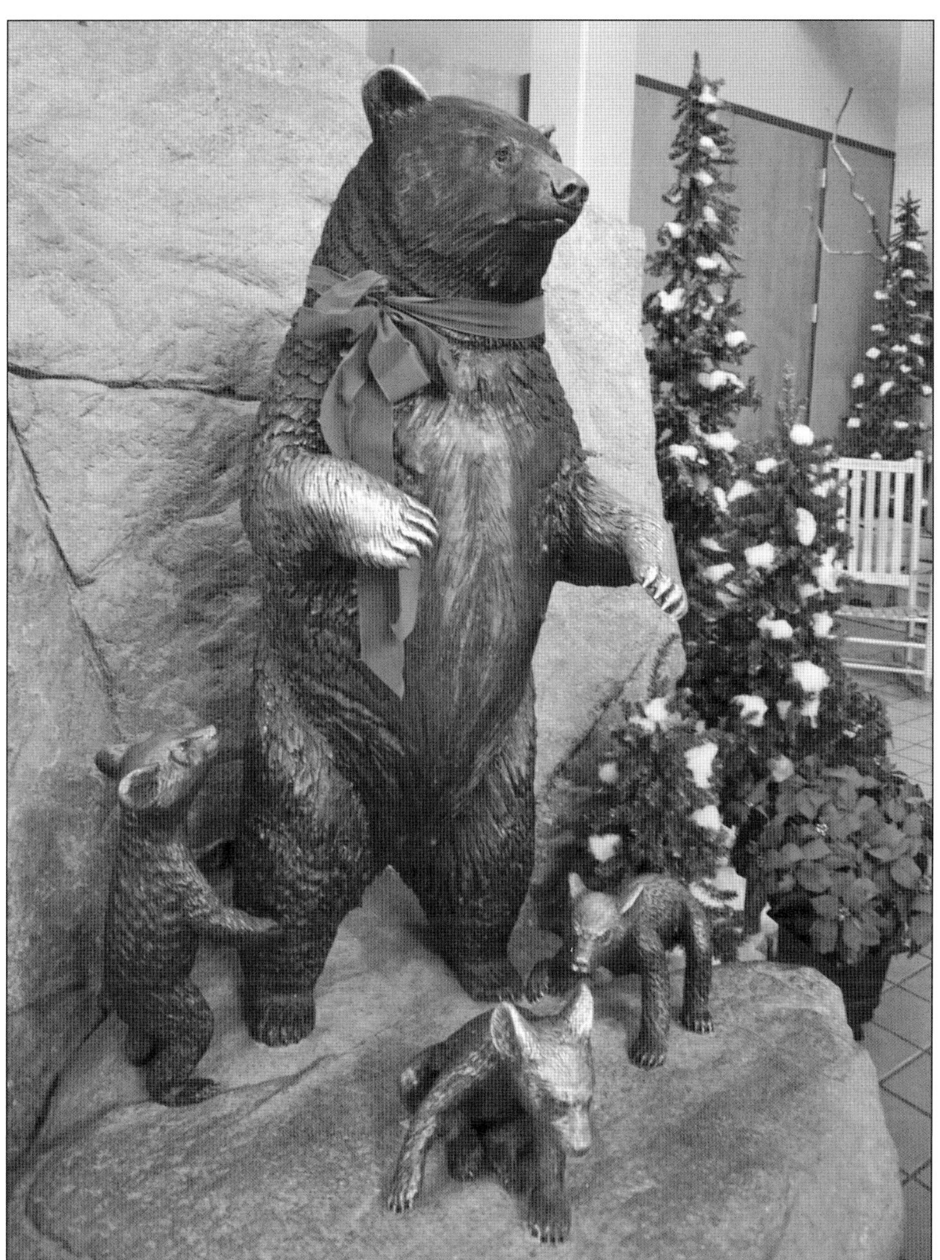

The bronze statue of Mildred the Bear, joined by her cubs, greets visitors in the Nature Museum and was designed by renowned sculptor Johnpaul Harris. According to one account, upon being presented with one of the bronze cubs, Mildred actually licked the statue on the nose. Harris also created the statue of Charlie "Choo Choo" Justice at the University of North Carolina at Chapel Hill, the statue of Atlanta mayor Andrew Young in Georgia, and the white rhino at the North Carolina Zoo. While the original Mildred the Bear has been gone for many years, her bronze look-a-like still stands at the Nature Museum, ready to greet the thousands who pass her way every year. Like the first Mildred, the bronze replica is a favorite photograph opportunity; visitors love to pose with her, and countless children have clamored up to join the cubs under Mildred's care. (Courtesy of Michael Hardy.)

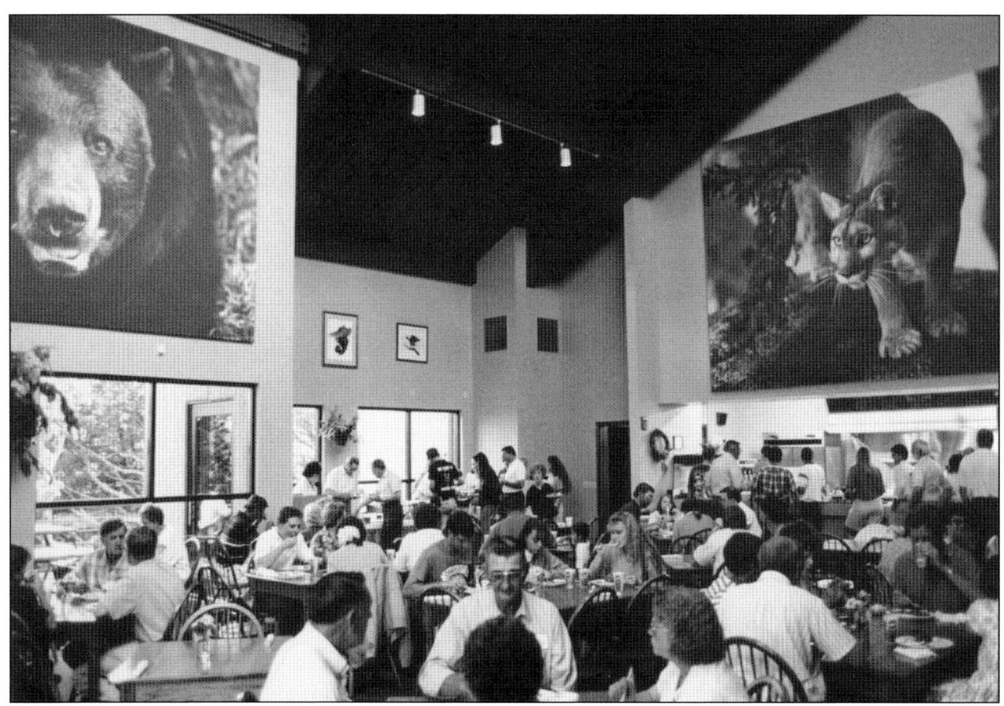

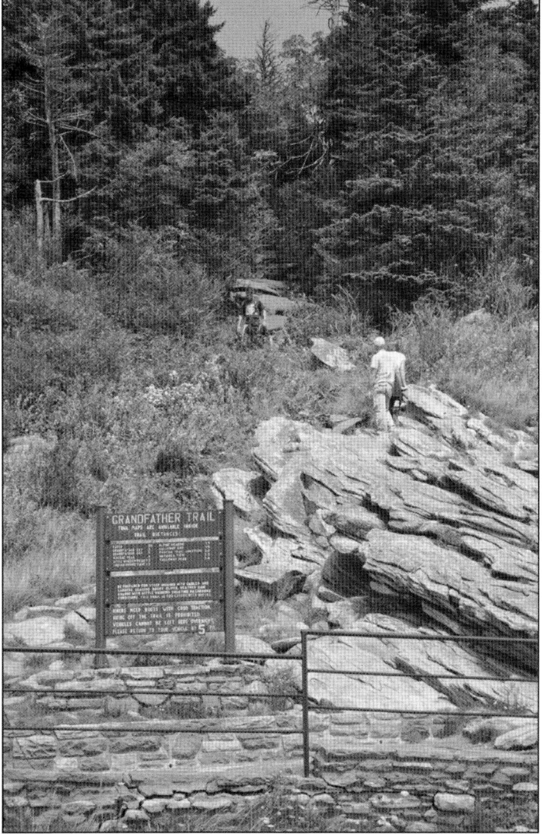

Included within the Nature Museum is Mildred's Grill. While many visitors grab a bite to fuel themselves for further exploring of Grandfather Mountain, the grill is also a great place to view a few of the wonderful images that Hugh Morton took of the attraction that he created. (Courtesy of Avery County Historical Museum.)

The Grandfather Trail is a 4.8-mile round-trip hike that leads to Calloway Peak. Local hiking guides rate the trail as strenuous as hikers traverse over peaks using ladders and cables. The trail begins opposite the Top Shop, passes under Head Bumpin' Rock, over MacRae Peak, through MacRae Gap, over a boulder known as the Subway, through Calloway Gap, and ends at Calloway Peak. (Courtesy of Michael Hardy.)

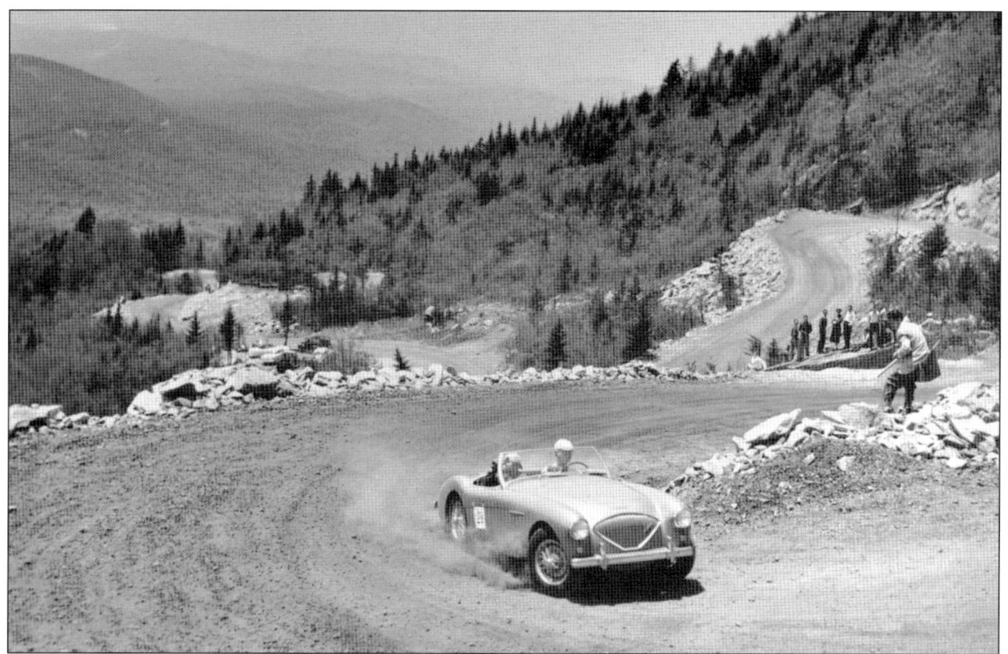

In the 1950s and early 1960s, Grandfather Mountain hosted an annual hill climb. Cars raced on the gravel road from the bottom to the top of the mountain, competing against the clock. There were all kinds of cars, including Porsches, MGs, Jaguars, Austin-Healeys, and Volkswagens. (Courtesy of Sebastian Sommer and Patricia Combs.)

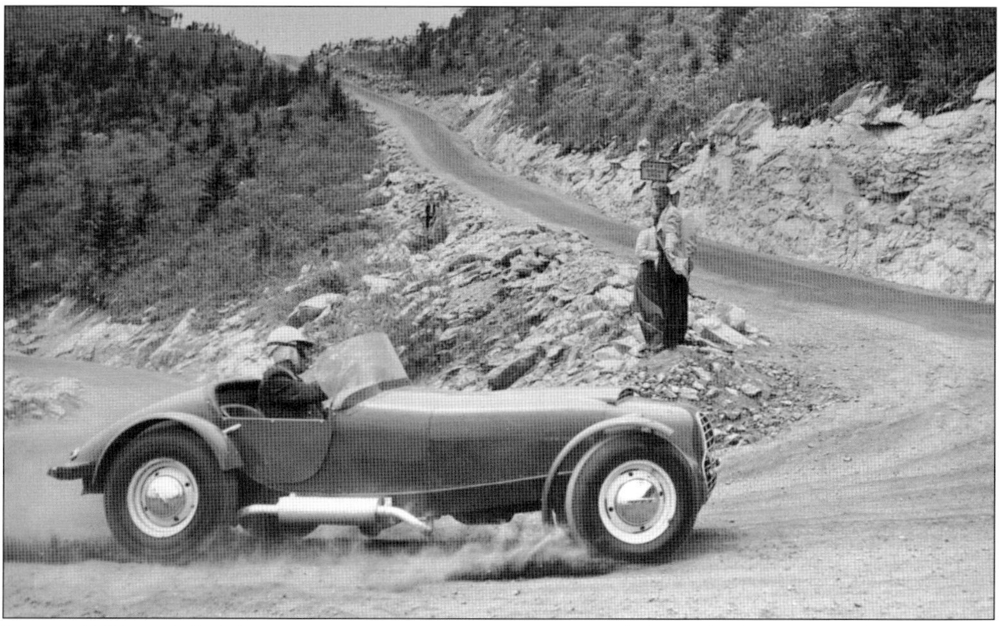

In the 1950s and 1960s, sports car races on mountains and through the streets of towns were all the rage. Grandfather Mountain held such races during the time, with competitors racing two and a half miles up the mountain, against the clock. In 1954, there were 34 competing cars and more than 1,000 spectators at the event. (Courtesy of Patricia Combs; photograph by Sebastian Sommer.)

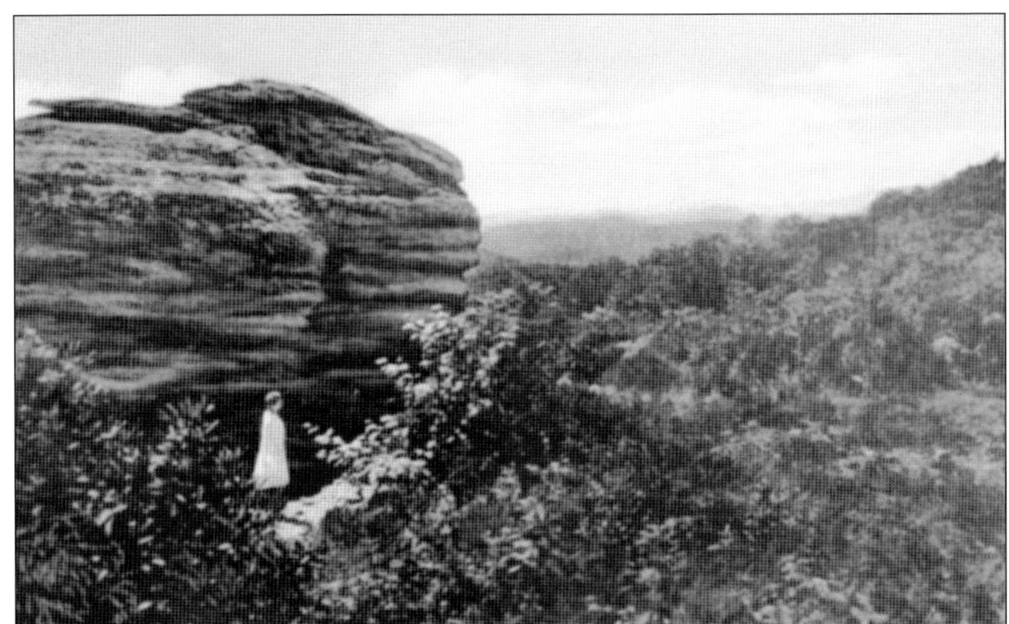

This early postcard depicts a young lady standing near the Sphinx Rock before the construction of the road that takes visitors to either the observation deck or the Mile-High Swinging Bridge. (Courtesy of Michael Hardy.)

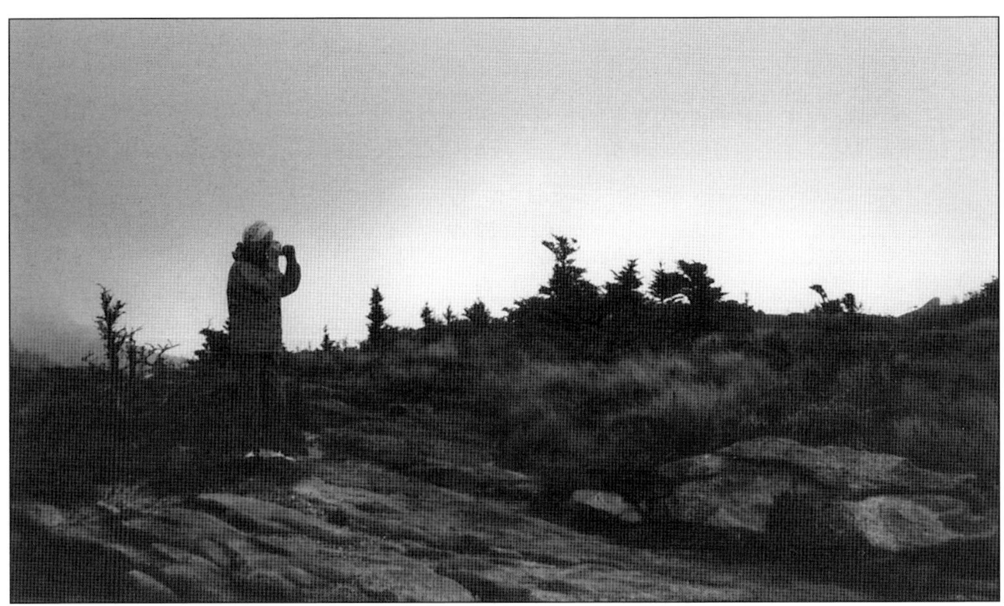

Barbara Cooney, pictured here taking in the sights on Grandfather Mountain, was a writer and illustrator of more than 200 children's books published over a span of 60 years. Twice, she won the Caldecott Medal, which recognizes the best illustrator any given year. She illustrated the award-winning *The Year of the Perfect Christmas Tree: An Appalachian Story* by Gloria Houston. (Courtesy of Gloria Houston.)

In this c. 1925 photograph, Retta Jarrett Gibson poses with Grandfather Mountain as her background and sports daring but practical hiking attire. (Courtesy of Vern and Shirley Thomas.)

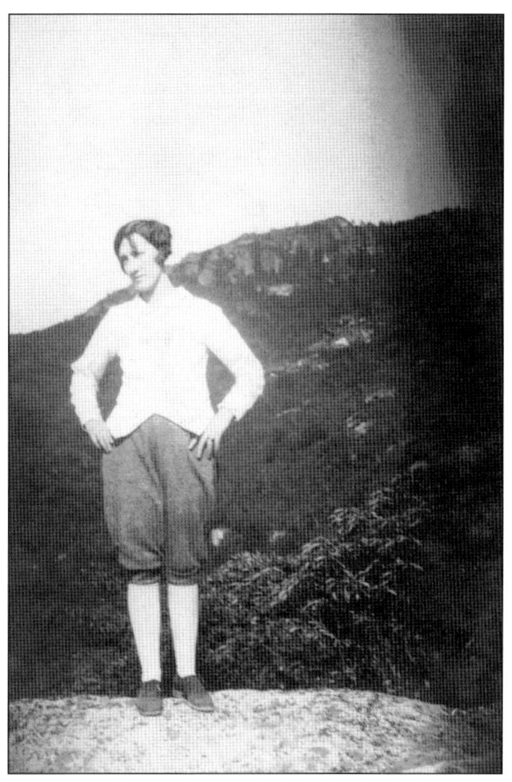

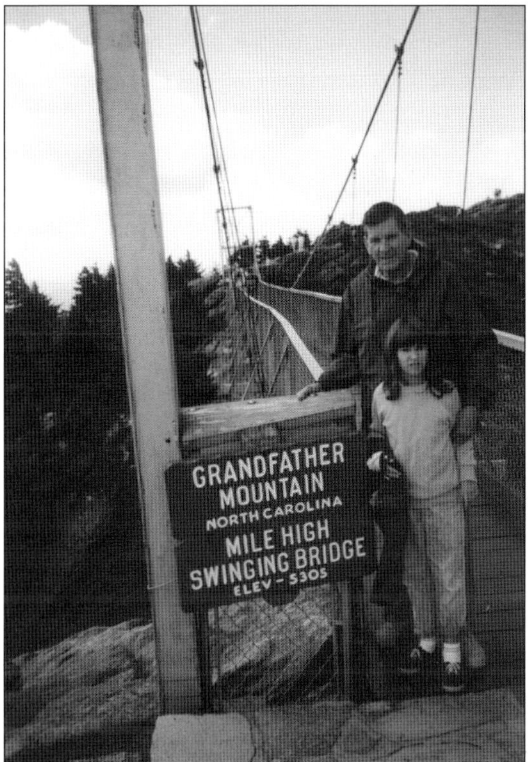

Vern Thomas, with his granddaughter, poses by the familiar Mile-High Swinging Bridge sign in 1990. After the bridge was rebuilt of galvanized steel in 1999, it was often called a "Singing Bridge." This is because the span now moves less and instead makes musical sounds as the winds blow through it. (Courtesy of Vern and Shirley Thomas.)

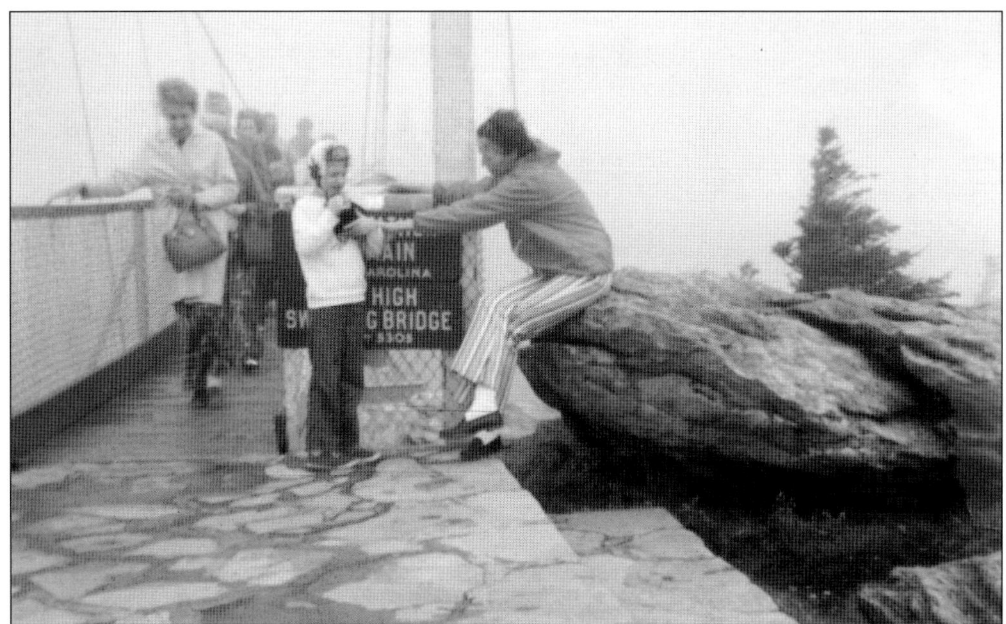

This picture was taken around 1968, and given the attire of the other ladies in the background, it was obviously a cool, windy, foggy day at Grandfather Mountain when Shirley Thomas, with her daughter Lisa, came for a visit. The windy conditions on Grandfather account for the unusual shapes of the trees, which have been shaped by the stiff air currents. (Courtesy of Vern and Shirley Thomas.)

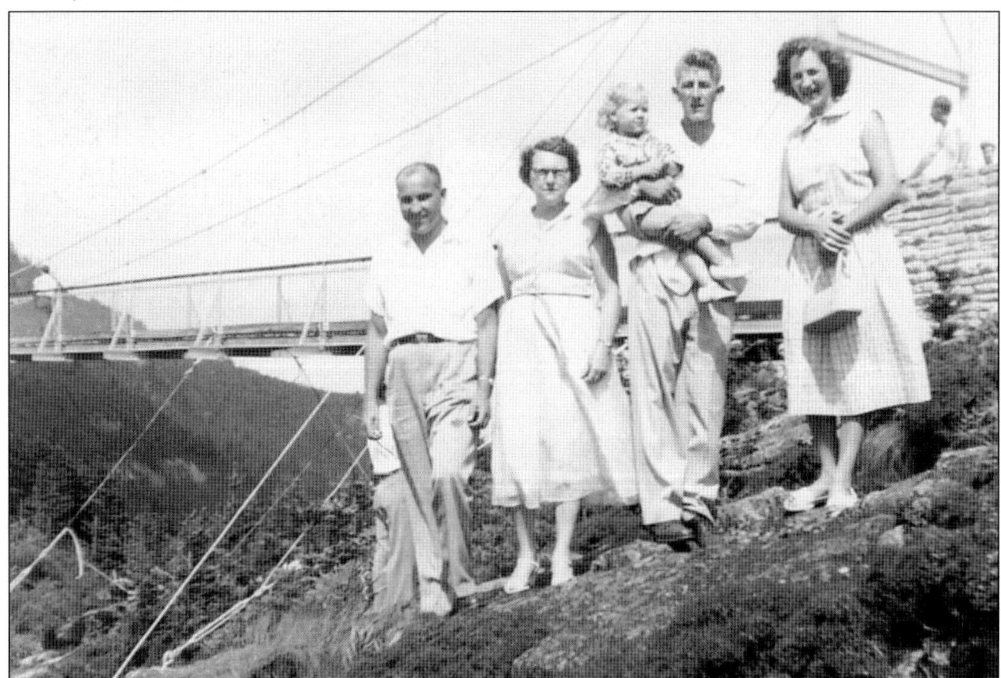

Taken in 1955, this photograph shows, from left to right, Tyson and Ruby Buchanan, Teresa Buckner, and Hershal and Amy Buckner beside the Mile-High Swinging Bridge at Grandfather Mountain. (Courtesy of Beth Davis.)

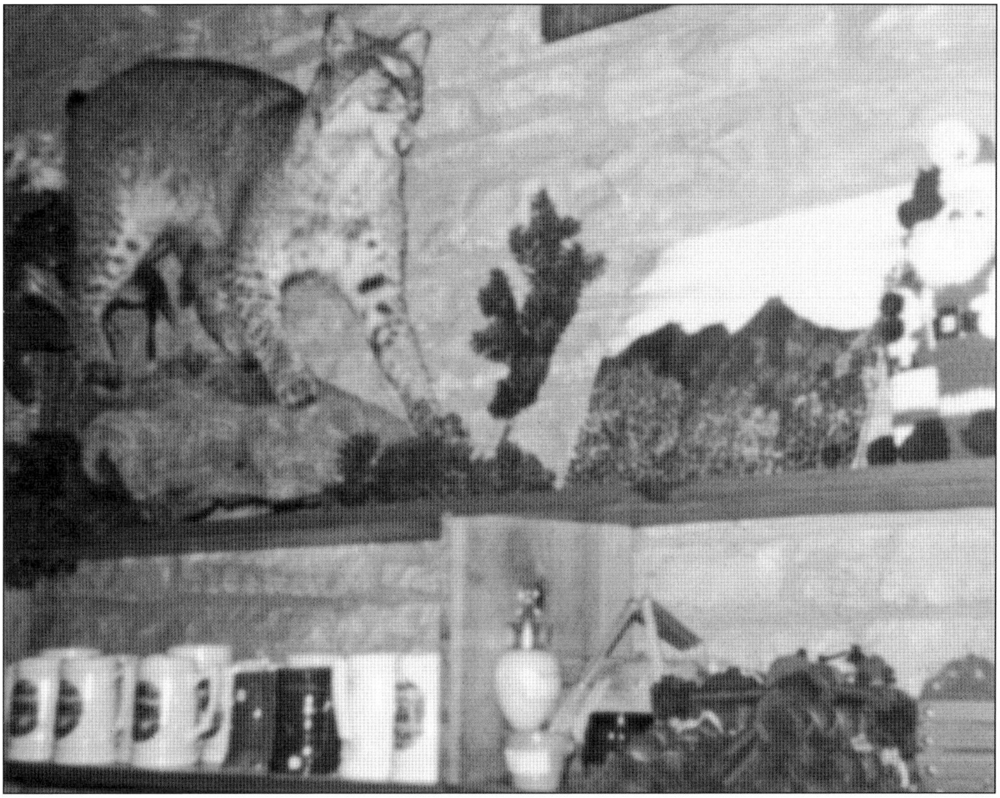

Visitors to the Top Shop in 1972 could purchase souvenir mugs, pennants, shot glasses, and postcards, not only of the Mile-High Swinging Bridge, but also of Grandfather Mountain itself. This photograph shows a small portion of the items in the Top Shop. The taxidermy bobcat was not for sale. (Courtesy of Suzanne Tucker.)

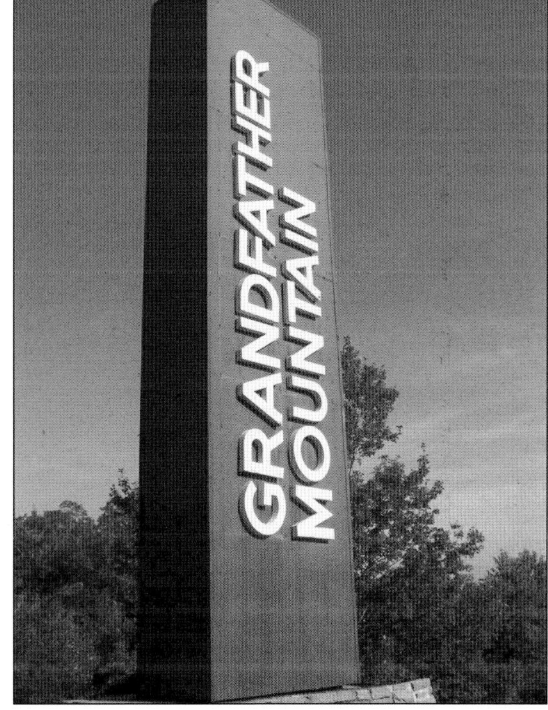

This sign, along US 221, or the Yohanlassee Road, greets visitors at the entrance of Grandfather Mountain and, with its vertical structure, echoes the mountain's towering presence. (Courtesy of Tim Bullard.)

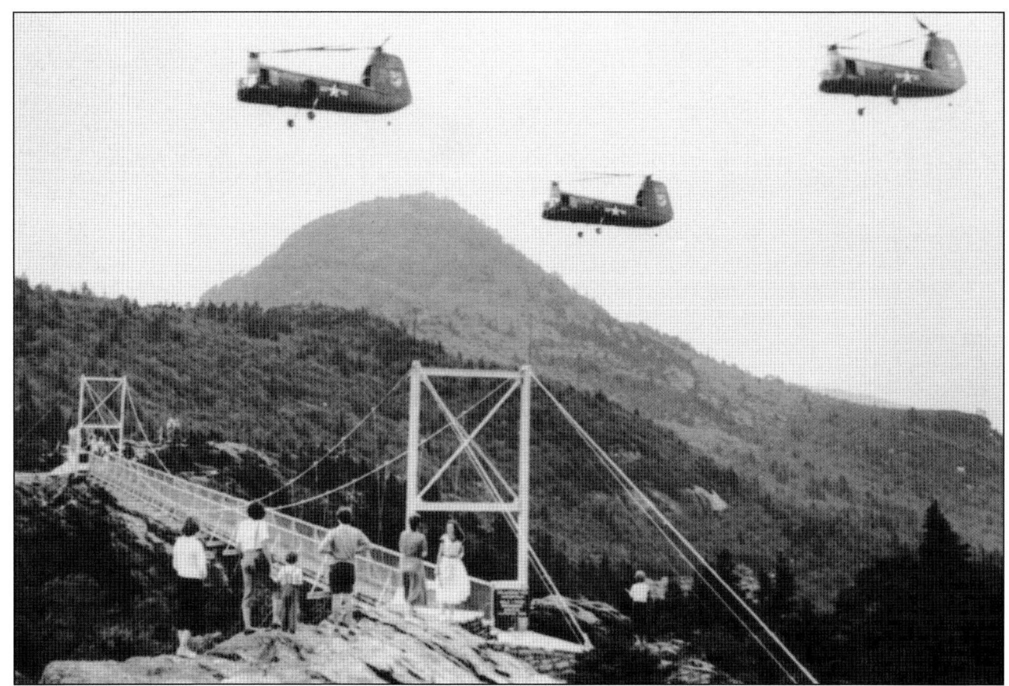

From time to time, different branches of the US military have used the Grandfather Mountain area for training. Hugh Morton allowed the military aviators, preparing for Vietnam, to train at high altitudes by landing their helicopters in the parking lot of the Mile-High Swinging Bridge. (Courtesy of Grandfather Mountain.)

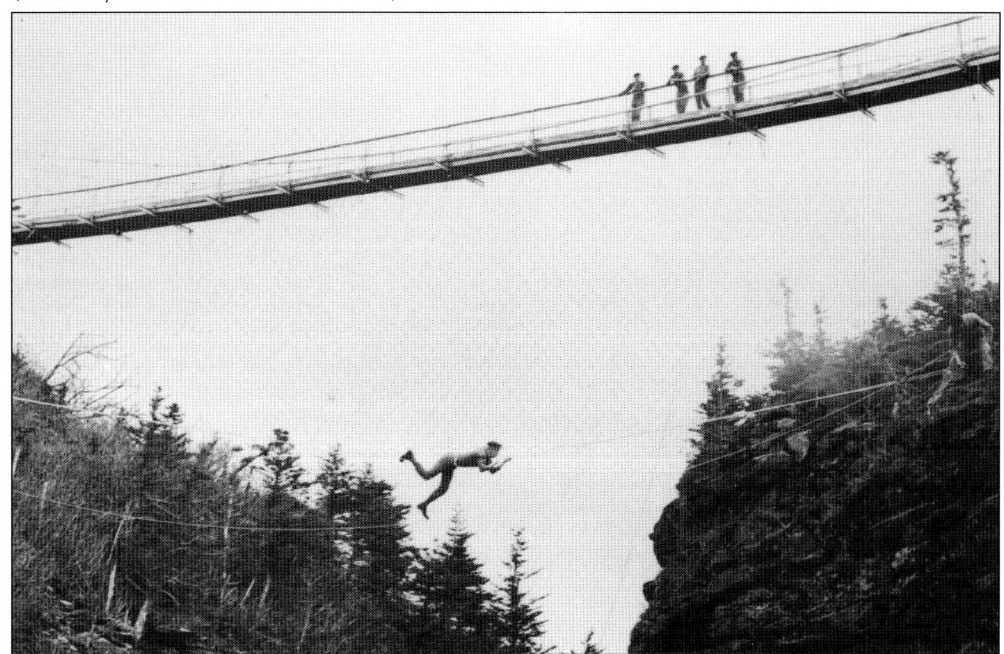

In May 1966, a detachment of Army Special Forces, members of the famed Green Berets, took time to train at Grandfather Mountain. The Green Berets were instrumental in training indigenous forces to fight in places like Vietnam. (Courtesy of Grandfather Mountain.)

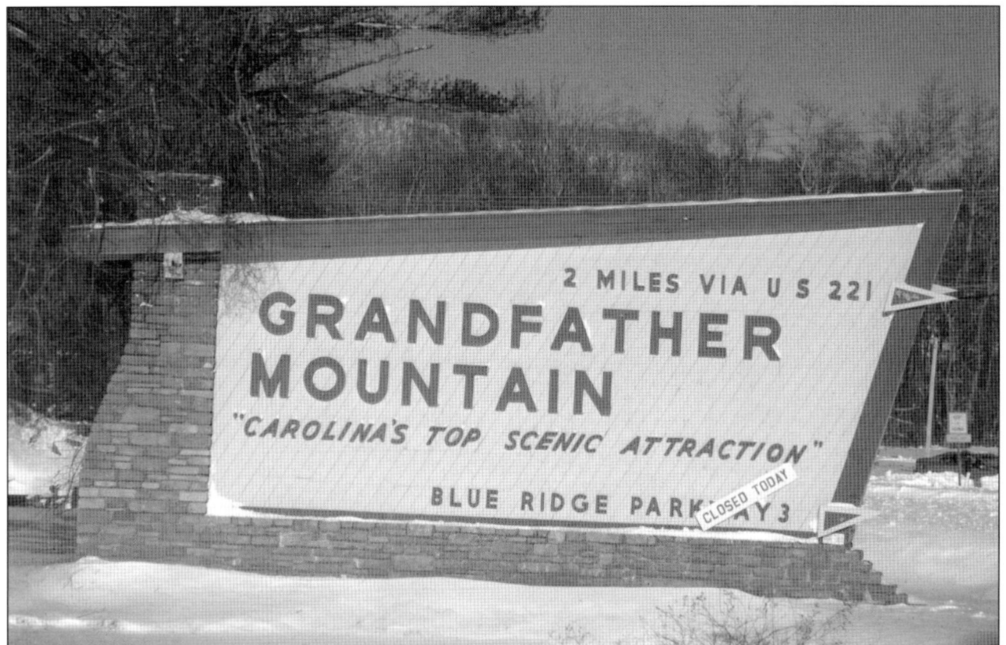

For the first few decades of the Grandfather Mountain attraction, everything closed during the winter months. Later on, the attraction stayed open during the winter, only closing when snow and ice made the roads impassable. Often, the lower half of the facilities remain open, while the Mile-High Swinging Bridge area closes. (Courtesy of Michael Hardy.)

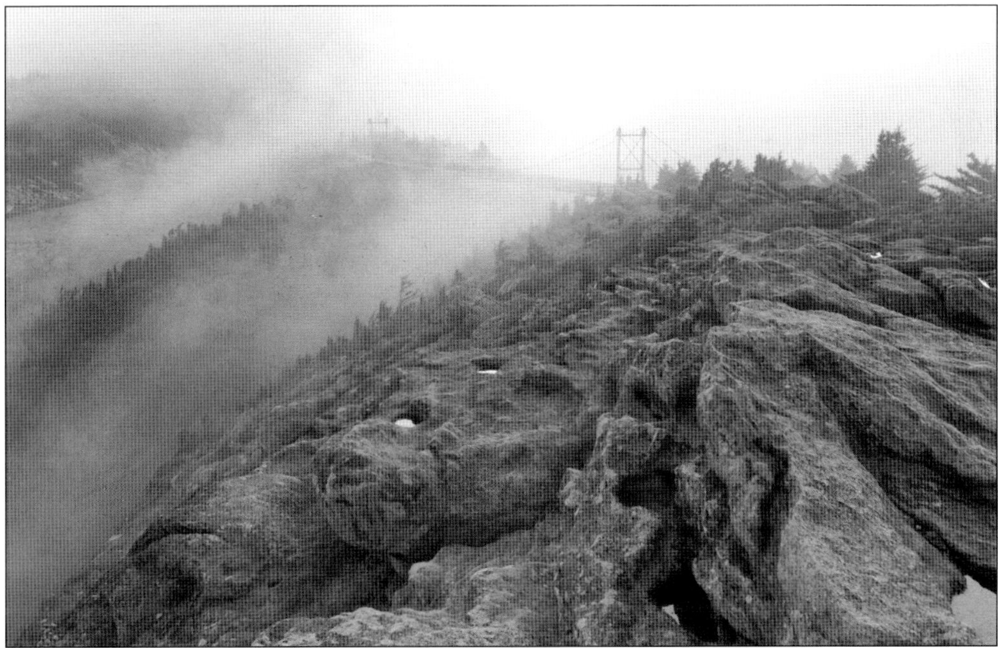

Weather conditions change frequently on Grandfather Mountain. On some days, the different peaks poke above the lower level of clouds. On other days, the top of the mountain is encased in fog, while the sun shines at lower levels. In the winter, ice often covers the top of the mountain (Courtesy of *Avery Journal-Times*.)

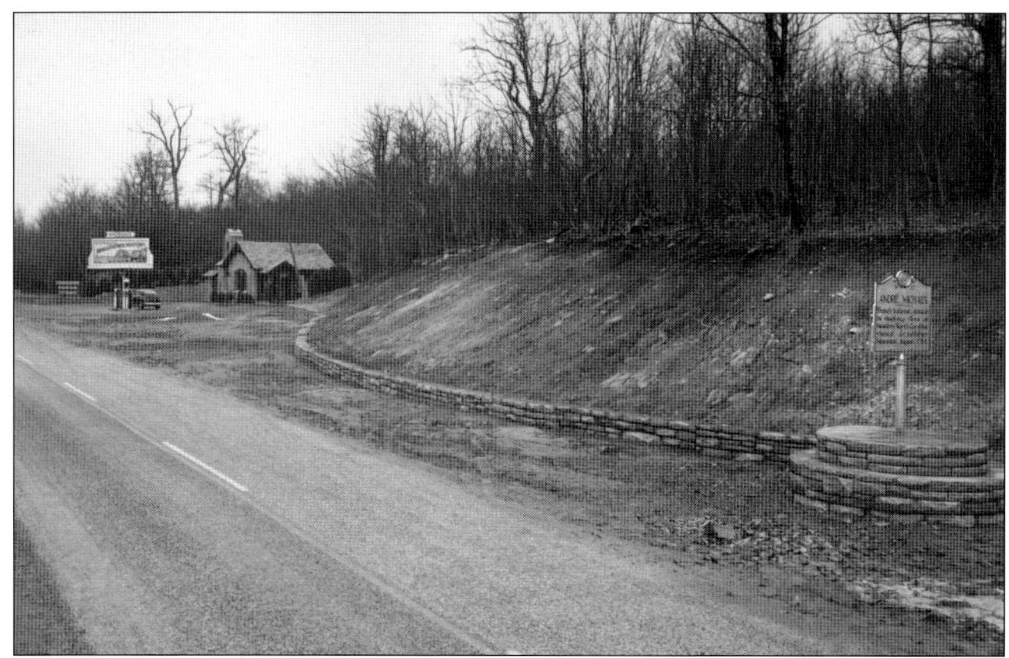

For many years, there was an Esso gas station located at the entrance of Grandfather Mountain. While the pumps are long gone, the stone building survives. The entrance where the fee is paid (originally the toll) has been expanded. (Courtesy of Avery County Historical Museum.)

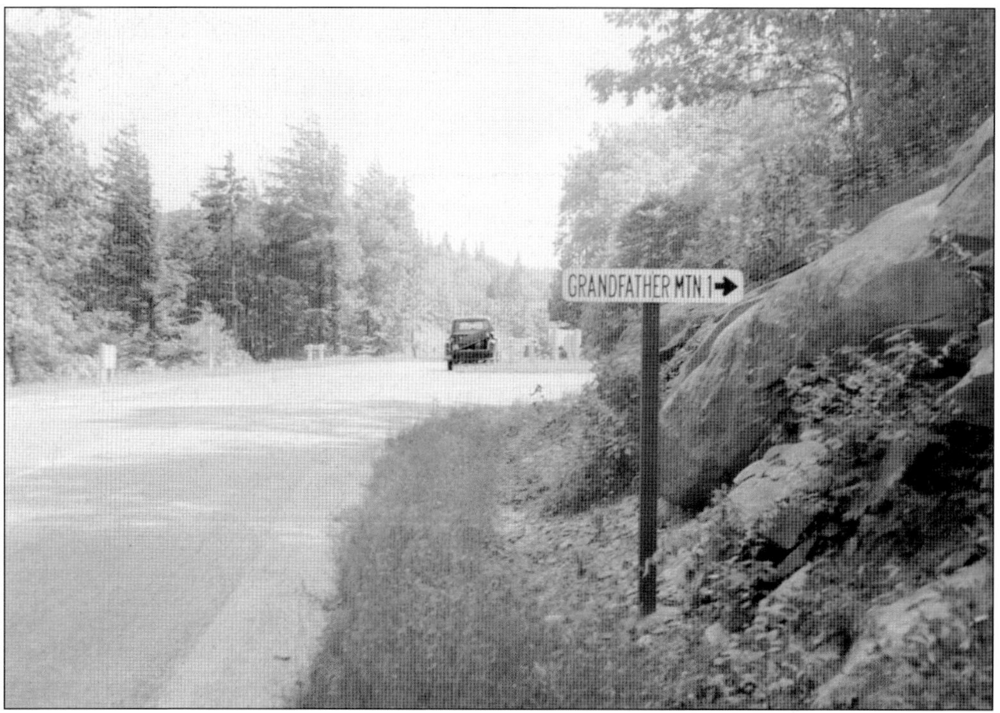

Signage along the Blue Ridge Parkway is rare. The National Park Service wants the area to remain as pristine as possible. This small sign signaled Blue Ridge Parkway motorists that the Grandfather Mountain attraction was just a mile away. (Courtesy of Blue Ridge Parkway.)

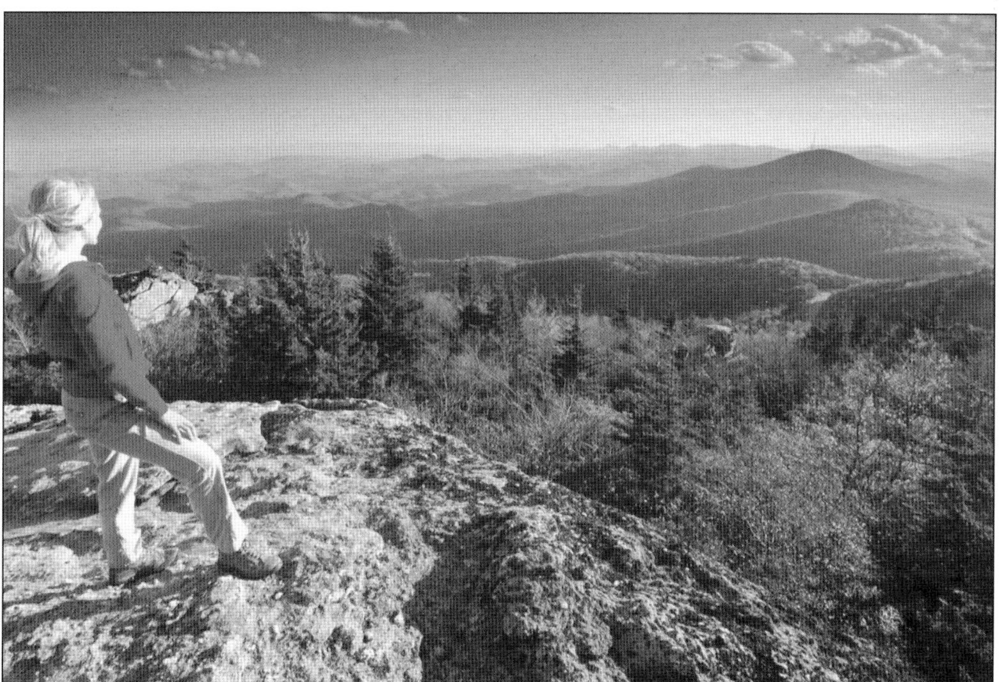

The rocks and crags of the different peaks that make up Grandfather Mountain provide incredible panoramic views of the surrounding countryside. (Courtesy of *Avery Journal-Times*.)

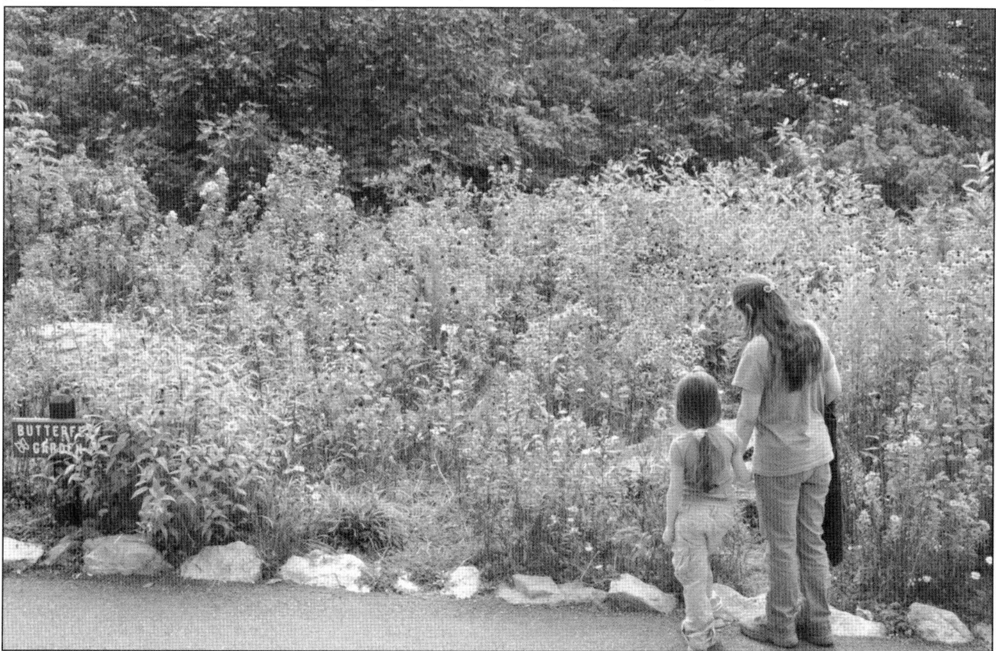

Grandfather Mountain's beautiful butterfly garden features a variety of native plants, such as evening primrose, Joe Pye weed, coneflowers, and milkweed. The monarch butterfly, in particular, feeds only on milkweed during its caterpillar stage, and adult monarchs enjoy the nectar of all of the flowers here. In the late summer and early fall, the monarchs can be seen on their legendary migration to Mexico. (Courtesy of Michael Hardy.)

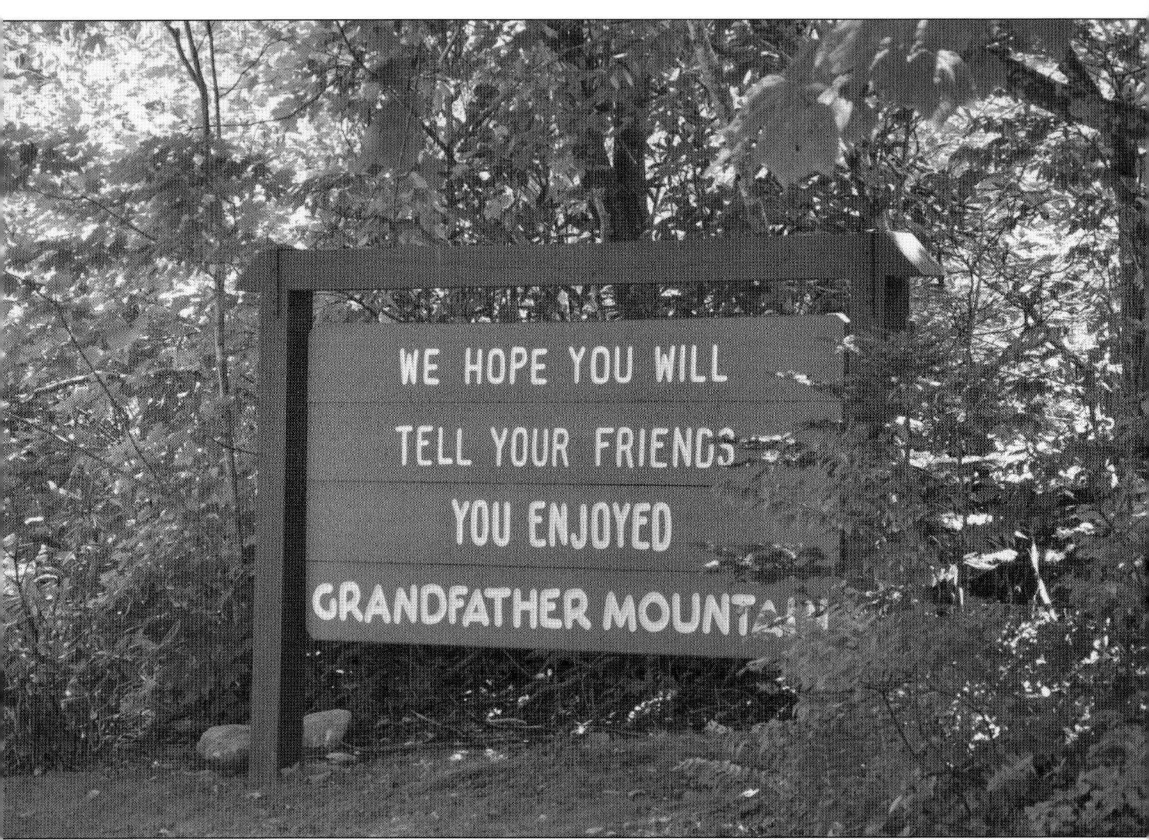

Thousands of people visit Grandfather Mountain each year. While some are from nearby communities, others travel from around the country and the world. They come to see the animals and learn about native biodiversity; they learn from the displays, films, and special programs in the nature museum; they hike trails that range from the easy to the extreme; they brave the Mile-High Swinging Bridge or just watch others doing so; and they have picnics, gather with friends and family, and enjoy the spectacular views. In addition to everyday visits, guests also congregate for special events like Kids' Day, the Singing on the Mountain, Scout events, and the Grandfather Mountain Highland Games. This sign at the Grandfather Mountain attraction bids those visitors to return soon and to spread the word about Western North Carolina's "grand old man" so that many more can come under Grandfather Mountain's spell. (Courtesy of Michael Hardy.)

Bibliography

Covington, Howard E., Jr. *Linville: A Mountain Home for 100 Years*. Dallas, TX: Taylor Publishing, 1992.

Dugger, Shepherd Monroe. *The Balsam Groves of the Grandfather Mountain*. [n.p.], 1934.

Hardy, Michael C. *Remembering Avery County: Old Tales from North Carolina's Youngest County*. Charleston, SC: The History Press, 2007.

Johnson, Randy. *Hiking the Blue Ridge Parkway*. Guilford, CT: Globe Pequot Press, 2003, 2010.

MacDonald, Donald. *America's Braemar: Grandfather Mountain and the Re-birth of Scottish Identity Across the U.S.A.* Madison, GA: Southern Lion Books, 2007.

Stewart, Kevin G., and Mary-Russell Roberson. *Exploring the Geology of the Carolinas*. Chapel Hill, NC: University of North Carolina Press, 2007.

Tager, Miles. *Grandfather Mountain: A Profile*. Boone, NC: Parkway Publishers, 1999.

Waite, John R. *The Blue Ridge Stemwinder*. Johnson City, TN: The Overmountain Press, 2003.

Whisnant, Anne Mitchell. *Super-Scenic Motorway: A Blue Ridge Parkway History*. Chapel Hill, NC: University of North Carolina Press, 2006.